The Last Days of
CHARLES I

GRAHAM EDWARDS

SUTTON PUBLISHING

First published in 1999 by
Sutton Publishing Limited · Phoenix Mill
Thrupp · Stroud · Gloucestershire GL5 2BU

Reprinted 1999

British Library Cataloguing in Publication Data
A catalogue record for this book is available from the British Library

ISBN 0 7509 2079 3

For Margaret,
with love

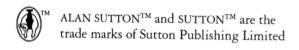
ALAN SUTTON™ and SUTTON™ are the
trade marks of Sutton Publishing Limited

Typeset in 11/14pt Garamond.
Typesetting and origination by
Sutton Publishing Limited.
Printed in Great Britain by
Butler & Tanner, Frome, Somerset.

Contents

Contents

Foreword

The troubled 1640s culminated in January 1649 with the trial and public execution of Charles I as 'that man of blood' who made war upon his own people. Graham Edwards provides a poignant narrative and a shrewd commentary upon the closing days of a king who, if he hardly knew how to rule, found at the moment of truth a marvellous capacity to die. Thoroughly researched, written with clarity and force, backed by copious contemporary illustrations, this book is a strikingly apt commemoration of the extraordinary and still controversial events of 350 years ago. I commend it.

Ivan Roots
Emeritus Professor of History
University of Exeter

Acknowledgements

I wish to thank many people for their kind and generous help.

My warmest thanks are to Professor Ivan Roots, who first fired my interest in this period of English history fifty years ago, for his great encouragement and invaluable help in preparing this book.

Without the assistance of two libraries the task would have been impossible. I am most grateful to, firstly, in the Somerset County Library Service, Mr David Bromwich of the Somerset Studies Library and, secondly, the ladies of Priorswood Library in Taunton. They have been of the greatest help in advising me and obtaining the relevant documents and books. The University of Exeter Library Staff have been highly co-operative, guiding me to the wealth of their comprehensive microfilm library of essential Thomason Tracts and other seventeenth-century material.

Particular thanks are due to Gareth Simon, the publisher of Pallas Armata, 98 Priory Road, Tonbridge, Kent. His unfailing help in discovering and reprinting long out-of-print books and documents of this and other historical periods has been of inestimable value to me and others, but of significant financial cost to himself. I am grateful to Robin Lewando of Langport without whose tuition on the word processor, this book would have been written in longhand.

I wish to thank Jane Crompton and Alison Flowers for the kind and thoughtful way in which they have edited the book, avoiding any possible bruising of the author's *amour propre* as, with much delicacy, they suggested changes to his deathless prose.

Finally, I owe many thanks to my assiduous proofreader, spelling-corrector and wife, Margaret, who has long been tolerant of my obsession with the Civil War period.

The majority of the illustrations are taken from prints in my collection.

Chronology

1600	*19 November*. Charles, second son of King James VI of Scotland, is born.
1603	*31 March*. King James VI of Scotland succeeds Queen Elizabeth I as King James I of England.
1605	Charles is created Duke of York.
	5 November. The Gunpowder Plot is discovered.
1610	King James introduces bishops into the Presbyterian Kirk of Scotland.
1611	Princess Elizabeth, King James's daughter, is betrothed to Frederick V, the Elector Palatine.
1612	Henry, Prince of Wales, dies.
1616	Charles becomes Prince of Wales. George Villiers, King James's favourite, is created viscount.
1617	Villiers is created Earl of Buckingham.
1618	Buckingham is created Marquess.
1619	Elector Palatine accepts the throne of Bohemia; he is defeated in the Battle of White Mountain and loses Bohemia and the Palatinate.
1620	Negotiations begin with Spain for Charles's marriage to the Infanta Maria.
1621	Parliament opposes the Spanish marriage and presents the Grand Protestation asserting its rights.
1622	Charles and Buckingham travel incognito to Spain to woo the Infanta. King James dissolves Parliament.
1623	Marriage negotiations with Spain fail. Buckingham is created Duke.
1624	Negotiations begin with France for Charles's marriage to Princess Henrietta Maria, sister of Louis XIII.
1625	*27 March*. King James dies. Charles succeeds as King Charles I.
	11 May. King Charles marries Henrietta Maria by proxy.
	12 June. Henrietta Maria arrives in England, discontented.

18 June. King Charles opens his first Parliament, which wants redress of grievances before voting him money.

August. Parliament dissolved.

October. The expedition organised by Buckingham against Spain fails at Cadiz.

1626   *2 February.* King Charles is crowned King of England at Westminster.

5 February. Second Parliament is opened. Buckingham's dismissal is demanded as the price for voting funds.

1 May. Parliament impeaches Buckingham on five charges. The King defends him.

15 June. Parliament dissolved without voting money. The King resorts to other means to raise funds, tonnage and poundage levies; demands financial gifts from wealthy; imposes forced loans.

7 August. Exasperated by the demands of the Queen's large French entourage, the King expells them from England, while Buckingham prepares to support French Protestants (Huguenots) in western Brittany in their fight against King Louis XIII.

1627   War with France. The expedition to the Isle de Rhé, off La Rochelle, fails.

1628   *17 March.* Third Parliament is opened.

28 May. Petition of Right lists Parliament's grievances.

23 August. Buckingham is murdered at Portsmouth by John Felton.

October. Parliament is prorogued.

1629   *5 March.* Charles orders the arrest of nine Parliamentarians.

10 March. The King dissolves Parliament and begins eleven years of personal rule.

1630   The King raises money by means of Distraint of Knighthood.

29 May. Charles (later Charles II) is born.

1631   Princess Mary is born.

1633   King Charles I is crowned in Edinburgh. William Laud becomes Archbishop of Canterbury.

October. James, Duke of York (later James II), is born.

1634   Ship Money tax is imposed on inland areas.

1636   William Juxon becomes Bishop of London.

1637   John Hampden is convicted of refusing to pay Ship Money.

1638   The Solemn League and Covenant is signed in Scotland. Covenanter Army assembles under Alexander Leslie. The Scottish Kirk abolishes bishops.

1639   The First Bishops' War with Scotland.

June. The King agrees terms with the Scots at Berwick.

1640   Thomas Wentworth is created Earl of Strafford and made the King's chief adviser.

April–May. The Short Parliament is called and dissolved.

August. The Second Bishops' War with Scotland. The King is defeated at Newburn.

28 October. Treaty of Ripon. The King agrees to pay the Scots £850 a day until settlement is agreed.

1641   Princess Mary marries Prince William II of Orange.

March. The Earl of Strafford is impeached by Parliament.

12 May. Strafford is executed.

October. Rebellion in Ireland.

1642   *4 January.* The King fails to arrest five MPs and Lord Kimbolton.

10 January. The King withdraws from London.

22 August. The Royal Standard is raised at Nottingham. Civil war between the King and Parliament becomes imminent.

23 October. Indecisive major battle at Edgehill.

12 November. The King's march on London is halted at Turnham Green.

1643–4 The Civil War continues with fluctuating fortunes for the King as well as for Parliament and its Scots allies.

1645   *10 January.* Parliament beheads Archbishop Laud, the King's close ally in his religious policies.

2 February. Montrose is victorious at Inverlochy in Scotland.

3 April. Parliament passes Self-denying Ordinance.

April. Parliament's New Model Army musters under Fairfax.

1 May. Montrose is victorious at Auldearn.

14 June. The King is heavily defeated at Naseby by New Model Army. He then goes to South Wales to raise more troops.

18 June. Fairfax takes Leicester.

10 July. A Royalist Army is defeated at Langport, Somerset.

July onward. The Royalists in the West of England and Montrose in Scotland are defeated.

24 September. The Royalists are defeated at Rowton Heath, Cheshire after which the King returns to Oxford for the winter.

1646   *January–April.* Montereul, a French emissary, sees Scottish Commissioners in London and the King at Oxford proposing a Scottish settlement with the King. The French aim to split the Scots/English alliance. Royalist reverses continue.

1 April. Montereul tells the King that the Scots would welcome him.

27 April. The King leaves Oxford in disguise, and travels towards London and then northward.

5 May. King Charles joins the Scottish Army near Newark, then orders the Newark Royalists to surrender.

13 May. Charles arrives at Newcastle upon Tyne under Scots escort.

19 May. The English Parliament votes for the Scots Army's withdrawal from England.

24 July. Newcastle Propositions presented to the King.

September. The Scottish–Westminster discussions on the King's future. The Westminster Parliament raises loan to pay the Scots Army's arrears.

December. The Scots Army prepares to leave England.

1647   *30 January.* The English Parliament takes control of the King.

3 February. The journey to Holdenby House, Northants, begins; the King arrives on 17 February.

March–June. Protracted negotiations between the King and Parliament.

4 June. Joyce seizes King Charles at Holdenby House. The New Model Army takes control of the King's person.

June. The King is taken to several places, including Windsor and Caversham, near Reading. Eleven MPs are denounced by the Army.

14 August. The King arrives at Hampton Court, now attended by Legge, Berkeley and Ashburnham.

August–November. Many people visit the King. The Army suspects intrigue and there are rumours of possible threats to the King's life.

11 November. The King escapes to the South Coast; he fails to find a ship.

13 November. The King is taken to Carisbrooke Castle, Isle of Wight.

26 November. The King signs 'Engagement' with the Scots who accept temporary religious settlement. This divides the Scottish nation. 'Engagers' undertake military aid for the King.

December. The Westminster Parliament demands a settlement with the King; he rejects their proposals.

1648   *January.* Parliament votes to end all negotiations with the King.

March–August. The Second Civil War breaks out in Wales, Norfolk, Essex and Kent.

17–19 August. Royalists and Scots are defeated at Preston, Lancs.

18 September. Parliament opens treaty discussions with the King at Newport, Isle of Wight.

20 November. Army Remonstrance presented to Parliament.

29 November. The Newport Treaty ends with the basis for settlement agreed.

30 November. The Army removes the King to Hurst Castle, Hampshire.

2 December. The Army marches from Windsor into London.

5 December. Parliament votes acceptance of the Newport Treaty.

6 December. 'Pride's Purge'.

December. The Army and remaining MPs (The Rump) consider trial of the King.

18 December. The King is taken to Windsor Castle.

28 December. The Commons Ordinance for trial is approved and Commissioners for the High Court of Justice are named.

1649   *1 January.* The House of Lords rejects the Ordinance, adjourning for seven days, trying to delay matters.

6 January. The Commons ignores the Lords and approves the Ordinance for trial by twenty-nine votes to twenty-six.

8–19 January. The High Court of Justice plans the King's trial.

20 January. The trial begins.

27 January. King Charles is sentenced to death.

28 January. The King composes himself at St James's Palace.

29 January. The royal children say farewell to their father.

30 January. King Charles I is executed at Whitehall.

1–6 February. The King's body lies at St James's Palace.

5 February. Scots proclaim the Prince of Wales as King Charles II.

7 February. Charles I is buried at St George's Chapel, Windsor.

16 March. English Parliament abolishes the monarchy and the Lords. A Commonwealth is proclaimed.

1650   *22 July.* Cromwell, Lord General after Fairfax's resignation, leads a pre-emptive invasion of Scotland.

3 September. After setbacks, he wins a major battle at Dunbar.

24 December. Edinburgh Castle surrenders to the English.

1651   *1 January.* King Charles II is crowned in Scotland.

3 September. Charles II and the Scots are defeated at Worcester.

1653   *December.* Cromwell establishes the Protectorate.

1658   Cromwell dies. His son Richard becomes Protector.

1660   *May.* King Charles II is restored to the English throne. Retribution for the Regicides begins.

Portrait of King Charles I.

Introduction

Since the death of King Harold at the Battle of Hastings several monarchs in Britain have died from acts of violence, some at the hands of their own people. William I's second son King William Rufus was mysteriously killed by an arrow in the New Forest while hunting. Edward II was foully murdered at Berkeley Castle in Gloucestershire in September 1327. Richard II starved to death in captivity at Pontefract Castle in January 1400, and Henry VI was fatally stabbed while a prisoner in the Tower of London seventy-one years later. Edward V, one of the 'Princes in the Tower' was, it was claimed, murdered there and his uncle Richard III was killed at the Battle of Bosworth Field in 1485. Mary Queen of Scots was executed, not by her own people, but on the orders of Queen Elizabeth I.

To Mary Queen of Scots' grandson, King Charles I, fell the dubious distinction of being the only monarch who was publicly tried and executed by some of his subjects.

This book provides a general account of the circumstances leading to that fateful day, the background to these events and the personalities involved. Its publication marks the 350th anniversary of King Charles's death on 30 January 1649.

The early chapters consider the King as a person, including his relationships with his family. His dealings with his subjects, mainly the Scots and the English, during the last two years of his life are also examined. The events and circumstances of the final three months of Charles I's reign, culminating in his execution, are explained in detail.

There are many mysteries that still surround the circumstances of the events which led to his death, some of which are explored in these pages. It is generally assumed that the King's execution was ordered by his rebellious English and Scottish Parliaments. But this was not so.

Why did he leave Oxford secretly and meet the Scottish Army at Newark? Did the Scots sell him to his English Parliamentary enemies, their allies? Who kidnapped the King from Holdenby House? The reasons behind his departure from Hampton Court Palace are not clear, neither is his proposed destination. Why after escaping from one form of Army custody did he enter another one on the Isle of Wight? How loyal were his trusted attendants? Were all his plans known to his enemies?

The question whether the King had to be condemned to death is one which is still asked. Other uncertainties have never been satisfactorily explained. Who were the ladies who interrupted the King's trial and what became of them? The identities of the actual headsman and his assistant have still not been clarified although many have been accused of wielding the axe. These, among others, are the issues which are considered. It is not only a historical 'Who Done It?', it is also a 'Why Done It?' How it was done is very well known.

This book is largely based on contemporary documents and accounts. In the seventeenth century the new year began on 25 March, which can cause confusion for those studying the writings of the time. For example, the King's execution under the old Julian calendar would have been recorded as 30 January 1648, and dates are often written as 1648/9 in an attempt to reconcile the two calendars. In this account all dates are in accordance with the Gregorian system of the New Year starting on 1 January. In quotations from documents unusual seventeenth-century spelling has also been updated.

It is very likely that the only archaic thinking is that of the author.

CHAPTER ONE

The King

. . . the most worthy of the title of an honest man
Edward Hyde, 1st Earl of Clarendon

His Majesty King Charles I is easily recognisable through the many pictures of him which have been published, notably those by Sir Anthony van Dyke. However, these only convey, as they were meant to do, the detached aloofness of the monarch rather than the person behind the kingly pose.

The portraits depict a man with fine features, delicate hands and a steadfast gaze, either immaculately and fashionably dressed or appearing warlike in armour, seated or mounted on a powerful charger. None of these pictures show that he was quite the reverse, and in fact a small man. The artist took great care not to place the King next to anything which might indicate that he was not of majestic proportions. The King stood, it appears, about 5 ft 4 in tall, as his suit of armour in the Tower Armoury indicates.

He was the second son of King James VI of Scotland and his Queen, Anne of Denmark. He was born at Dunfermline Palace in Scotland on 19 November 1600, six years after his elder brother Henry. Charles was reported to have been a sickly child, who was unable to walk or talk even at the age of three. When his father succeeded Queen Elizabeth I to the English throne, as well as retaining the throne of Scotland, the infant Charles was thought unfit to travel to London. He remained in Scotland in the care of nurses and other servants while the rest of his family journeyed to London. He joined them in the summer of 1604, having travelled south in short managable stages.[1]

As Charles grew he strengthened under the dedicated care of Lady Cary, the governess appointed to supervise his upbringing by the King. Lady Cary's husband Sir Robert had carried the news to

King James I and VI, father of Charles I.

Scotland of James's accession to the English throne as James I. Sir Robert, in his memoirs, wrote of his wife's resistance to the King's plans for his son, 'that the string under his tongue should be cut, for he was so long in beginning to speak . . . Then he would have him put in iron boots, to strengthen his sinews and joints, but my wife protested so much against them both, as she got the victory, and the King was fain to yield.'[2]

Anne of Denmark, mother of Charles I.

The young Charles was not strong enough to participate in many physical activities in his early years, but benefited from enjoyable study under the continued guidance of the Scottish tutor Thomas Murray, also appointed by his father. As he grew he was considered to be mild in temper, quiet and serious-minded. He suffered from a speech impediment, a hesitation which had almost disappeared by the time he was grown up. Charles admired his elder brother, who at that time was all that he was not. Henry was sturdy, active and outgoing, whereas Charles was shy, diffident and unsure of himself when speaking or in the presence of others. Henry, although popular, was not above baiting his younger brother about his physique, 'until he made him weep, telling him that he should be a bishop, a gown being fittest to hide his legs'.[3] This does not seem to have diminished Charles's love for his elder brother as affectionate letters written by Charles to Henry show.[4]

Charles was created Duke of York when he was five years old, but seven years later Prince Henry died of a fever and the younger son became the heir apparent. At this time Charles also lost the company of his sister, his beloved Elizabeth who left for Germany to marry Frederick, the Elector Palatine. Charles was now the sole royal child in Britain and as his physical strength had increased he was determined to excel at some sort of sport or hobby.

He was said by the Venetian ambassador to have become 'the best marksman and the most graceful manager of the great horse in the three kingdoms'. He was of a fearless nature and was to distinguish himself at the jousting tournament held in Whitehall in 1620 to commemorate the anniversary of his father's accession to the English throne. He ran for pleasure in the area around St James's Palace on most days and made every effort to cure his stammer. He conquered this last problem to a large extent by thinking out each sentence carefully before speaking it.

These early experiences contributed to the formation of Charles's character. Edward Hyde, later the Earl of Clarendon and Chancellor of the Exchequer, that most loyal of supporters and dedicated historian, thought that the King, as he was to become, 'had a tenderness and compassion of nature, which restrained him from ever doing a hard-hearted thing'. He was still as reticent and wary as he had been in childhood for, 'He saw and observed men long before he received any about his person, and did not love strangers, nor very confident men.' He was most temperate in his habits, 'he abhorred all debauchery' and drank wine only in moderation.[5]

Just before his sixteenth birthday Charles became Prince of Wales and this required him to attend Court more regularly, a society in which he was ill-at-ease. He became more reserved and shy, blushing when addressed by people he did not know well. Beneath this hesitant manner, however, there was evidence of a hard determination, as can be seen by his efforts to improve his physique, become competent at certain pursuits and to overcome his speech handicap. His shyness and unease at Court were increased by his dislike of the drunkenness and lewd, discourteous behaviour which prevailed there with his father's tacit consent and even his participating endorsement.

By 1620, as Charles was now approaching adulthood, plans for his marriage were being discussed. These were, as was usual, motivated by dynastic and diplomatic concerns. Now he was the only son the future of the Stuart dynasty was his responsibility. His mother was over forty years old and his father displayed more of an interest in young men than producing another son. The marriage of the Prince of Wales was also important in terms of confirming an alliance with and enlisting the support of a powerful European monarch for the foreign policy that the King wished to pursue.

Henry, Prince of Wales, elder brother of Charles I.

Soon after ascending the English throne James had, sensibly, made peace with Spain. He had also mediated between the Protestant Dutch and their Catholic Spanish overlords to end the prolonged revolt in the Netherlands. James considered himself capable of playing a far more important role on the international stage than the strength of his small kingdoms might merit. As his daughter had married a Protestant ruler, it would benefit his aims to provide the balance between the more powerful Protestant and Catholic states. This could be achieved if his son were to marry a Catholic princess, which would demonstrate his impartiality in matters of diplomacy. When the King's intentions became more widely known there was much opposition, especially in Parliament, to any alliance with a Catholic power. The country's most powerful enemies were the Catholic powers of Europe and tales of religious persecution under the Catholic Queen Mary were engraved in the folk memory. The religious and political menace of the Catholic states was viewed as an ever-present threat to the safety of England.

In 1618 a major war began in Germany between the Catholic and Protestant countries on the Continent. This, the Thirty Years' War, was to see King James's Protestant son-in-law, the Elector Palatine, defeated and ousted from his throne. The King would later need money to pay for an army of 4,000 men to help his son-in-law to recover the Palatinate. Chronically short of finance, he summoned a Parliament to raise the essential funds. This and other matters increased the tension and there were angry exchanges before James adjourned Parliament without the funds being voted. One major cause of this tension was the King's determination that Parliament should have no influence over his foreign policy.

The prevailing and increasing anti-Catholic attitude did not deter the King in his search for a Spanish bride for his son. Much has been written about the circumstances of Prince Charles's secret visit to Madrid, accompanied by the Duke of Buckingham. The venture failed mainly because the Spanish demanded that Charles become a Catholic and Britain return to the old faith.

Anti-Spanish feeling was running high and negotiations began to promote alliances with the Dutch and the French, both of whom opposed the Habsburg policies for Germany.

Parliament pressed for a naval war against Britain's traditional enemy Spain, which only thirty-three years earlier and well within living memory, had sent the Armada against England. They also demanded fresh action against the English Catholics as one of the conditions for voting the sum of £300,000 for military preparations.

In the meantime while the King's thoughts turned towards negotiation for a French daughter-in-law, it was evident that the Prince was learning from his experiences. Charles was no longer a diffident young man, but had become more self-assured and he was not slow to assert himself. The princess being considered as Charles's bride was fourteen-year-old Henrietta Maria, the sixth and youngest daughter of the late King Henri IV, Henri of Navarre, and Marie de Medici. She was small, dark and not unattractive.

Discussion of the possible marriage was, of necessity, more of a treaty negotiation than a wooing and although neither of the principals expressed personal revulsion, the fact that they were of different religious faiths was politically significant. The French wanted to obtain more concessions for the English Catholics, just as the English required

King Charles I and Queen
Henrietta Maria.

more practical assistance in their bid to free the Palatinate and to
restore the Elector and his wife to their lost throne. Neither side was
prepared to concede much and negotiations were becoming stagnant by
1625 when, on 27 March, King James died and his son ascended the
throne as King Charles I of England, Scotland and Ireland.

The new King wasted little time. He undertook, secretly, to
guarantee English Catholics the right of freedom of worship and also
to allow his proposed wife, Henrietta Maria, to continue to practise
her faith. The new Queen should also have the responsibility for the
education of their children until they were thirteen years old; have
her own chapel and religious confessors; and be attended by an
entourage of about a hundred French Catholics. The marriage was
agreed on these conditions, and on 1 May 1625 it took place outside
the West Door of Notre Dame Cathedral in Paris by proxy. The Duc
de Chevreuse took the place of the absent King Charles.

Some days later the Duke of Buckingham, arrayed in
magnificence, arrived to escort the new Queen to England. He did
not value the new alliance with France and his behaviour towards
Charles's French Queen was at best unseemly and at worst
disturbing. Alexander Dumas's story, *The Three Musketeers*, gave
details of their alleged relationship, and implied it was based on
romance. This, however, obscured the political damage his attitude
towards the Queen was to cause.

Henrietta Maria's journey to her new country was uncomfortable.
The Channel crossing was rough and took twenty-four hours. The

George Villiers, Duke of
Buckingham.

Dover Castle, where the fifteen-year-old Henrietta Maria spent her first stormy rain-swept night in England.

weather in June was predictable – heavy rain. On arrival she was taken to Dover Castle where it is likely this fifteen-year-old girl spent an unhappy night, tired from her experiences and worried at the prospect of meeting this unknown man who was now her husband. Members of her entourage were also unimpressed by the reception their Princess received. There had been no ceremonial arrival. There was no King to greet his Queen, and their lodgings were in a fortress built more to withstand attack than to create an opulent environment. There seemed little prospect of a wealthy and comfortable life for the Queen in England.

Henrietta Maria's first meeting with King Charles the following morning smacked of a poorly rehearsed ceremony, and was only saved from disaster by the kindliness of the bridegroom. When she hurried from her breakfast to greet him and nervousness ruined her little formal speech of fealty, Charles put his arms about her and comforted his weeping young wife with kisses and gentle words.[6] The King seemed to be enchanted by her, as were the people who saw them later as they rode to Canterbury Cathedral for their second marriage ceremony.

The royal party's approach to London was ultimately by barge along the Thames, the banks of which were lined with cheering people. Their journey continued past the Tower and London Bridge to the Queen's home at Somerset House, a temporary arrangement while St James's Palace was being restored. London was not a

Old London Bridge viewed from Southwark in the time of Charles I.

cheerful place in the height of summer, and plague was rife at that time.

Despite this, and the mournful fact that their new Queen was a Catholic, the people were reported to have high hopes that she would soon settle and being young adapt quickly to their ways. It was widely rumoured that when someone asked her if she could tolerate Protestants, she replied, 'Why not? Was not my father one?' This anecdote implies contrivance and an attempt to reconcile the people to the fact that their Queen practised the hated papist religion. Her father had been a leader of the French Protestants in the French Wars

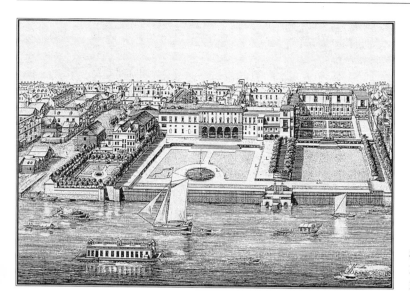

Somerset Palace, Henrietta
Maria's temporary London
home.

of Religion during the sixteenth century, but had become a Catholic
to gain the French throne, uttering the eminently realistic comment
that 'Paris was well worth a Mass'.

Henrietta Maria, however, adhered firmly to her Catholic faith.
Her youth and lack of experience did little to cure her uncertainty or
to help her homesickness. The constant complaints to members of
her entourage about England, the English, their weather and the
apparent lack of warmth in their reception of her, unadorned as it
had been with magnificent ceremony, hardly encouraged the Queen
to adapt positively. She sulked, taking little trouble to hide her
dissatisfaction with all she saw around her. She was sullen in her
meetings with prominent people and unsmiling during public
appearances. Despite the Queen's Catholicism, the English people
were prepared to accept her but her obvious distaste for her new life
caused much of the early goodwill towards her to evaporate and she
acquired the scornful nickname, 'the popish brat'.

The early period of the King and Queen's marriage was not a
happy one. The King, himself new to direct responsibility for
government, was beset by problems concerning money, politics and
religion. He would undoubtedly have welcomed his marriage as a
refuge of peace and tranquility centred around a cheerful loving wife.
Instead, he was confronted by quarrels about proposed advantages for
members of her retinue, criticism of everything English and, at one
time, contradiction in public by his inexperienced Queen.

Charles himself, obviously exasperated by the situation, was hardly a model of reticence, tact or good taste in this instance. He spoke and even wrote to Buckingham about his wife's shortcomings and Buckingham with his dislike for the alliance was not slow to gossip about these confidences. The King could not help but be aware of the adverse influence her French companions had on his young, impressionable Queen and after about a year of reluctant tolerance, he decided to expel them all from the kingdom. Domestic tantrums followed, but the King was adamant. Even so, a month later the French were still in London, using as many pretexts as they could to delay their departure. Finally, Charles ordered their immediate expulsion, but following his wife's entreaties relented enough to allow her to retain two religious confessors, one English, one Scottish, as well as three women attendants who spoke French.

Fashionable dress of the nobility, *c.* 1640.

The King's assertion of his power in his own house changed the domestic situation, but the Queen disliked Buckingham's influence over her husband and this continued to be a source of tension in their relationship. In 1627 Buckingham was pursuing a policy of support for the beleaguered French Protestants, the Huguenots, at La Rochelle in western Brittany, a policy doubly unpopular with the Queen for its anti-French and anti-Catholic feeling. The immediate problems caused by Buckingham were, however, removed when he was killed in August 1628. An unemployed officer, John Felton, stabbed Buckingham to death at Portsmouth while he was preparing another expedition to the area of La Rochelle.

The death of Buckingham brought the King and Queen closer together and in the following months the foundations for a happy marriage began to be laid. Evidence of this shift in attitude came when news emerged of the Queen's pregnancy. The baby boy's delivery was a breech birth and his chances of survival so uncertain that he was immediately baptised James Charles. He died an hour or so later and was buried in Westminster Abbey at the side of his grandfather, King James I.

Later that year Henrietta Maria became pregnant again and this time, at St James's Palace on 29 May 1630, she gave birth to a strong, healthy, vigorous son, who later became King Charles II. Although upset that her son had been baptised according to the rites of the Anglican Church, she drew some comfort that with his dark colouring, black eyes and general bearing he reminded her of her father.

The royal marriage settled down to happiness and children were born with some regularity. Princess Mary arrived in November 1631;

The royal Children, *c.* 1641. From left to right: Princess Mary, Prince James (later James II), Prince Charles (later Charles II), Princess Elizabeth and Prince Henry of Gloucester.

James, Duke of York (later King James II) in October 1633; Elizabeth in December 1635; Anne in March 1637; Katherine born and died in January 1639; Henry, Duke of Gloucester in July 1640. Finally, in 1644, Princess Henrietta Anne was born in Exeter at the height of the first Civil War.

King Charles was now not only a loving husband, he was a devoted and responsible father, who was to feel deeply the sorrow of separation which the approaching Civil War was to bring. Of necessity the royal family was separated as the war continued beyond the very early optimistic forecasts of victory for the King. The acute shortage of money for the Royalist war efforts caused the Queen to travel to France to raise funds, weapons and, if she could, men to fight against the rebels.

The two eldest boys, Prince Charles, the Prince of Wales and James, Duke of York spent most of the time with their father at the Royalist headquarters at Oxford and elsewhere until early 1645. Then the King reluctantly decided to send his eldest son, with carefully selected advisers, to the West of England to bring some order to the significant Royalist forces there, whose commanders continually bickered among themselves. This would give the fifteen-

Frederic, the Elector Palatine, the erstwhile King of Bohemia and his wife, Elizabeth, sister to Charles I.

year-old Prince direct responsibility, 'to unboy him'[7] as he so charmingly wrote; this is perhaps also a sly witty reference to Prince Rupert's poodle, 'Boy', as young Charles idolised Rupert, his dashing older cousin. Gentle, wry wit has seldom been attributed to the serious-minded King Charles.

There was a further reason for this separation, since the King was concerned lest both he and his heir should fall into rebel hands. He was also aware that should Prince Charles be captured, the Parliamentarians could, and probably would, use him as a pawn in a constitutional gambit and force him to replace his father on the throne. The West of England was overwhelmingly but not entirely Royalist and promised greater safety for his beloved son and heir.

King Charles's personal unhappiness was increased by the knowledge that two of his youngest children, Princess Elizabeth and Prince Henry, were, by 1645, in the hands of the rebels. This was made even worse by the fact that they were in the care and control of Algernon Percy, the tenth Earl of Northumberland, and his wife. The Percys were very much *personae non grata* in royal eyes. Lucy Percy, Countess of Carlisle, had been a lady-in-waiting to the Queen and, hearing, in January 1642, of the King's plans to arrest five Members of the House of Commons and one of the Lords, for opposing his wishes, had warned her friend John Pym of this. Pym and the others were able to escape before the King arrived at the Commons with his soldiers.

This was not the only odious act committed by the Percys in Charles's eyes. Algernon, a former Lord High Admiral before the

Civil War, was the leader of the body which directed the strategy of the Parliamentarians, the Committee of Both Kingdoms. Among its members were commissioners from the Scottish Parliament, which was then in alliance with the English Parliament against the King. It was some small consolation to the King to know that his younger children were being treated with kindness and consideration.

After the Royalist surrender, James and Henry, with their sister Elizabeth, were being cared for by the Northumberlands. Henrietta, the youngest child, was in France with her mother and the Prince of Wales had left the mainland first for the Scilly Isles, then Jersey and then to France at the end of June 1646.

Although the King was a loving, faithful husband who did not have mistresses, as others did, and although he was a loving, caring father who worried about his children as his letters show,[8] he was even more conscious of the responsibilities of his family to the monarchy. This emerges in the instructions he gave to his two eldest sons when, after successive defeats and reverses in June, July and September of 1645, he began for the first time to show less optimism for the future of his cause. The King ordered Prince Charles to 'go over sea' rather than be taken by the rebels. He consigned him to the care of his mother in Paris, who was to take responsibility for him in all matters except those of religion, and ordered that the Prince was to maintain his religious allegiance to the Church of England.

At Hereford the King heard that his trusted nephew and lieutenant-general of all the Royalist forces, Prince Rupert, had surrendered the vital port, fortress and armoury of Bristol to Sir Thomas Fairfax and the New Model Army after a very short fight in September 1645. He had sent a message to the eleven-year-old Duke of York, who was at Oxford, saying that the King would prefer to hear that his son had been knocked on the head than to learn that he had committed such a weak and cowardly act as that of Rupert, the former idol who had, according to the King, feet of 'treasonable clay'.

The King's bitter reaction to Rupert's treachery, as he saw it, was most uncharacteristic and did not accord with his previous practice of intense loyalty to his friends and supporters whatever the circumstances. He had persistently defended the flamboyant and self-seeking Buckingham against attacks by Parliament. He had also backed Thomas Wentworth, the Earl of Strafford, his Lord Deputy in Ireland, when he was accused by Parliament of High Treason on the probably false pretext of planning to bring Irish troops across to subdue Members. In this instance the King was mortified to find

Prince Rupert, son of the Elector Palatine and his wife Elizabeth, and nephew to Charles I. He was Royalist lieutenant-general.

that he had offered his supporter more than he could deliver. He had written to Strafford on 23 April 1641: 'I cannot satisfy myself in honour or conscience without assuring you (now in the middle of your troubles), that upon the word of a king, you shall not suffer in life, honour, or fortune.'[9]

Less than three weeks later the King had signed his consent for the Act of Attainder that condemned Strafford to death; he was duly executed on 12 May. The King's justification for signing was evident in his ultimately ironic statement to the Privy Council, 'If my own person only were in danger, I would gladly venture it to save Lord Strafford's life, but seeing my wife, children and all my kingdom are concerned . . . I am forced to give way . . .'.[10] Clarendon knew the King well and, in an attempt to justify his actions over Strafford, considered that '. . . he was, if any, the most worthy of the title of an honest man; so great a lover of justice, that no temptation could dispose him to a wrongful action, except it were so disguised to him that he believed it to be just. He had a tenderness and compassion of nature, which restrained him from ever doing a hard-hearted thing; and therefore was apt to grant pardon to malefactors.'[11]

Thomas Wentworth, Earl of Strafford, executed in 1641.

Lest it should be thought that King Charles was beyond error, there are a number of examples of his tendency to act without thoroughly considering the consequences. As preparations were being made for battle at Edgehill there was dispute between the King's Commander-in-Chief, Robert Bertie, the Earl of Lindsey, and Prince Rupert, the son of the King's beloved sister, Elizabeth of Bohemia. This concerned the way in which the footsoldiers of the royal Army should be deployed. The King, learning of this difference of opinion, sided with his 24-year-old kinsman against his experienced Commander-in-Chief. Lindsey promptly resigned his office and took part in the battle at the head of his regiment of foot; he was to die of the wounds he received. His death was no fault of the King, but to precipitate the loss of his most senior general barely minutes before a major battle could hardly be considered forward planning.

The second example of this royal trait occurred in 1645 when, in order to appease resentment in South Wales, he replaced his commander in the area, General Gerard. As compensation the King created him Lord Gerard of Brandon. Sir Edward Walker, the King's Secretary at War, commented on the possible slight this act could have conveyed when he wrote, '. . . within three days after Sir Thomas Glemham came thither, General Gerard was made Lord

The death of Robert Bertie, Earl of Lindsey after the Battle of Edgehill, October, 1642. A Victorian impression.

Gerard of Brandon, in Suffolk, a Town wherein Sir Thomas Glemham hath both Interest, and is an Heir of the Family of Brandon, by which Name the other [Gerard] affected to be called. This would have troubled another Man . . .'.[12] Glemham, who had defended Carlisle against the Scottish Army and after surrender had marched loyally to South Wales to join the King, remained firm in his allegiance. There were certainly times when the King did not deserve the loyalty he received.

These decisions serve to illustrate another of the King's characteristics that had been observed by Clarendon. His Majesty, he wrote, '. . . had an excellent understanding, but was not confident enough of it; which made him oftentimes change his own opinion for a worse, and follow the advice of a man that did not judge so well as himself. And this made him more irresolute than the conjuncture of his affairs would admit. If he had been of a rougher and more imperious nature, he would have found more respect and duty.'[13]

This reliance on the advice of others can be seen clearly after the Battle of Naseby, when the King could have taken one of two main courses of action to gather together a replacement army for that destroyed in the battle. He could have travelled to the West of England to join Prince Charles who was trying to recruit an army there. This was a course recommended, *ex post facto*, by Sir Edward Walker and by Edward Hyde, both of whom wrote with the benefit of hindsight. The King, armed with the promise by the Earl of Glamorgan that the men of South Wales would raise 4,000 foot-soldiers for his cause, decided to go there. Glamorgan's promise was an empty one. In South Wales the King found resentment, obstruction and demands from the local leaders, whose people were tired of the war and its impositions. His decision to go to South Wales is very understandable, despite the cavilling of Walker and Hyde. The responsibility for raising troops in the West of England lay with his son, and so it would have been neglecting an opportunity not to travel to an area which seemed to promise many new recruits for his army. He had, however, taken advice which proved to be unsound.

The King's personal characteristics have been outlined, but yet to be considered are the firmly held beliefs and other personal traits which influenced or brought about the momentous events during his reign. These tenets of faith and characteristics affected and even governed his actions as the sovereign of three distinct and separate kingdoms, England with Wales, Scotland and Ireland. Here we are concerned mainly with the events in England and Scotland during the last period of the reign of King Charles I.

CHAPTER TWO

The King and the Conflicts

He that complies against his will,
Is of his own opinion still.

Samuel Butler, *Hudibras*

This loving family man, fastidious in dress and manners, abstemious at a time of widespread excesses in drink and debauchery, punctilious in his religious devotions, had faults as a monarch which even his most ardent supporters could not overlook. Clarendon considered that 'His kingly virtues had some mixture and allay [alloy] that hindered them from shining in full lustre . . .'.[1] Among these alloys which caused flaws in His Majesty's kingship was the perception that 'He was not in his nature bountiful', especially after the death of Buckingham, and that 'he paused too long in giving, which made those to whom he gave less sensible of the benefit'.[2]

Clarendon's claim, that the King 'was a patient hearer of causes, which he frequently accustomed himself to, at the Council board; and judged very well, and was dextrous in the mediating part; so that he often put an end to causes by persuasion, which the stubbornness of men's humours made dilatory in courts of justice', needs to be considered with much caution. Events proved that on certain issues the King may have been a patient hearer and may have been dextrous in the mediating part when trying to solve the problems of others. He was certainly not prepared to concede anything he held dear to help to resolve his own difficulties.

There were three matters in particular on which King Charles was stubborn and inflexible in dealings with his subjects. First and

Sir Edward Hyde, 1st Earl of Clarendon, Chancellor of the Royal Exchequer and historian.

King Charles raising the Royal
Standard at Nottingham in
1642. A Victorian
interpretation.

foremost he was adamant that, '. . . princes are not bound to give
account of their actions, but to God alone'.[3] This belief in his divine
right to rule unchallenged and uncriticised was the bedrock of his
political beliefs.

Time and again this unshakeable view led him into conflict with
his subjects and, while in conflict, bolstered his determination never
to compromise but always ultimately to reject any attempt to lessen
his royal rights and prerogatives. Challenges to these rights brought
in the first eighteen years of his reign precipitate action to end the
immediate dissension. This can be seen in several instances, among
them his peremptory dissolution of the four Parliaments he had
called to raise funds to finance his government; his hasty gathering of
an army to solve the dispute with the Scots over bishops; his entry
into Parliament with armed men to arrest the five Members of the
House of Commons and the Earl of Manchester, at the time Lord
Kimbolton; and finally by raising the Royal Standard at Nottingham
and issuing Commissions of Array to recruit soldiers. This latter act
gave his enemies the chance to claim that it was the King who had
first declared war on his people, although he was to dispute this
assertion.

During the Civil Wars and up to 1649, although he engaged in
negotiations with his enemies, the determination to maintain his

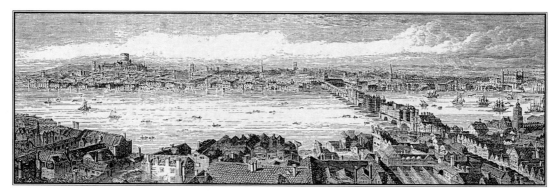

A panoramic view of London
in 1649.

royal secular and religious prerogatives underlay all discussions, even
when he appeared to be considering concessions.

Opportunities of challenging the King's power presented
themselves when the other two matters which were central to the
monarchy were raised. The first was the King's chronic need for
money. On his accession the royal exchequer was in a parlous state.
King James I had spent liberally and the wars with Spain and France,
combined with the vain efforts to restore the Palatinate, had taken
their financial toll. Buckingham, who was instrumental in
instigating the conflicts with Spain and France, was himself also a
drain on potential royal funds, holding as he did many lucrative
monopolies and financial customs concessions granted to him by
James I.

Much of the wealth of the three kingdoms, which comprised
7.5 million people, was not in the hands of the King. It was held by
the Church, by landowners and by the merchants, particularly those
who traded in textiles. For example, in 1640 the total value of
exports from England was almost £1.5 million, of which nearly £1.1
million was exported from London.[4] This was at a time when a farm
labourer on the 'Dorset rate' earned 8 old pence a day (about 3.33
new pence, or under 2 US cents a day at the present sterling/dollar
exchange rate). Some owners of that wealth were beginning seriously
to agitate for a role in government, demands which brought them
into collision with the King's adamant rejection of moves which
threatened any part of his royal prerogative.

The King was determined not to rely solely on Parliament for the
supply of finance, especially as Parliament was not only reluctant to
vote money but collection was also notoriously slow, even when such
a vote had been passed. To raise the necessary cash to pay for

government, defence and the protection of overseas trade, he employed several methods. Some of these were dubious, others hardly legal. When in 1629 Parliament challenged the King's right to customs dues for the whole of his reign and instead offered him a limited period, he dissolved Parliament and reigned without the doubtful assistance of that body for eleven years.

In 1625 Parliament had not voted the Crown the income from tonnage and poundage taxes on imports and exports. In 1626 the King levied these dues. He also ordered Justices of the Peace to request free gifts from the wealthy in the country and later raised forced loans from those on the Parliamentary subsidy lists. The legality of these forced loans was challenged in the courts by five knights who had been imprisoned for refusing to pay. They had not been charged with any offence and so judges declared that their arrest was a matter of state. As the King had the right to imprison without charge in matters of state, their arrest was not illegal. Such a ruling, which ignored the forced loan aspect of the dispute, served to inflame rather than lessen opposition.

Far more public outcry arose when later, while no Parliament was sitting, the King extended the tax of 'Ship Money' to inland areas. The tax was raised to build up the strength of the Navy, not only against European enemies but also against the 'Turkish'. These were actually Algerian pirates who infested the English Channel, capturing ships, consigning their crews to galley slavery and disrupting the trade which was essential to the wealth of Charles's kingdom. This tax had previously been a levy on maritime counties only, but the royal proclamation announced, with irrefutable logic, '. . . that charge of defence which concerneth all men ought to be supported by all, as by the laws and customs of the kingdom of England hath accustomed to be done . . .'.[5]

The legality of the proclamation and the tax it proposed was questioned by a leading Parliamentarian, John Hampden, who refused to pay. He was arrested and tried. He lost, but the opportunity to stir up further discontent was worth the effort as it helped to crystallise opposition to the King's policy of overriding Parliament and its vociferous supporters at very little financial or other costs.

Issues of practicality soon become matters of principle. Once this stage is reached entrenchment begins, especially when one of the antagonists, the King, is clearly determined not to give way, except on minor points, that in themselves become seen as sops to placate,

John Hampden, the MP who opposed Ship Money.

or as crumbs to take the edge off any political hunger rather than real concessions.

The third major issue of contention between King Charles and his political opponents, in England as well as in Scotland, was that of religion. This comprised the forms of church organisation as well as the theological aspects as expressed in church doctrine. This factor, added to the political and financial disputes, was to compound the conflict between the King and his people. The problems of Ireland, with the presence of Protestant colonists in Ulster and the aggressive political aspirations of the native, Catholic Irish chieftains, were a further ingredient in an already extremely combustible situation.

King Charles's own devotions followed the patterns of the Anglican High Church, which reflected the Roman Catholic doctrine from which it was derived. The major difference between the Church of England and the Church of Rome, apart from that of theological interpretation of the meaning of the acts of Communion, lay in the Anglican rejection of the Pope as head of their Church. This had occurred as a result of King Henry VIII's wish to divorce Queen Catherine of Aragon and the Pope's refusal to sanction it; this ultimately led to the separation of the Church of England from the Church of Rome. King Charles had inherited, with his throne, the position of Supreme Head of the Anglican Church. There was deep distrust of those English families who remained Catholic, since England's main enemies abroad were the powerful Catholic states of the Habsburg Empire, France and particularly Spain.

The religious situation in England, where many Anglicans held views about forms of worship which had moved further away from those of the Roman Church and the High Anglican Protestants, was further complicated within Protestantism by the emergence of an increasing number of non-conformist or Puritan sects, often referred to as Independents.

The religious situation in Scotland was also highly complex. The Scottish Reformation of the sixteenth century took as its theological driving force the doctrines and church organisation of John Calvin, who was bitterly opposed to all aspects of the Roman Church. Under the leadership of John Knox the reformed Calvinistic Kirk of Scotland rejected the espiscopalian form of government by bishops and had adopted a system of government by elders, all of equal status, in hierarchical Assemblies. This was known as Presbyterianism.

King James I (and VI) had, against much opposition from clergy and some nobles, reimposed church government by bishops in

John Knox, the Calvinist leader of the Scottish Reformation.

Newcastle upon Tyne.

Scotland in 1610, the year before the appearance of the Authorised Version of the Holy Bible. This version, produced remarkably by a committee after seven years' work, was intended as a major step towards uniformity in religion in the kingdom.

King Charles also wanted uniformity of religious practices in his kingdoms and in 1637 he ordered the introduction of a Book of Common Prayer into the Scottish Church. There was immediate, widespread and even violent opposition among Scottish congregations. Nobles, clergy and the people all rallied to the defence of the reformed religion. They drew up the Solemn League and Covenant which was generally signed throughout the country and the Covenanter movement was born. When the King threatened to impose his will, the Covenanters mustered an army to oppose him.

Ultimately the King failed in his efforts, having suffered military reverses in the so-called First Bishops' War in 1639. The following year, when there was still no resolution of the dispute, the Scots' Army crossed the border, occupied Newcastle upon Tyne and Durham, then defeated the English Army at Newburn. In order to raise the funds to finance the campaign and to meet all the expenses of government, Charles was forced to recall the English Parliament.

This need for finance gave rise to the opportunities sought by some for redress of their political grievances. The King, aware that funds were not to be voted without conditions, dissolved this Short Parliament on 5 May 1640 after only three weeks.

Denzil Hollis, another leading MP who opposed the King.

The Scots, declaring parliamentary independence from the need for Royal Assent to their Acts, sent an army to besiege Newcastle upon Tyne. An armistice was agreed at Ripon provided the Scots received £850 a day from the King until matters between them were settled.

This placed even greater financial pressure on the monarch, who then called another, his fifth, Parliament, known as the Long Parliament, in November 1640. For the next two years the conflict between the King and Parliament intensified. There were increasing demands by Parliament for a say in government as the price for their financial support, while an escalating, frustrated anger coloured the King's attitude to his unco-operative subjects.

John Pym, MP, the Parliamentarian who opposed the King.

On 4 January 1642 in an exasperated but rash venture, King Charles entered the Commons supported by troops to arrest five of the Members he regarded as the most rebellious in their opposition to him. His targets, John Pym, John Hampden, Denzil Holles, Sir Arthur Haselrig and William Strode, along with Lord Kimbolton, later the Earl of Manchester, were forewarned and had taken refuge elsewhere. The King had failed in his effort to decapitate the rebellious Commons, but he had used military force to intimidate his people. After this events proceeded inexorably towards bitter, bloody and costly civil war.

There are very many excellent books that cover the course of the war and therefore the battles, sieges and skirmishes need not be detailed here. There are, however, some developments which need explanation in order fully to appreciate the significance of certain events which led to the death of the King.

Under the ancient constitution military and political decisions were the prerogative of the King. At the outbreak of the Civil War in 1642 the responsibility for Parliamentary military and political decisions was vested in a small body of influential Members of both Houses of Parliament. There was no separation of military from political decision-making. The Parliamentary conduct of the war was placed in the hands of the Earl of Essex as Lord General and he was supported by forces raised by the towns, cities and counties under officers appointed by the authorities in those places, but funded by monthly levies authorised by Parliamentary Ordinances and raised throughout the areas under its control. The war, apart from major encounters, was fought within regions. Mrs John Hutchinson, wife of the Nottingham Parliamentary commander, observed that each county had its own civil war.[6] There was also, therefore, little overall strategic planning.

Lord Kimbolton, later Earl of Manchester, whom the King tried to arrest in early 1642.

The situation became even more complex when the Scottish Covenanters allied themselves with the English Parliament and sent a large army into northern England to fight the King and a smaller force to Ireland to support fellow Protestants there. The English Parliament undertook to pay for both Scottish forces. The intervention of the Scots resulted in a change in the way Parliament directed the war with the establishment of the Committee of Both Kingdoms, which was composed of Members of both the English and Scottish Parliaments. It was, however, very much under the control of those who held English military commands.

As the war continued with inconclusive results, two requirements became clear. First, the need for a centralised field army under the control of Parliament itself. As the Parliamentary general, Sir William Waller, put it in a letter to Derby House in July 1644, 'My Lords, . . . till you have an army merely your own, that you may command it is . . . impossible to do anything of importance'.[7] Second, there was some agitation for a change of senior commanders. Not all Members of Parliament urged the removal of Essex and the Earl of Manchester, who commanded the largest force in Essex's army, that of the Eastern Association (comprising the counties of East Anglia). However, a hardcore, led by Oliver Cromwell, Manchester's lieutenant-general of horse, desired and worked for a change of leadership.

Many of those who favoured change were Puritan in their religious affiliations. Many Members of Parliament, in both the Lords and Commons, were inclined to the Presbyterian persuasion, which reinforced Scottish Covenanter support against the King. These religious distinctions, however, quickly became matters of political rather than theological identification.

Parliament was also divided in another way. Many Members wished to negotiate a settlement with the King. Others, including most of the Independents, favoured decisive military victory before any settlement with His Majesty was agreed.

The device used to remove the senior military leaders, most of whom were also Members of Parliament (either by election to the Commons or by birthright part of the House of Lords), was the introduction of a Self-Denying Ordinance.

Under this, no Member of Parliament of either House would be permitted to hold any military or civilian governmental post. As can be imagined, there was opposition to this proposal, especially from the supporters of some of the current military leaders and from those

Sir William Waller, a Parliamentary general who called for a change of army organisation.

Robert Devereux, Earl of Essex, Parliamentary Lord General until April 1645.

sitting in the House of Lords who could not resign their seats in Parliament. Members of the Commons, Oliver Cromwell included, could resign their parliamentary seats and therefore be eligible to hold high civil or military office. At the same time as the preparation of this Ordinance, Cromwell had charged Manchester with prosecuting the war reluctantly and incompetently. Cromwell had also warned Parliament that the people of the country were disillusioned and that there was a widespread feeling that Members of Parliament were prolonging the struggle solely for personal aggrandisement.

Robert Rich, Earl of Warwick, Lord High Admiral of the Parliament's Navy.

The outcome of these machinations was the resignation from military command of Essex, Manchester, William Waller, the Earl of Warwick (the Lord Admiral of the Navy, which had almost wholly supported Parliament), and several other less senior military commanders. The decision to remodel the militia was also implemented and the New Model Army came into being, commanded by Sir Thomas Fairfax, a 33-year-old experienced soldier from Yorkshire. In the field this army carried all before it, defeating the Royalists at the Battles of Naseby and Langport in 1645 and Torrington in 1646 as well as reducing many Royalist fortresses and garrisons by siege and assault during that period.

During the forty days allowed for parliamentary resignations from command, Fairfax obtained parliamentary authority for Cromwell to take up the post of lieutenant-general of horse in the New Model Army for a limited period of just weeks at first. As the war progressed this authority was extended several times for longer periods until it became virtually permanent.

The effect of the Self-Denying Ordinance was to create a clear division between the political and the military leaders in Parliament's prosecution of the war, with, initially, the military subordinated to the political leadership. Several of the displaced commanders, including Essex, Manchester, William Waller and his cousin, Hardress Waller, remained members of the Committee of Both Kingdoms and therefore were still very involved in military decision-making.

This was the situation in 1646 after the defeat of King Charles's forces. Parliament and its Scottish allies had gained complete military victory. After the Royalist defeat at Rowton Heath near Chester on 24 September 1645 the King had returned to his headquarters in Christ Church College, Oxford, where he stayed, contemplating his future action. Royalist hopes in Scotland had also been dashed by the

Sir Thomas Fairfax, Lord General of the New Model Army.

defeat on 11 September 1645 of the King's Captain-General there, James Graham, the Marquess of Montrose. He had, with small resources, conducted a brilliant campaign, winning several victories against the Covenanters ranged against him until a force under David Leslie was sent from the Scots Army in England. Montrose was surprised at Philiphaugh in the Borders and put to rout.

It is important to appreciate that in the struggle between the King and the Westminster Parliament the majority of the population did not actively take sides. For example, in Yorkshire 240 of the 680 gentry families remained neutral during the war. In Cheshire the recorded number of neutral gentry families was 104 from a total of 200, while it was estimated that 60 per cent of such Lancastrian families remained

James Graham, Marquess of Montrose, the King's Captain-General in Scotland.

Oliver Cromwell, MP for Huntingdon, Lieutenant-General of the New Model Army, later Lord Protector.

uncommitted. Of the merchants of Bristol it is thought that about 85 per cent offered dedicated support to neither side, a remarkable figure for a city considered to be of vital importance by both. There were very few ordinary people who were fervent in support for either cause, only participating as followers of local gentry or as impressed men, forcibly conscripted by the soldier-hungry armies.[8]

The armies of both sides were regarded by civilians, with very good cause, as predatory. Before Fairfax took charge of the New Model Army and exercised firm control, the Parliamentarians vied with the Royalists in their ill-treatment of the local populations. Eventually this gave rise to the Peace Associations, or the Clubmen as they were called. These were formed by large numbers of local men who banded together to oppose the depradations of the soldiers of whichever side and to try to bring about peace through negotiation; the associations kept order locally. The movement had spread by late 1645 and was active in South Wales and in the counties of Hereford, Worcester, Somerset, Wiltshire, Dorset, Hampshire and Sussex. The victories of the Parliamentarians brought the peace that these associations sought, but the very existence of these groups forced the leaders of both sides to take note of and action against them in some of these areas, as they were seen as an illegal challenge to lawful authority.

The end of fighting would bring a measure of relief to the beleaguered people of the country, especially as there were bad harvests to come for the five years after 1646.[9] There was little relief, however, for the King who now faced the distasteful prospect of having to treat with rebels.

He had written to the Speaker of the House of Lords on 29 January 1646 offering concessions, including the right of Parliament to nominate officers for the army, navy and government posts as well as judges for specific periods. He suggested the disbandment of all forces either in garrisons or elsewhere and a freedom for all to worship as their consciences directed if they were unable to accept Presbyterianism. He offered an Act of Oblivion, or free pardon, for England as well as Scotland. These offers, renewed in March, were ignored by his enemies as they were no longer threatened by Royalist forces. It is significant that this letter was addressed to the Speaker of the House of Lords rather than to the House of Commons. By this time the Speaker of the Lords was the Earl of Manchester who, as ever, was ready to negotiate. This was a method of communication which irritated the Commons, as they showed later.[10] Although this is probably why the King acted in this way.

While King Charles appeared to make many concessions to the hated rebels, the final paragraph of this letter is significant as it reveals that fundamentally he was determined to preserve his major prerogatives. He concluded, with some defiance: 'And now, His Majesty having so fully and clearly expressed his intentions and desired of making a happy and well-grounded peace; if any person shall decline that happiness, by opposing so apparent a way of attaining it, he will sufficiently demonstrate to all the world, his intention and design can be no other than the total subversion and change of the ancient and happy government of this kingdom, under which the English nation hath so long flourished.'[11] It seems clear from this that King Charles was well aware of the divisions which existed in the ranks of his enemies. He knew of the desire for peace among many in Parliament, especially the majority group, the Presbyterians.

So, having failed to achieve his ends through military means, the King was planning to divide his enemies politically by careful, crafty and selective negotiation. There certainly were divisions he could exploit. Tension existed between the Lords and the Commons and between the Scots and their English allies. The Scots were unhappy with the Westminster Parliament, which was particularly slow in providing its contracted regular supply of money, just as there was delay in imposing the Presbyterian religion in England as had been agreed when the English Parliament accepted the Covenant. They were also well aware of the increasingly active Independents who advocated freedom of worship and were opposed to the imposition of Presbyterianism on the English.

On this topic the Independents' thoughts were similar to those of the King, who wrote to his wife on 19 February, 'For I assure thee, I put little or no difference between setting up the Presbyterian government, or submitting to the Church of Rome.' He went on to confess that he had made concessions to the rebels 'for public respects' and 'that a relapse now would be insufferable'.[12] By 'relapse' he meant a weakening of his resolve to gain what he wanted. In fact he demonstrated in a postscript to the same letter that he had by no means given up the fight. He wrote, 'For God's sake, as thou lovest me, see what may be done for the landing of the 5,000 men [from Ireland], at the place and by the time as I wrote to thee the 1st February, and with them as much money as possibly thou canst. I assure thee that the well-doing of this is likely to save both my crown and liberty.'

Through the agency of the Queen, who was still in Paris, and the efforts of the French Court to try to obtain a settlement in Britain which would be to their advantage, a French diplomatist, Jean de Montereul (whose name is often given as Montreuil), had been sent to undertake secret negotiations with the Scots for the resolution of their dispute with King Charles. This, combined with the King's continued quarrel with the English Parliament, threatened to

Oxford, where the King had
his headquarters in the 1640s.

perpetuate a disunited Britain which would pose less of a threat to
French interests in the future.

Montereul, a Paris lawyer in his early thirties, found those
Commissioners of the Scottish Parliament resident in London
receptive to his idea of negotiation with the King. However, he
wrote that he could not understand their fixation with the
replacement of the Anglican form of worship with their Presbyterian
model in face of opposition from the King and many English people.
It is possible that as a Catholic Montereul considered both forms of
religion to be heretically irrelevant. He discounted the claim that if
both countries had the same religion it would lessen the Scots' fears
of future aggression from their old enemy. A common religion had
hardly ever prevented countries going to war in the past.[13]

The French envoy had discussed matters with the King at Oxford
in January and he was dismayed at the King's adamant refusal to
countenance the Anglican Church being replaced by Presbyterianism
in England. He reported that the King had said that, '. . . conscience
would not allow him to consent to the ruin of the religion he had
sworn to maintain, and that he would rather lose his crown than his
soul'.[14] Montereul, the worldly wise pragmatist, was astonished at
this statement and it was probably his incredulity at the religious
stubbornness of both parties which led to the ultimate failure of his
efforts to bring about a settlement.

After discussions with the Scots Commissioners in London, he
travelled to the area of Newark where the Earl of Leven's Covenanter
Army was assisting the Parliamentarians in the siege of that Royalist
stronghold. There he had talks with the senior officers, subsequently,
on 1 April, telling the King that should he decide to come to the
Scots he would be received 'as their natural sovereign and that he
shall be with them in all freedom of his conscience and honour'.[15]

The King's plan to travel to the Scots Army was evident in a letter he sent to James Butler, the Marquess of Ormond, his Lord Deputy and Commander-in-Chief in Ireland, on 13 April. He wrote, repeating almost verbatim the Scottish promises which Montereul had recorded in his letter, 'Having lately received very good Security that we and all that do or shall adhere to us, shall be safe in our Persons, Honours and Consciences in the Scottish Army; and that they shall really and effectually join with us, . . . and shall employ their Armies and Forces to assist us to the procuring of a happy and well-grounded peace . . .'. He continued, '. . . We are resolved to use our best Endeavour with their Assistance, and with the Conjunction of the Forces under the Marquess of Montrose, and such as of our well-affected Subjects of England, shall rise for us to procure, if it may be, an honourable and Speedy Peace.'[16]

It also would appear from these extracts that the King was only too well aware of the weakness of his current position. It would be far preferable to be able to negotiate from strength. Even so, King Charles must have realised that if he were with the Scots that very fact would tend to increase the distrust which seemed to be growing in the enemy alliance.

There was also a pressing need for the King to leave Oxford before the full strength of the New Model Army completely encircled the city. At 2 a.m. on 27 April 1646, disguised as the servant of John Ashburnham, his Groom of the Bedchamber, and guided by a clergyman, Dr Michael Hudson, who was familiar with the proposed route, the King left Oxford for the last time.

There is, in contemporary accounts, some uncertainty about his intended destination. Clarendon considers that the King himself was unsure of what to do. It is possible that he might have considered going to London to 'lie there concealed till he might choose that which was best . . .'.[17] The evidence of the King's letter to Ormond may seem to argue against this, even though when Hudson was subsequently questioned he said that their route had been to Henley, Harrow in the Hill and Brentford, as though the King might enter London; then north to St Albans and on to (Market) Harborough where Montereul was to have met them with a Scottish escort. The Frenchman did not appear and so they went to Stamford in Lincolnshire. From there they rode to Downham in Norfolk where the King 'lay at a petty Ale-House'.[18]

At Baldock, in Hertfordshire, the King had sent Hudson ahead to make contact with Montereul. Hudson failed to do so at the planned

King Charles I as portrayed by
van Dyke in 1640.

rendezvous at Market Harborough and rode on to Southwell, where
he found the Frenchman at the Scots Army headquarters, the Scots
having refused to send a cavalry escort for the King. This, and
subsequent days of uncertainty over the King's whereabouts, caused
Montereul much concern.

In Norfolk the King declined as too uncertain Ashburnham's
advice to find a sea-going vessel which would take him to Scotland
to join with Montrose. This would also sow the seeds of suspicion in
the minds of the Covenanters at a time when the most productive
way of continuing negotiations was to join Montereul, who was still
with the Scottish Army. In the meantime, Hudson discovered that

the Scots would not commit to paper any of the conditions on which they were prepared to receive the King. They did, however, allow him to record the following to avoid any misunderstanding;

1. That they should secure the King in his person and honour. 2. That they should press the King to do nothing contrary to his conscience. 3. That Mr. Ashburnham and I should be protected. 4. That if Parliament refused, upon a message from the King, to restore the King to his rights and prerogatives, they should declare for the King, and take all the King's friends into their protection. And if the Parliament did condescend to restore the King . . . not above four of them [Royalists] should suffer banishment; and none at all death. . . .[19]

Montereul was surprised that these conditions were far more generous than the Scottish Commissioners in London had been prepared to grant, but he assured Hudson that the Scots were serious in their intention to keep to them and he wrote a note to that effect. Armed with these written details, Hudson returned to the King, obviously at a pre-arranged rendezvous, and His Majesty decided on the strength of these assurances to ride to the Scottish Army.

Clarendon later wrote of the King, 'He was always an immoderate lover of the Scottish nation, having not only been born there, but educated by that people, and besieged by them always, having few English about him until he was king; and the major number of his servants being still of those, who he thought could never fail him. . . .'[20] Events were to test this sentiment very severely. The King was never again to be a completely free man.

CHAPTER THREE

The King and the Scots

. . . the stubborn they chastise

George Crabbe, *The Library*

The Scots had been aware since shortly after Montereul came to them that the King might join them at their headquarters. Alexander Leslie, the Earl of Leven and their Army commander, had travelled from Newcastle to Newark in anticipation of the King's arrival. On 4 May instructions had been sent to Sir James Lumsden, still at Newcastle, to make arrangements there to receive the King. Even so, when the King appeared at Newark it came as a surprise.

On the morning of Tuesday 5 May 'General Leven having Intelligence that His Majesty was come into their Garrison, for some officers that were upon the Guard that saw Him, and had some suspicion of Him that it was the King, . . . a search was made three hours before they could hear where he was'.[1] At about noon the King sent a message to Leven telling him that he was with Montereul at Southwell. The General then alerted the Scottish Commissioners who always accompanied the Army and together they went to meet their King.

For greater safety they took King Charles to David Leslie's camp at Kelham, where 'there was much amazement to see into how low a condition His Majesty was brought'. The King's appearance after travelling and hiding disguised as a servant for nine days was startling. He was dishevelled, having slept in his clothes the previous night, and further, 'His beard was shaved and His Locks cut.'[2] At Kelham Sir James Turner reported that the Earl of Lothian, as President of the Scottish Commissioners with the Army,

> . . . to his eternal reproach, imperiously require his Majesty (before he had either drunk, refreshed or reposed himself), to command

Alexander Leslie, Earl of Leven, commanding general of the Scots Covenanter Army in England.

my Lord Bellasis to deliver up Newark to the Parliament's forces, to sign the Covenant, to order the establishment of presbyterian government in England and Ireland, and to command James Graham (for so he called Great Montrose), to lay down arms; all which the King stoutly refused; telling him that he who had made him an Earl had made James Graham a Marquess. Barbarously used he was, strong guards put upon him, and sentinels at all his windows.[3]

William Kerr, Earl of Lothian, Scottish Comissioner who bullied the King at Newark.

There was no excuse for Lothian's rudeness. It was, as the account shows, counter-productive, since it drew an indirect but nevertheless sharp reminder from the King that his intemperate subject owed his present status to His Majesty and that Montrose, to whom Lothian referred without courtesy, was his superior in rank. The aggressive tone which Hudson described, coupled with the lack of personal consideration for his immediate needs, aroused the royal anger and increased the King's determination to resist such importuning. This early exchange did not augur well for the forthcoming negotiations.

This censure of the Scots' precautions of strong guards and sentinels as implied insults and further discourtesy to the King overlooks the Scots' concern that one of two parties might attempt to take the King from their control. They were clearly worried about the reaction of their English allies, whose strong forces around Newark might try to capture the monarch, and there was always the chance that Lord Bellasis and the Royalist garrison of Newark might attack to release the King, if he should let them know that he had changed his mind. These eventualities had obviously been considered at the planning stage before the King arrived. The immediate move from Southwell to Kelham, where there was a strong concentration of Scottish troops, was one indication of this, as was the plan to take the King to Newcastle for which orders were issued the day before he arrived.

The Earl of Lothian was careful on the very day of the King's arrival to inform the English Commissioners who were with the Scottish Army of the event which 'having overtaken us unexpectedly hath filled us with amazement and made us like men that dream'.[4] He went on to assure their allies that it was unlikely that the King should have come to them unless he had the intention 'to give full satisfaction to both kingdoms in their just and reasonable demand in all those things which concern religion and righteousness'. He also stressed that whatever the outcome the alliance with England, 'the Solemn League and Covenant', was strong.

The remains of the castle at Newark-on-Trent, a Royalist stronghold.

This letter is a fine example of the old adage that a half-truth is like a half-brick; it goes further. Lothian does not actually lie, neither does he reveal the whole truth. The Scots were well aware that the King planned to come to them, but the timing of the royal arrival came as a surprise. However, the secret negotiations, with Montereul and through him with the King, remain undisclosed. It is no surprise that the King obviously thought long and hard before he finally committed himself into the hands of his Scottish Covenanter subjects. Montereul had had some misgivings about their reliability.

One of Leven's secretaries was sent as a messenger to the Scottish Commissioners resident in London with an account of His Majesty's arrival. This would have enabled the Scots to inform their allies, the English Parliament, of developments to allay the suspicion that the Scots were negotiating a separate peace with the King. News of these latest events could have added to the unease which was already present in England.

On 5 May, after further discussion with the Earl of Leven, the King agreed to order Bellasis and the Royalist garrison to negotiate an immediate surrender upon reasonable terms. There were three

John, Lord Bellasis, the Royalist Commander and Governor of Newark.

factors which could have contributed to the Scottish insistence on the surrender of Newark. It made sense from a military point of view to capture a very strong Royalist fortification. Also they wanted to increase their control of the King by moving him to Newcastle, which was nearer Scotland and in a region which could be even more strongly garrisoned if the whole of their Army were there. Finally, while having successfully moved the King, they would have wished to have avoided the charge of deserting their allies, the English Parliamentary troops, by leaving them unsupported before a large garrison of a strongly held Royalist town in order to further their own, Scottish, ends.

David Leslie, later Earl of Newark, Lieutenant-General of the Scots Covenanter Army.

On 6 May Bellasis obeyed the King's order to surrender Newark and the following afternoon the Scottish Army began its march north, the King riding with the lieutenant-general, David Leslie, and the cavalry. The Scottish efforts to co-operate with their English allies drew approval from, it seems, one of the English Commissioners who resided with the Scottish Army. A letter to London written from Newark on 7 May said that the King had, '. . . marched away Northwards with all the Scots Army, . . . we believe it is only into fresh Quarters, till the desires of the Parliament may be signified unto them, how they would have the Army disposed of. We have found a very exceeding fair correspondence with the old Scots General and all the Commissioners, who have been ready to comply with us in all reasonable demands.'[5]

As long as the King remained with the Scots, however, there would be English uncertainty about the intentions of their allies, especially after the Scots had taken him northwards.

There was another more mercenary reason than the religious and political arguments given by the Scottish Parliament and its Commissioners to substantiate their alliance with the English Parliament. The Scots Armies in England and Ireland had not received the agreed pay from London for many months and even those now in immediate attendance on King Charles 'were long since in rags'.[6] If the alliance were to rupture, the Scots would most likely never receive the money owed to them.

Writing in his memoirs in 1670, ten years after the Restoration and possibly allowing his memory to portray events in a more favourable light, Sir James Turner, the experienced soldier who was Adjutant-General to the Scots Army, related how on the march to Newcastle the King 'bade me tell him the sense of our army concerning him. I did so, and withall assured him he was a prisoner, and therefore prayed him to think of his escape, offering him all the service I could do him . . . but our conversation was interrupted very uncivilly . . . neither was I ever permitted afterward to speak with him'.[7] When the Scots left Durham on 13 May Leven ordered his army to have nothing to do with any persons who had formerly fought against the English Parliament, neither were they to accept 'any gift, pension, or mark of honour from his Majesty'.

Sir James Turner, Adjutant-General in the Scots Army in England, who warned the King that he was a prisoner.

One of the King's plans was to dispute matters of religion with the Scottish Presbyterian clergy, to challenge their doctrine. He began this en route to Newcastle and, having reached Durham on 12 May, he debated with some of the most able ministers who accompanied the Scottish Army.

The King's arrival at Newcastle on 13 May, escorted by a detachment of some 300 horse, was without ceremony. 'Some that attended upon his Majesty rode before all bare[headed], then his Majesty marched with the General, and some other Scottish officers, divers of who also that were near the King rode bare'.[8] There was no civic reception committee, as the local dignitaries had been forbidden to make any such arrangements and known Royalists had been forbidden to enter the city. The King is quoted as seeming 'melancholy and very grey with cares', the nature of the reception

Anderson Place, Newcastle upon Tyne, where the King was held by the Covenanters.

apparently confirming to him Turner's view that he was a prisoner, especially when a guard of musketeers was mounted at his quarters. Other trustworthy guardians were appointed from the city's population to take note of all people entering or leaving. No one was allowed to enter without an official pass.

There now began a period of weeks in which the King was subjected to many and continuous demands to accept the Covenant and to replace the episcopacy of the Church of England with the Calvinistic theology and organisation of Presbyterianism. It should not be assumed that the King resented these pressures. He seemed to relish the opportunity to convert the Scottish theologians to his own view of religion. Shortly after his arrival, he asked that the foremost theologian of the day, Alexander Henderson, be summoned from Edinburgh to debate with him those religious principles which, in his innermost heart, he was determined to defend.

Alexander Henderson, eminent Scottish theologian, with whom the King debated.

As was to be expected, while these events took place in the north and news of the King's action was digested, the Parliament at Westminster was in a state of confusion. Suspicion of the Scots' motives deepened and there were calls for the withdrawal of the Covenanter Army from England now that the Royalists were beaten. Parliament also wished to reduce the size and costs of their own army, which was becoming increasingly politically and professionally restless.

For the English Presbyterians the withdrawal of the Scots Army was essential before any disbandment of Fairfax's troops could be ordered. It would have been foolish to reduce the English forces while the army of another nation, no matter how friendly its protestations, remained on English soil. Another reason to hasten the Scots' withdrawal was the constant complaint of northcountrymen about the demanding behaviour of the Scottish soldiers. Of increasing concern to the Presbyterian majority in the Houses of Parliament was evidence of the influence that the Independent faction had already established within the New Model Army. This influence had always been markedly present in some regiments, especially in the Horse, as indicated by the critical Presbyterian observation, 'Look on Col. Fleetwood's regiment with his Major Harrison, what a cluster of preaching officers and troopers there is'.[9] The distinction between Presbyterian and Independent was becoming more of a political than a religious issue. From the Presbyterians' point of view the sooner some of the more politically active of Fairfax's regiments were disbanded, the better.

On 19 May the House of Commons had voted 'That this Kingdom hath no further Use of the Continuing of the Scots Army within the Kingdom of England'.[10] There would be a price attached to this resolution, however, as it was realised that in order to encourage the Scots to leave the English would have to face the daunting prospect of paying the arrears owed.

The King was not slow to add a little fuel to the debate. On 18 May he wrote to the English recommending a speedy settling of the religious question by taking the advice of the clergy of both kingdoms assembled at Westminster.[11] He also offered the Lords and Commons the right to name all military commanders for a period of seven years after which the responsibility for this would be shared by the King and Parliament. He proposed the same terms to the Scottish Parliament.

In the meantime the King's personal isolation deepened with the departure of John Ashburnham by sea for Holland and the detention of Dr Michael Hudson, despite previous Scottish promises to the contrary. Hudson was then sent to London for questioning as had been requested earlier by the Parliament.

One cannot but appreciate the stresses and strains to which the King was now being subjected. He was now not only far away from his beloved family, but he no longer had the company of loyal friends following the departure of his two companions. All Royalist sympathisers had been excluded from him and he was surrounded by watchful guards. Further, he was being increasingly harassed by Scottish visitors who demanded concessions of policy in beliefs he considered sacrosanct. He lacked most of the attendance to which he was accustomed and resented the way in which his captors treated him.

It says a great deal for the King and his determined character that he was able to resist the many pressures being exerted upon him by the Parliaments of Scotland and England. The quiet, reserved, hesitant young boy had developed an inflexible will and nerves of steel, based upon an unshakeable religious faith and concept of kingship. These ideals, allied with his continual efforts to exploit divisions among his adversaries, made him a formidable opponent. Clarendon's assessment that Charles was a shrewd judge of situations but that he often lacked confidence in his own judgment and deferred to the inferior advice of others would seem to be confirmed. Now the King had no one, inferior or superior in intelligence, to advise him. He was alone and would have to rely on his own skills in debate and discussion. He was to give a good account of himself, determined never to yield to his enemies.

With a view to further dividing his enemies, the King wrote to the Lord Mayor of the City of London and to the Lord Provost of Edinburgh, telling them that he was ready 'to comply with our Parliaments in everything for settling truth and peace'. This was a clever move as the City of London was the English Parliamentary banker and played a vital role when the monthly 'contributions' demanded from the counties, cities, towns and other places were slow in arriving, which they invariably were. The City of London had also raised the loan of £80,000 necessary to pay for the establishment of the New Model Army, its men, weapons, equipment, uniforms, horses and food. The monthly cost of the Army was over £53,000 – a massive bill at this time.

If King Charles could undermine the confidence which the mainly Presbyterian-inclined City of London had in the Parliament, he would deal his enemies a serious blow. Also, if he hoped to re-establish royal control in Scotland, the support of Edinburgh would be vital. There is guile in his careful selection of the phrase 'truth and peace', which was open to wide interpretation. It could mean granting everything the Parliaments wanted, or, as it certainly meant, settling matters based on the King's version of truth. In most matters of negotiation with His Majesty it was absolutely necessary to understand what he meant by his choice of particular words and phrases. Such differences in interpretation increased a belief that the King's word could never be trusted.

Rumours were rife in London that the Scots had made an agreement with the King to the exclusion of the English Parliament. When this news reached Newcastle in late May the Scots hurriedly issued a public Declaration of Denial, saying that it was always their intention to maintain the Covenant between the two kingdoms and that 'they abhorred all public and private Ways tending to violate the same, or to create a Misunderstanding between the two nations'.[12]

One can visualise the King's secret smile, reflecting a deep sense of pleasure, when he heard of this heavily defensive declaration. It amounted to a firm public denial that smacked of guilt. Even if the Scots had not actually concluded an agreement with the King, the vehemence of their defence could have indicated to their suspicious Parliamentary allies that it might have been in their minds to do so. If King Charles could not engineer a positive fracture between his main enemies, he could heighten their mutual distrust by exploiting the circumstances, by giving one of them 'something to deny'.[13]

His captors allowed His Majesty to write letters, especially if the contents of these appeared to aid their cause. There are records at this time of letters to his faithful supporters at Oxford, Sir Edward Nicholas the Secretary of State and Sir Thomas Glemham, now the city's governor, instructing them to secure good terms for the surrender of the former Royalist headquarters, disband their forces and, if possible, arrange for young James, Duke of York to join him in Newcastle. He also wrote to the Prince of Wales 'to tell you where I am' and ordering him to obey his mother, the Queen, in all things except in matters of religion.[14] Later, he wrote to Montrose commanding him to lay down his arms and subsequently to the Earl of Antrim, who had been reported as landing with Irish troops in Scotland, ordering him to follow Montrose's example and end the fight. These letters must have been a pleasure to the Covenanters, as there now would be no Royalist forces active in Scotland.

Sir Edward Nicholas, the King's Secretary of State.

On 17 June he wrote to Henrietta Maria giving her a serio-comic analysis of Scottish political groupings. He wrote, 'I divide them into four factions: Montrose, the neutrals, the Hamiltons, and the Campbells. The second hath no declared head, but Callander may be said to be chief of them; as for the others, it is ignorance to ask who were theirs. The first three seem to correspond, the last two are avowed enemies, the second keeps fair quarter with all, and none of them trusts one another.' He continues by discussing individual nobles, their characteristics and their attitudes towards him, some hostile, others ingratiating. He ends with the revealing sentence, 'I hope God hath sent me hither for the last punishment that He will inflict upon me for my sins, for assuredly no honest man can prosper in these people's company.'[15]

Consideration of the King's situation and his reactions to it leads one to visualise a small, but determined spider with larger, seemingly more powerful insects buzzing dangerously around, while the tiny insect-eater manipulates a slender and inadequate web, gaining minor triumphs against its numerous adversaries.

Charles's defiance and a further example of his willingness to respond on being harassed over religious matters were evident in an exchange between him and a Scottish minister. Having preached at the King, the minister closed his harangue with a call for the 52nd Psalm, which begins, 'Why boastest thou thyself in mischief, O mighty man?' At which His Majesty stood up and responded with

Archibald Campbell, Earl of Argyle, leader of the Scottish Covenanters.

the opening verse of Psalm 56, 'Be merciful unto me, O God: for man would swallow me up; the fighting daily oppresseth me.'[16]

The King was soon to be further oppressed when the English Parliament, after consultation with its Scottish allies, sent Commissioners to him with proposals for a settlement which became known as the Newcastle Propositions.[17] These very comprehensive terms included all that had been put forward by Parliament at the treaty talks at Uxbridge in late 1644–5.[18] The King had firmly rejected these at the time. The latest version of these conditions was even stricter because of the King's weakened situation.

The Parliamentary Commissioners presented the document to the King on 24 July, telling him that they were only able to remain at Newcastle for ten days. The Scottish Lord Chancellor, the Earl of Loudon, urged the King to accept these proposals. On 1 August the King replied that they involved so great a change in the government of Church and both kingdoms that further explanation and discussion were required. He suggested that he should be allowed to go to London to 'have those Doubts cleared and those Difficulties explained to him'. He assured them, 'That as he could never condescend to what was absolutely destructive to that just Power which by the Laws of God and the land he was born unto, so he would cheerfully grant and give Assent to all such Bills as should be really for the Good and Peace of his People, not having regard to his own particular.'[19]

This was clearly a delaying tactic and as such gave some satisfaction to the Independents in England, who did not want a settlement which imposed the Presbyterian Church throughout their country. The King's wish to negotiate in London was his attempt to be able to influence more people in his favour and also to have greater opportunity to foster quarrels among his enemies. He had long realised in his struggles that his main enemy was the Westminster Parliament, which controlled the greater wealth.

At about this time the Scottish Commissioners in London passed on the offer to withdraw their army from England, provided they received all arrears of money due to them. They also suggested further talks as a result of the King's failure to accept the Newcastle Propositions.

A prolonged and unseemly haggle over the amount of money due to the Scots ensued. The Scots submitted a claim for £2 million; the English Parliament offered £200,000. The Scots retorted with a request for £500,000; Parliament bid £300,000. The Scots said they

James Livingstone, Earl of Callander, notional leader of the neutrals in Scotland.

would accept £400,000, to which Parliament agreed, but only if half was paid when the Scots Army departed and the balance made as instalments at various specified times. It was this financial transaction which led to Montrose's claim in November 1649 that the Scots had sold the King to Parliament in England for the sum of £400,000. There appears to be no written evidence to support this assertion, just as there is none to disprove it, at least in part. It is possible that the prospect of money had an influence upon the King's removal to England, but it is certain that this money was not in direct payment for the transfer of the King.

The Scots, even after the financial agreement about the withdrawal of their army, still continued to press the King to accept the Newcastle Propositions. It was even arranged for Scotland's premier duke, James, Duke of Hamilton to be released from imprisonment at St Michael's Mount in Cornwall so that he and others could plead with King Charles to accept these terms. If the Scots had sold the King and he had, as a result of their pleas, then changed his mind and accepted the terms offered, this would have invalidated any cash contract with the English Parliament and the Scots would not have been paid. Therefore, the Scots' persistent efforts to reach a settlement would indicate that the payment they were to receive was truly for the costs their army had incurred in England.

The removal of the King to England after the financial agreement has given rise to the belief that '*post hoc ergo propter hoc*' – that as the event came after the financial agreement, it came about because of that agreement.

The King told Hamilton and the others that he had not rejected the proposals, but had merely asked for a clear explanation of them. The following day in another attempt to divide his enemies he offered a concession on the religious dispute over the bishops of the Episcopal Church. He wrote saying that he would be content to keep bishops in some dioceses, naming Oxford, Winchester, Bristol, Bath and Wells, and Exeter, leaving the rest of England to Presbyterian government, 'with the strictest clauses they could think upon against Papists and Independents'.[20] Such a suggestion might find favour with the Presbyterians but would certainly anger the Independents, who favoured a greater freedom of worship than the Presbyterians would allow, although this did not extend to Catholics.

In September the Westminster Parliament, agreeing that the King's future should be a matter decided by both the Lords and Commons, began discussions with the Scots. The view of the two

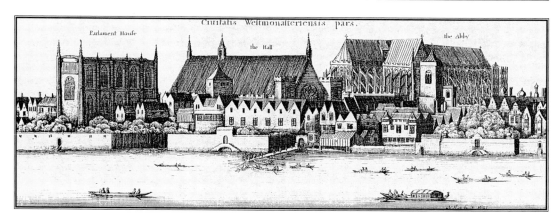

A view of Westminster, the centre of English Parliamentary activity, 1647.

allies differed. The Scots asserted that as Charles was King of both countries his future personal status, detained or free, should be a matter for both particularly as they had a common interest through the Covenant.

The English replied that as the King was in England decisions about his future role were matters for them alone. Although he had retired to the Scots Army, this force, paid for by the Westminster Parliament, was not independent but an auxiliary of the New Model Army. Therefore, it was as if the King had come to the Parliamentary Army, of which the Scots were merely a part.

The Scottish Lord Chancellor, Loudon, proposed that as it was too dangerous for the King to live free in Scotland because of the continued threat of Royalist intervention from the Highlands or Ireland, he should be allowed to live free in London, or one of the royal palaces, while negotiations were ongoing. He believed that if the King continued to be a prisoner in the south there might be intervention by foreign rulers, instigated by the Prince of Wales or by Queen Henrietta Maria with her influence in mainly Catholic Europe. Loudon must have been aware that there was no chance that the King would be allowed to live unrestrained once he was in the power of the English. If he were free there would be no reason to expect the King not to flee if his aims were completely thwarted. Loudon's comments appear to be a justification for handing the King over to the English while still insisting that any decisions should be jointly made and that no one country had the right to arrive at a settlement unilaterally.

The English Parliament was experiencing difficulties in raising the money to pay the Scots for the withdrawal of their army and so

John Campbell, 1st Earl of Loudon, Chancellor of Scotland who urged the King to agree a settlement.

the City of London was asked for a loan of £200,000. The interest charged was 8 per cent and the principal guaranteed from the general excise and the sale of land held by bishops. This latter decision resulted in the hasty sequestering of the lands concerned and a committee was appointed to arrange their early disposal.

In December while the Scottish Parliament declared that it supported the monarchy in the person of the King and his just title to the throne of England, the General Assembly of the Church of Scotland made a powerful statement. It ruled that as long as the King did not approve in his heart and seal with his own hand the League and Covenant, he could not be received in Scotland without exposing that kingdom to fresh troubles. On receipt of this clerical blast, the Scottish Parliament fell into line, refusing permission for the King to come to Scotland unless he accepted in full the Newcastle Propositions and the Covenant. Such was the power of the Kirk in Scotland.

As the Scots Army was preparing to leave England, with some of its arrears in hand, there was nowhere for the King to go but into the orbit of the Westminster Parliament. He himself was content to leave Scottish control and, as he hoped, to go to London to negotiate. He was to be disappointed. The Lords voted that he should go to Newmarket, but the Commons ruled that he should go to Holdenby (sometimes called Holmby) House in Northamptonshire. A Parliamentary Commission was appointed to bring the King to the south, consisting of three Members of the Lords and six Members of the House of Commons, including Philip Herbert, Earl of Pembroke and Basil Feilding, Earl of Denbigh. On 23 January they arrived at Newcastle and a week later on 30 January 1647 the King was escorted by them out of the hands of his Scottish subjects.

No doubt His Majesty viewed with anticipation the prospect of negotiations where he might be able to influence wider English opinion on his behalf. He had during his stay in Newcastle successfully resisted all pressure to compromise his deeply held beliefs. While he may have congratulated himself, it is likely that he did not appreciate that although his determination not to compromise may have brought him a limited satisfaction, his continued stubbornness might do much more to exasperate and thus erode any support from those of his opponents who held moderate, conciliatory opinions.

Philip Herbert, Earl of Pembroke and Montgomery, one of the Parliamentary Commissioners to the King in Newcastle upon Tyne.

Basil Feilding, Earl of Denbigh, a Parliamentary general and Commissioner to the King at Newcastle upon Tyne.

CHAPTER FOUR

The King and the English

With long arrears to make good
When the English began to hate
Rudyard Kipling, *The Beginnings*

Had the King extended his amusing analysis of the Scottish political situation to that in England, he would have produced a veritable spectrum of fractured and fracturing policies with shifting alliances, rather than the simple four-segmented picture of Scottish groupings and personalities he outlined for the Queen.[1]

Initially it is difficult to understand complex matters unless one starts from the simple, almost the simplistic facts and then analyses further. The simple labelling of groups, people or ideas is a human trait which helps understanding but, more often than not, leads to mistaken assumptions and wrong conclusions. The patterns of human aims and endeavours are seldom neat, tidy or easily understood. So it was when the King was escorted south to Holdenby House.

Superficially the political circumstances facing the King were straightforward. There were three major political groupings in England: those who were for him; those who opposed him; and the neutrals, or 'neuters' as they were sometimes scornfully called.

In 1647 the Royalists, although severely shaken by military defeat, were by no means completely conquered even if increasing numbers of them were 'compounding', that is, paying fines to Parliament as penalties for their active support of the King and to recover confiscated lands and property. The neutrals, many of whom

Holdenby (Holmby) House,
Northamptonshire, where the
English Parliament held the
King.

had been robbed, pillaged and taxed beyond forbearance, were
themselves divided by inclination. Some, as in Wiltshire, Dorset and
East Somerset, had according to Sir Thomas Fairfax been 'ready to
declare for the King' in 1645.[2] Others, about 6,000 in number, from
Gloucestershire and other parts of Somerset and Wiltshire, had
assisted Fairfax in his successful siege and storming of Bristol. Many
others kept strictly to themselves, merely attempting to live
peacefully although surrounded by threat and turmoil. In every
upheaval of general human conflict there have been some who were
concerned only to cultivate their gardens, or develop their skills in
some interest, determinedly disregarding the events around them as
they struggled to survive insanity. There have always been others
who know or care about nothing apart from their own immediate
concerns. While some try to rest from the heavy demands of political
life by 'getting away from it all', other folk live there.[3]

The most complex patterns of difference could be found among
the King's English opponents. They were made up of three main
groupings: the Members of Parliament; men of influence outside
Parliament, such as the leaders of the City of London or the County
Committees; and finally, the victorious Parliamentary armies.

Parliament was divided between the House of Lords and the House of Commons, each of which had its own internal divisions that were mainly based on the broad religious labels of Presbyterian and Independent. These categories themselves concealed distinctions. Some Presbyterians were closer to the Scottish Calvinistic theological belief in predestination than many others were, while the term Independent covered a growing number of religious sects. The challenge to the social and religious authority of the established church, the Church of England, brought forth many Biblical interpretations, or political tenets justified by Biblical reference around which adherents might form a sect. These sects and the more radical political concepts that were evolving played a major role in establishing the context in which future events took place, although they actually had little direct involvement in these events. Active roles were reserved for determined pragmatists, who may or may not have shared the beliefs of their supporters.

In the House of Lords there was a marked Presbyterian majority, initially under the leadership of the well-respected but ailing former Lord General of the Parliamentary Armies, Robert Devereux, the Earl of Essex. His death on 14 September 1646 was to prove a serious blow to their cause. In the Commons too the Presbyterians had a significant numerical advantage over the Independents.

These divisions were also increasingly present among the officers and soldiers of the Parliamentary forces, particularly in the New Model Army, which was not the only army under Parliamentary command when the war ended. In the north was the force under Major-General Sydenham Poyntz, the victor of Rowton Heath, an army about 10,000 strong. There were also about 3,000 men of the Western Association Brigade. Their wayward behaviour was causing much distress in the western counties in the absence of their former commander Edward Massey. He had been elected as a Recruiter to Parliament as the MP for Wootton Bassett. As with all the Parliamentary forces, the Western Association Brigade's arrears of pay were long overdue. That, and a not unconnected lack of discipline, made this formation notorious for its acts of lawlessness and depredations upon the local people.

By the end of 1646 the Parliamentary armies' arrears of pay amounted to nearly £3 million. The monthly pay bill for the New Model Army alone was about £45,000.[4] Anger over the arrears, concern about current pay and future uncertainty meant that discontent was festering.

A Trooper of Horse of the New Model Army.

The factors which influenced this situation were three-fold. First there was Parliament's very pressing need to save money now that the war in England and Wales had ended. Arrears had to be paid and the many loans repaid. Then there was an urgent need for an army to be sent to Ireland to resolve the problems there. The Royalist truce agreed by the Marquess of Ormond with the native Irish chieftains posed an acute threat to English rule and to the Parliamentary supporters in Ulster and elsewhere. Finally, and most importantly in the longer term but slightly less pressing now that the King was in Parliament's hands, there was the necessity for a satisfactory constitutional settlement that would also resolve the religious differences to the satisfaction of all concerned, including His Majesty.

The most obvious but, as it was to turn out, not the quickest way to save money was to reduce the costs of the Parliamentary armies by a major disbandment. The agreement for the withdrawal of the Scots Army, while costly, had weakened some of the justification for keeping the Parliamentary forces at their wartime strength. The Presbyterians would have viewed the departure of the Scots, the determined advocates of Presbyterianism, with mixed feelings. Neither would it have been wholly welcomed by the Independents, since with no Scots Army on English soil one reason for delaying the reduction of the New Model Army had disappeared. Serving New Model soldiers currently in their units provided active, vocal and more central support for the Independent cause. Wholesale release from the Army would disperse this advocacy and make it far less effective in London, the main centre of English political power. The plan to dismiss many of the regiments of the armies was not universally acceptable, except in the case of the Western Brigade, which was disbanded without great difficulty by Fairfax and Cromwell later in 1646.

The Self-Denying Ordinance of early 1645 had separated the military from the political authorities with the prospect of subordinating the military to political control. Now, after the war, there were empty seats in the Commons, vacated by MPs who had sided with the King since 1642 and by the deaths of sitting Parliamentary supporters. Recruiter elections ensured the arrival of many Army officers in those empty seats. The subordination of the military to the political authorities was therefore being eroded just as the New Model Army, professionally discontented, was increasingly involving itself in politics.

By a special dispensation Oliver Cromwell had retained his seat in Parliament while he commanded the cavalry of the New Model

Army. Among other officers who joined him at Westminster were Henry Ireton, soon to be his son-in-law, who was elected for Appleby in Yorkshire, Thomas Harrison for Wendover, George Fleetwood for Buckinghamshire, Edmund Ludlow for Wiltshire and John Hutchinson for Nottinghamshire.[5]

The King's journey south from Newcastle was, in one way, a continuation of the conflict through different means. The Parliamentary Commissioners had brought with them two Presbyterian chaplains whose main task was to convert the King to their form of worship and induce him to sign the Covenant which would establish Presbyterianism throughout England and Wales. His Majesty adamantly refused to hear them preach. He was reluctantly prepared to hear sermons from Scottish ministers when he was with the Scots because the dispute over religious matters in that country had long been settled. He showed his determination in this matter even before leaving Newcastle when he granted permission for the Commissioners to hold a service conducted by these two chaplains. Having obtained his agreement, the Commissioners provided a seat for the King to occupy during the celebration. It remained empty throughout – King Charles simply did not attend.[6]

When the journey began it was more like a royal progress than the march of a captive. Although the King was, as he saw it, in the hands of men who behaved as if they were his enemies, those enemies were trying to reach a settlement which acknowledged that the monarch had rights. They proposed that in future the constitution should comprise the King in Parliament, rather than the King, supreme and unchallenged, enforcing a Divine Right to rule as the Lord's Anointed. Moderate opinion had always granted respect to the King and the monarchy. The Parliament had always claimed throughout the war that it had fought 'For King and Parliament' and that His Majesty had been led astray by 'evil counsellors'.

The royal procession that set out from Newcastle on Wednesday 3 February was headed by two equerries, Sir Robert Pye and Colonel Titus, with three led horses. Next rode the King, carrying a military baton. He was followed by the Parliamentary Commissioners and the rest of the entourage. The King was escorted by two regiments of horse, those of Sir Robert Pye and Colonel Richard Graves, another experienced New Model Army soldier, who was in command of all the troops.

By 5 February the King had reached Richmond in North Yorkshire and had been greeted by large numbers of people who left their homes to see him pass. News of his approach invariably drew the local folk on to the roadside to greet him. The numbers varied according to, among other things, the political inclination of the area and its inhabitants.

On Sunday 7 February the King was at Ripon where he still refused to allow the chaplains, the Reverends Marshall and Caryl, to preach or conduct the service. He is reported as having said that 'he could not join in saying Amen to such praying as it is against his conscience'. At Leeds the following day thousands appeared to line the route for about 2 miles, cheering for His Majesty which, it was said, gave much offence to the soldiers of his escort. The journey continued through Wakefield and Rotherham on the next two days, heading for Nottingham.

On the approach to Nottingham the royal column was met by Sir Thomas Fairfax, who had come to pay his respects to the King. When His Majesty was near, Fairfax dismounted and kissed the King's hand in silence. His Majesty was also silent, but later remarked to one of the Commissioners that Fairfax 'was a man of honour, that he hath been faithful to his trust and kept his word with him'. This was a marked change in royal attitude to Sir Thomas, whom the King had described at the setting up of the New Model Army as 'their brutish new general'. Fairfax accompanied the King into Nottingham and the following morning escorted him for 2 miles along the road to Leicester, where King Charles was accommodated at the Angel Inn until Monday 15 February. On the Sunday, determined to the last, Marshall and Caryl preached at the inn, but in His Majesty's equally determined absence.

A musketeer preparing to reload.

On the way to Holdenby the following day word came that the house was not quite ready to receive the King and so he stayed the night at Market Harborough, sleeping, appropriately, at The Crown. The next day saw the last stage of the fourteen-day journey as the King rode through Northampton. The area had been staunchly for Parliament during the war, but this did not prevent the inhabitants and many gentlemen in the vicinity from appearing to greet the King with shouts of 'God Bless Your Majesty!'. This delighted the King who, on hearing the church bells ring and the cannon firing in salute, expressed the view that he hoped this journey would prove to be a prosperous voyage for him and for his posterity.

The King approached Holdenby through the beautiful surrounding countryside. This Elizabethan house had been built for Sir Christopher Hatton, the old Queen's Chancellor and the man who financed Sir Francis Drake's circumnavigation of the globe. Drake's ship, the *Pelican*, had been renamed in Hatton's honour *The Golden Hind*, the animal which figured on Sir Christopher's coat of arms. King James I, King Charles's father, had bought the house in 1607 as a summer residence removed from the hot stench of London and, although little of it now remains, it was celebrated in its day for, among other things, its famous herb garden.

The day after his arrival the King sent Thomas Herbert to Parliament to ask for the attendance of two chaplains, to be selected from a list of twelve names he sent. Parliament, no doubt irritated by the King's attitude to Marshall and Caryl, refused his request. Therefore, there were no religious services at Holdenby, although the King continued to his own devotions.

Life in Northamptonshire was far less lonely and spartan than it had been with the Scots at Newcastle. Here His Majesty was allowed a modicum of state ceremony. He had pages and other Court officials in attendance; the Parliamentary Commissioners waited behind the King's chair at mealtimes and, although he was denied music, trumpets were sounded at the start of meals. Colonel Graves, the commander of the escort, was in constant attendance to ensure not only the King's safety but also to guard against his escape. The vast majority of the escort who were not on duty were quartered some distance away.

Other than matters concerning the negotiations, there was little to do. There was no hunting, field sports, tennis, or any of the games which the King enjoyed until the weather improved in April. Then three days a week he walked to nearby Althorp, later the childhood home and final resting place of Princess Diana, the Princess of Wales.

The embargo on the King sending and receiving letters, other than to and from Parliament, was more rigorously applied by the Parliamentary Commissioners than it had been by the Scots. At Newcastle he had been able to send letters to the Queen as well as to the Lords Jermyn and Culpepper, and to the faithful Ashburnham who was now in Paris with other exiled Royalists. Despite the embargo, individuals made several attempts to pass letters to the King. On one such occasion when the King was walking to Althorp to play bowls accompanied by the Parliamentary Commissioners, a packet of letters from the Queen and others in France was pressed into his hand. The man who made the delivery appeared to be a countryman merely out fishing, but he was reported to be a Major Bosvile of Lord Cleveland's Royalist regiment of horse. Arrested for

Queen Henrietta Maria, who
was in Paris during the King's
captivity.

his trouble, he could have been Major Humphrey Boswell who was
known to be a royal courier from the Continent at that time and
regarded by Parliament as 'a very dangerous person'. Later, in 1652,
acting as courier for the Lord Percy, he was arrested in London and
committed to the Tower.[7]

Although Boswell was apprehended when he gave the letters to
the King, the Commissioners did not dare to take the bundle from
His Majesty. Later, another attempt to smuggle a letter to him from
the Queen failed when a servant of Lady Cave was caught in the act.
Lady Cave herself was subsequently imprisoned in Northampton

Castle for her part in the effort. It was reported that 'those that carried her away were stricken to blushes by her beauty, boldness and carriage . . . the letter was found very obscure'. It was no doubt in code, as were so many of the royal letters.

The King, playing for time, his usual tactic to give his enemies the opportunity of quarrelling, wrote to Parliament saying that he had not been able to respond fully to the Newcastle Propositions because he had expected them to send him some clarification.[8] He had understood that the initial delay had been caused by the tardy arrival from Scotland of the Earl of Lauderdale, the chief Scottish Commissioner in London. As Lauderdale had now been in the capital for ten days, he queried why there was still no communication. He went on to say that despite Parliament's delay he did not think that he, personally, should be required to negotiate in the conditions under which he was presently being held. His servants were denied access to him, except those few authorised to be with him. It was a crime for anyone but the Commissioners to speak to him and he was not allowed freely to send or receive letters.

John Maitland, Earl of Lauderdale, chief Scottish Commissioner in London, who visited King Charles at Hampton Court.

In such circumstances 'may he not say that he is not in case fit to make confessions [*sic*] [concessions?] or give answers, since he is not master of those ordinary actions which are the undoubted rights of every free-born man, how mean soever his birth be'. Still defiant and very much on his regal dignity, he wrote that he intended to remain silent until the conditions under which he existed were improved. Despite this, he continued to write that he had done much to try to understand and satisfy his conscience to enable him to give answers to the Propositions which would be 'most agreeable to his Parliaments' but try as he might, he could not approve all of them.

Charles underlined his honesty for, as he wrote, he could agree to all and then break his word. However, such actions he regarded as 'unlawful for any man and most base in a King'. He stressed again the need for him to travel to London to negotiate with Parliament in person. He then made some concessions. He offered to agree to a Presbyterian government for the Church for three years, providing he and his household, presumably the Queen and her Catholic attendants included, should have freedom of worship. During that time there should be debates and discussions about a long-term settlement in the Assembly of Divines, to which should be added twenty clergymen of his nomination.

The King wanted to defer his answer on the introduction of the Covenant throughout his kingdoms, but he agreed that Catholics should be subjected to stricter laws and that their children should be brought up in the Protestant faith on pain of fining. He queried the level of fines which Parliament proposed for failure to comply. He agreed to an Act for the due observation of the Lord's Day and to another for the suppression of religious innovations, as well as those concerning the preaching of God's Word. He agreed that the clergy should be punished for non-residence in their livings and that no clergyman might hold more than one living.

Future control of the military was another area where the King could not agree with the Propositions: 'because thereby . . . he wholly parts with the power of the sword entrusted to him by God and the laws of the land for the protection and government of his people . . . which is absolutely necessary to the kingly office . . .'.[9] The use of particular phrases and words in this passage is revealing. In the King's belief not only is the sword necessary for the protection of his people, but also for their government. His most recent attempts to use the sword to govern had proved both useless and costly. The emphasis that the sword was entrusted to him by God demonstrates yet again the strength of his concept of the Divine Right by which he ruled – and hardly reflected the point of view of one attempting to reach a compromise, as Clarendon claimed.

While this form of slow-motion negotiation went on between the King and the Presbyterian majority in Parliament, the Army, especially many of its senior officers, was expressing its deep discontent for two reasons. First there was widespread resentment at the policy which Parliament was following concerning the Army. The soldiers had petitioned for the granting of immunity from prosecution for their wartime actions as soldiers; for the payment of arrears (which in total equated to about fifty-six months' pay for everyone); for impressment (i.e., forced enlistment, or conscription) to end; for relief for widows and maimed soldiers and finally for pay to continue until actual disbandment. Parliament was extremely slow to address these matters, and the mere size of the bill for arrears was probably enough to shock the Members into inactivity.

Further discontent was caused by the announcement that Major-General Philip Skippon and Major-General Edward Massey were to command the army being prepared for service in Ireland. Skippon was an extremely well-respected and popular New Model Army general who had been wounded at Naseby. Massey had never served in the New Model Army, although his Western Association Brigade had operated with the New Model soldiers in the successful 1645

Commissary-General Henry
Ireton, an extremely active
politician, second-in-
command of the Horse
regiments of the New Model
Army and Oliver Cromwell's
son-in-law.

campaign in the West of England. Massey was not trusted because of
his Presbyterian leanings and was unpopular with the New Model
Army because of the complaints he made, although with some
justification, during the Western Campaign. With the announcement that Massey would be the lieutenant-general of horse in
Ireland, the Army protested loudly, calling for Fairfax, Cromwell and
Skippon to lead the force and for Massey to be removed. Eventually
Cromwell was appointed in June 1649, with Henry Ireton as his
lieutenant-general.

These grievances, coupled with an after-the-war truculence
sometimes found in victorious forces whose employment seems at an
end, caused the Army to prepare itself for protest to ensure that its
views were not only heard but acted upon. Each company of foot, or
dragoons, and each troop of horse nominated two of its number to
act, or 'agitate', on behalf of the others. These delegates, all of whom

were drawn from the ranks of ensign or cornet (the most junior commissioned rank in the infantry and cavalry respectively) and below, became known as 'Agitators'. They represented the views of their comrades to another body made up of generals, colonels and officers of the rank of captain and above. This body was called the Council of Officers.

Election or nomination to such bodies tends to result in the emergence of the dedicated activist, as the majority of people seldom wish to be bothered or are content to allow others to take on the responsibilities involved. This is what happened in the New Model Army, where some of the Agitators tended to demonstrate almost the modern, sometimes subversive meaning of that term. The presence of activists frequently leads to a greater political rather than practical involvement of the organisation. It often begins to act beyond its original purpose as a means to effective communication and starts actively to exert a great deal of pressure to originate policy.

The second major source of discontent, this time among the senior officers and those who supported Independency rather than Presbyterianism, was that the majority in Parliament planned to impose Presbyterianism throughout England and Wales, compelling all to subscribe to the Presbyterian Covenant insisted upon by the Scots. Also opposed to the introduction of Presbyterianism was King Charles, a rather odd ally. The Independents' concern regarding this issue was increased by the fact that His Majesty was in the hands of the majority, Presbyterian, Parliamentary group. The Independents had had little experience of the King's implacable resistance to the threats, pleadings, religious discussions and other methods employed by the Scots to try to get him to agree to their religious proposals. It was possible that his known opposition might weaken under the sustained political and religious pressure exerted jointly by the Scots and the English Presbyterians. There were some signs to indicate this in the small religious concessions already made through his letters of negotiation with the Parliament from Holdenby House. The Independent MPs would have noted these, however small, with some alarm. There was a way to prevent the King from making major concessions to the Presbyterians which would be to his own disadvantage as well as that of the Independents – this course of action was taken much to the surprise of the other protagonists.

On 3 June 1646 a force of 500 New Model Army horsemen, selected from several regiments, rode to Holdenby House to take control of the King's person. In other words, to kidnap him. They

Cornet Joyce kidnaps the King from Holdenby House. An impression by a Victorian artist.

were commanded by Cornet George Joyce of Colonel Edward Whalley's regiment. Although Whalley was Oliver Cromwell's cousin, he was reported to have been of Presbyterian leanings but he obviously agreed with the plan of action to take control of the King.

On learning that there was a strong force of horse in the neighbourhood planning to take the house and the King, the fifty guards at Holdenby were discreetly valorous. Their commander, Colonel Graves, was even more so. Probably aware that he was suspected by the Army of plotting with the King and the Scots, he left, quietly but hurriedly. When Joyce and some of his men entered the House the following morning, the guards offered no resistance. Joyce then delivered a written declaration to the Parliamentary Commissioners which claimed that others were plotting to 'take away the King, to the end that he might side with that intended army to be raised, which if effected, would be to the utter undoing of the Kingdom'.

The King appeared and the following exchange occurred.

The King: Mr Joyce . . . what authority do you have to take charge of my person and carry me away?

Joyce: I am sent by the Authority of the Army, to prevent the design of their enemies, who seek to involve the Kingdom a second time in blood.

The King:	That is no lawful authority. I know of none in England but mine, and after mine that of the Parliament. Have you any written commission from Sir Thomas Fairfax?
Joyce:	I have the authority of the Army, and the General is included in the Army.
The King:	That is no answer. The general is head of the Army. Have you any written commission?
Joyce:	I beseech your Majesty to ask me no more questions. There is my commission [pointing to the troopers . . .]
The King:	[with a smile] I have never before read such a commission; but it is written in characters fair and legible enough; a company of as handsome proper gentlemen as I have seen in a long while. But to remove me hence you must use absolute force unless you give me satisfaction as to those reasonable and just demands which I make: that I may be used with honour and respect, and that I may not be forced in anything against my conscience or my honour, though I hope that my resolution is so fixed that no force can cause me to do so base a thing. You are masters of my body, my soul is above your reach.[10]

This polite exchange between the King and Joyce, a former tailor, shows not only the King's innate courtesy but also his personal courage, surprised and confronted as he was in the very early morning by a group of heavily armed men. His sardonic humour is revealed, but above all this episode underlines his insistence on the observation of the laws of the land. This had been a recurring theme in His Majesty's dealings with his opponents and it was to persist.

The New Model Army had mustered at Newmarket and the captive King chose to be taken there. When Fairfax heard that Joyce had taken the King and was now at Hinchingbrooke, he sent Edward Whalley's regiment to guard and escort His Majesty back to Holdenby. When he refused to return there, he was quartered at Childerly. There, when Charles questioned them, Fairfax and Cromwell both denied the assertion that one or both of them had been responsible for his removal. The King's answer was, 'unless you hang up Joyce, I will not believe what you say'.[11]

The King was not returned to Holdenby, but was moved first to Windsor Castle then, on the following day, to Lord Craven's house at Caversham, near Reading. There the Army relaxed many restrictions,

The King greets his children at the Greyhound Inn at Maidenhead, Berkshire. A Victorian impression.

allowing him to have two of his chaplains to conduct services using the *Book of Common Prayer*, permitting him to receive letters from the Queen and granting free access to all who wished to attend on him. Above all, to his great delight, they brought the Duke of York, Princess Elizabeth and Prince Henry to meet him at the Greyhound Inn in Maidenhead. After father and children had dined together, they all returned to Caversham where the royal children stayed for two days.

A few days after the children had returned to St James's Palace in London, the King's location was changed three times until he finally arrived at Hampton Court on 14 August. There he was allowed a high degree of freedom, within broad limits. He hunted deer, played pell mell and real tennis in the court that is still in existence in the palace. The King was also allowed to make visits to other houses, particularly to Syon House, which was owned by the Earl of Northumberland and was now the home of his three children. Northumberland and his Countess were taking excellent care of the royal children, for which they received the King's heartfelt gratitude.

While the King was occupied with these activities, the conflict in Parliament between the Presbyterians and the Independents, with their Army backing, had been intensifying. The Council for the Army had prepared a 'Declaration for the Army', which set out

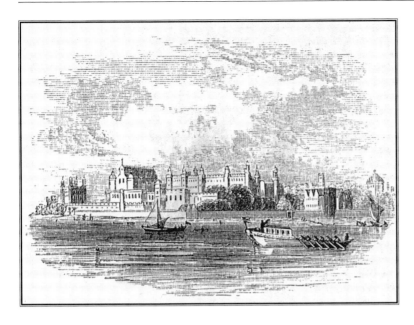

Hampton Court Palace, where
the King was detained.

political and constitutional aims, rather than concerning itself with
soldiers' grievances. These proposals, spearheaded by Henry Ireton,
Commissary General or Second-in-Command of Cromwell's cavalry,
created much dissension when tabled in the House of Commons. In
June eleven prominent Presbyterian leaders who opposed the paper
were denounced by the Army, which demanded their suspension
from Parliament. This was refused. Among the eleven were the most
influential leaders of their faction, including Denzil Holles, Philip
Stapleton, John Clotworthy, William Waller, John Maynard and
Edward Massey.

Edward Massey MP, former
General of Parliament's
Western Association Brigade.

In the ensuing quarrelling, during which the London mobs were
active, the Independents in Parliament were concerned for their
safety. Eight peers and fifty-seven Members of the Commons who
supported the Independent policies, along with the two Speakers, the
Earl of Manchester for the Lords and William Lenthall for the
Commons, took refuge with the Army. Early in August the Army
entered London to re-establish, in their eyes, the true Parliament. At
this the eleven Members withdrew, some of them fleeing to France.
This now gave the Independents the greater influence in both
Houses. The City of London was mainly Presbyterian in outlook, but
made more noise than effort in support of the Parliamentary
Members who shared their view. As was fairly normal in those times,
the apprentices of the City indulged in their usual demonstrations,

which were perhaps more to relieve boredom than to express deeply held political beliefs. Their activities were none the less threatening for that.

Fairfax had marched the Army to Hounslow at about the time the King arrived at Hampton Court, and in the weeks following His Majesty must have had high hopes that the Army, sharing his objections to Presbyterianism, might be his salvation. He had, personally, fared much better in Army hands than he had when under the control of either the Scots or the Parliamentary Commissioners at Holdenby.

A pikeman of a Foot regiment of Fairfax's Army.

Having arrived at Hampton Court he was even allowed to receive people who suffered from scrofula, a swelling of the glands similar to tuberculosis, which it was widely believed could be cured by the touch of God's anointed King. Many scoffed at this as mere superstition, but it is significant that in accordance with his beliefs the King was prepared to carry out the ceremony. He regretted that he had no gold or silver to give his unfortunate subjects, but he gave them what little he had as he laid hands on them in the sincere belief that they could be cured by that act. It says much for his kindness that he was prepared, in the midst of his troubles, to touch sufferers of the disease known as 'the King's Evil' because only the touch of a King could cure it. It was also, of course, a public act of defiance to his Parliamentary enemies who had declared the practice to be illegal and a re-affirmation of the divinity of his right to rule.

In July Queen Henrietta Maria, on learning that the King was now more at liberty than he had been and was permitted more attendants, ordered three Royalists who were with her in Paris to go to Hampton Court to be of service to the King. These were His Majesty's companion in his flight from Oxford, John Ashburnham, and Sir John Berkeley, the former Governor of Exeter, who had been instrumental in conducting the young Princess Henrietta to her mother. The third member of the party was Sir William Legge, the former Governor of Oxford, whom the King still viewed cautiously as Legge had been wrongly thought of as conspiring in treasonable acts with his great friend Prince Rupert after the latter's disgrace following his surrender of Bristol.

In addition to the senior Army officers, notably Cromwell, who visited and conversed with the King, there were many others who came to talk with him. Among these was James Butler, the Marquis of Ormond, who had surrendered Dublin on the King's orders and was now on his way to France. There were also visits from Arthur,

Lord Capel, who had travelled from Jersey via France to bring news and discuss matters with His Majesty, and the Earl of Lauderdale, the senior Scottish Commissioner in London. The Scots were disturbed by the current political superiority of the Independents and by the role which the Army had assumed, especially as the more extreme elements of the Army were calling for greater legal, political and social reforms. These, associated with the civilian radicals called (derisively) Levellers, appeared to be gaining more influence and their views were seen as a threat to the traditional constitutions of both countries.

The success of the Independents in Parliament and the growing assertiveness of the Army in political matters brought about a discernible change of attitude among the soldiers guarding the King. Courtesy was beginning to evaporate and some visitors were treated rudely. There were also hints about outside, unspecified threats to the safety of the King himself and these caused His Majesty some concern. He had taken the opportunity when seeing his children to emphasise that should anything ever happen to him they were to remain loyal to their brother Prince Charles or, if the Prince of Wales should die, their loyalty would be to the Duke of York. Prince Henry of Gloucester, who at this time was only seven years old, was repeatedly told by his father not to allow himself to be proclaimed king while either of his brothers was alive. The prospect of threats on the King's life also concerned the Scots, who, although demanding religious reform, did not seek a change in the monarchy.[12]

There was a suspicion in the minds of the Independent and Army leaders that the Scots and the King might be planning an alliance. Visits by senior officers to Hampton Court became less frequent and the general atmosphere of goodwill began to dwindle. This may also have been a response to the increase in the number of pro-Royalist and pro-Presbyterian newsheets and pamphlets that were then beginning to be published and distributed. This change of attitude, coupled with warning notes passed to the King, made him even more aware of the potential threats to his person and led him to make plans for escape. Colonel Whalley had doubled the guard, whether to increase the King's security, prevent any escape attempt or even to heighten the King's alarm and so stimulate an effort to escape it is not clear. King Charles had earlier withdrawn his parole not to escape.

On Thursday 11 November the King saw two letters that could have confirmed his fears. One, from Cromwell to Edward Whalley, wrote of 'some murderous design, or fear of it, against his Majesty'.[13] The Colonel showed this letter to the King. The other, signed cryptically 'E.R.', warned the King that the writer's brother had attended a meeting with 'eight or nine agitators, who, in debate of the obstacle which did most to hinder the speedy effecting of their designs, did conclude it was your Majesty and as long as your Majesty doth live you would be so. And therefore, resolved, for the good of the kingdom, to take your life away . . .'.[14]

It is unlikely that the sight of these letters would have panicked the King into precipitate action, but they may have caused him to bring forward his escape, for which planning was well in hand. That night, the King, having pretended to be indisposed during the day, stealthily left his apartment by a route that led to the garden, where Berkeley and Legge had brought horses. They rode to meet Ashburnham who was waiting for them at his house in Thames Ditton, then the four of them proceeded south, aiming for the coast.

CHAPTER FIVE

Conflicts Intensify

Stone Walls do not a prison make,
Nor Iron bars a cage.

Richard Lovelace, 'To Althea, From Prison'

The King's flight from Hampton Court was, as it was to turn out, more a result of ineptitude than a carefully organised escape. The King had confided his plans only to Ashburnham, who 'was as entirely trusted by the King as any man in England . . .'.[1] Berkeley and Legge had been ordered to be ready with the horses at the appointed time and place. As a Groom of the Bedchamber who had his own house nearby, Ashburnham would have had a greater freedom to make arrangements to further the King's plan. Only the King, and one must assume Ashburnham, knew of His Majesty's full intention and the planned destination.

Before leaving his apartment, the King had written three letters, one to Colonel Whalley, the second to Lord Montague, one of the Parliamentary Commissioners in residence at Hampton Court, and the third to the Speaker of the House of Commons, which he asked Montague to forward and also to send a copy of it to Sir Thomas Fairfax. He thanked Whalley for his unfailing courtesy to him and asked him to return several items, including a greyhound, to their former owners. He stressed in his letters to Whalley and to the Speaker that he was leaving because he was 'loath to be made a close prisoner'. In the Speaker's letter he expressed concern about the disturbing activities of the Levellers and their possible influence on policy towards him and also that there seemed to be no chance of him being heard by the Presbyterians, the Independents or the Army.

There is a view held by some that the reported threats to the King's life were spurious and that they, and his escape, were engineered by some of His Majesty's opponents, Cromwell and Whalley included. There is no doubt that at this stage it would have delighted the King's enemies if he were to flee abroad, giving them the powerful claim that he had deserted his peoples. Then they could introduce their constitutional and religious reforms without the obstruction of the King's determined opposition. Such a retreat by the King would also have damaged the increasing Royalist support that was becoming evident. Many in the kingdoms felt sympathy for the personal plight of the beleaguered, imprisoned King.

A pikeman adopting a defensive stance.

The stormy night and incompetent route-finding caused much delay and by daybreak the fugitive party had arrived only at Long Sutton, between Farnham and Basingstoke. There, obviously by prior arrangement, they changed horses. They had to hasten as the villagers were just stirring and the local inn was the headquarters of the Parliamentary Committee for the area. They headed for the New Forest and as they neared the coast the King sent Ashburnham to find the ship. Accounts of these events refer to 'the ship' rather than 'a ship' and this would seem to indicate some preparatory planning. It also strongly suggests that the King intended to leave the mainland. He could have intended to sail to the Continent, thus quitting his dominions, or to the Channel Islands, which would mean that he would not have left British soil. Sir Richard Bulstrode had no doubt that 'his Majesty missed his Design of going to Jersey'.[2] It is reasonably clear from subsequent events that he was not planning to cross to the Isle of Wight. Clarendon, that diligent researcher, did not identify the King's planned destination, but was sure that it was not where he finally arrived.

Ashburnham returned to the King unable to find the ship. He has been blamed by many for his totally inept organisation, including the delay on route and the change of horses almost under the noses of the enemy. In fairness, and this is complete conjecture, if the King had brought forward the plan for the escape, hatched after withdrawing his parole a fortnight earlier, it is hardly surprising that the essential parts of any pre-arranged plan might not mesh. That a ship engaged for some later date might, by chance, be available earlier was not too vain a hope, especially if the vessel was usually berthed in the area, which was very likely. Certainly His Majesty was no stranger to over-optimism, as his letters after the defeats at Naseby, Langport and Bristol show. Conversely the delay *en route* may have caused them to miss the sailing. Had they planned to reach the ship by dawn and only reached Long Sutton by this time, they would still have had over 40 miles to ride if the ship was to be boarded somewhere on the coast south of the New Forest.

No ship was available on 12 November and so the King decided they would seek temporary shelter at Tichfield, the house of the Earl of Southampton, whose mother was in residence. There they discussed what was to be done. It was suggested, apparently by Ashburnham, that the Isle of Wight could provide a refuge for the King, as its governor, the fine Parliamentary soldier Colonel Robert Hammond, was considered by Ashburnham to be a man 'of honour and generosity enough to trust the King's person to'.[3] The King himself knew Hammond, whose uncle was one of the Royal Chaplains. Further, Hammond had spoken with them all during visits he had made to Hampton Court. Ashburnham believed that he would be prepared to protect His Majesty from harm with all courtesy and entertain him as well as he could.

The King decided to send Ashburnham and Berkeley to discover if Hammond would agree not to surrender him to Parliament or to the Army, but to allow him later to go free. He stressed that his two emissaries should not tell Hammond where he was, but that they should return with the governor's reply. When Hammond was finally located and approached he agreed he would protect the King from any violence, but emphasised that he was a subordinate officer and subject to the orders of his superiors. He therefore could not guarantee to do more than guard the King in courtesy and to see to his immediate comfort. This was not the hoped-for answer and when the emissaries were asked where the King was, they remained silent but said that they would inform him of Hammond's reply. The governor suggested that Ashburnham should stay with him while Berkeley returned to the King. This was rejected as the sovereign would regard this as a sign of bad faith and would not put any further trust in Hammond.

After much further discussion, during which the two Royalists were assured that Hammond was prepared to be of service to the King, they agreed to take him and three or four others to see His Majesty. When the King heard that Hammond was at Tichfield, he cried out, 'Oh, Jack, thou has undone me!' Ashburnham, weeping, was prevented by the King from descending the stairs to kill Hammond. The King called the governor to him and tried to obtain the promise which had been previously refused. While Hammond was prepared to do all he could for His Majesty, he could not promise to do all that was being asked of him. However, he appeared to

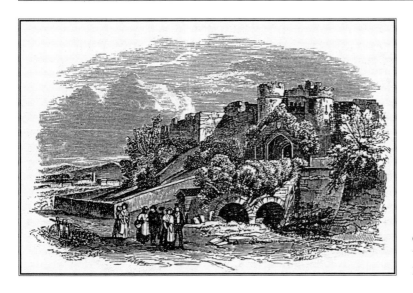

Carisbrooke Castle, Isle of Wight, where the King was held prisoner.

consider that King Charles was safe with the Army.[4] Seeing that further discussion would be pointless and realising that Hammond had enough men close by to foil another escape attempt, the King agreed to go with him to the Isle of Wight, where he was lodged in Carisbrooke Castle.

The episode illustrates that the King was very probably too trusting of his servants, even when they lacked sound judgment. He appears again to have confirmed Clarendon's assessment that he was unsure of his own powers of judgment and relied too often on that of men who were less capable than he. The King made no accusation that the faithful Ashburnham betrayed him, but many were puzzled by the latter's decison to take Hammond to where the King was hiding. There were some who claimed, Sir Marmaduke Langdale (later Lord Langdale) among them, that Ashburnham had always intended the King to flee to the Isle of Wight. Langdale often repeated that when in Ashburnham's room a few days before the escape he had seen a letter on the table which had recommended that very course of action.[5]

Bulstrode believed that Ashburnham and Berkeley had brought Hammond to the King, 'being loath to be taken into Custody, or for what other Reason none can tell'.[6] What is clear is that Ashburnham was not blamed or punished in any way, by the Army or Parliament, for his part in the King's escape from Hampton Court, although he and Berkeley became enemies as a result of their adventures together.

He continued to live in England and was later imprisoned by Cromwell. Released on the Protector's death, Ashburnham was well regarded at the Restoration. In 1667, however, he was expelled from his seat in Parliament for accepting a large bribe from a French merchant.

If Ashburnham was not guilty of betraying the King, his judgment had been extremely poor. It is almost inconceivable that he could believe that a man of Hammond's honour and probity would be prepared to go against those who had appointed him and those in the New Model Army with whom he had fought. Ashburnham must also have known that Hammond was the son-in-law of the late Parliamentary hero John Hampden, who was, in turn, a cousin of Oliver Cromwell. However, his faulty judgment was more than matched by the King's own poor assessment of his courtier's abilities.

Berkeley and Legge were later sent by the King from Carisbrooke to urge the Army to oppose the Presbyterian majority in Parliament. They were twice rebuffed. Berkeley went to France and later became the governor to the Duke of York. He also saw some campaigning with the French Army. He was created Lord Berkeley by the exiled Charles II in 1658. Legge plotted to free the King, but in May 1648 he was imprisoned in Arundel Castle. He compounded, went abroad, served in Ireland, was captured and detained at Exeter Castle, returned abroad and was again arrested for trying to raise Royalist support in England the year before the Restoration. He declined a peerage in 1660 because he could not afford to support the honour. His son was, however, created Baron Dartmouth in 1682.

At Carisbrooke, initially, true to his word, Hammond treated the King with much courtesy, allowing him almost as much liberty as he had had at the start of his stay at Hampton Court. He was able to visit places on the island, to be entertained to a banquet by local dignitaries and to receive visitors.

Parliament, now increasingly Independent with its Army support, dispensed with all pretence at negotiating with the King and in late December 1647, following a submission by him to them, Parliament returned four Bills for his agreement with all the hallmarks of an ultimatum. Two of them would have caused little problem, but the remaining two would, in effect, have stripped him and his heirs of two major powers – control and financing of the armed forces and the power to dissolve Parliament. King Charles rejected all four. Unsettled, he made plans to escape but was prevented from doing so by being placed in close confinement in the castle.

In the meantime, on 26 November 1647, the King had signed an 'Engagement' with the Scots. By this alliance he agreed to the introduction of Presbyterianism into England for a period of three years in return for their support. This agreement split the Scots: the faction which supported the 'Engagement' was led by the Duke of Hamilton; those who opposed it followed the lead of the Earl of Argyle. The alliance with the King made war inevitable between Parliamentary England and the 'Engagers'.

In January 1648 the English Parliament formally voted to break off all negotiations with the King, who still had not given up hope of escape. Hammond had been ordered to replace the royal attendants with, among others, Thomas Herbert, Anthony Mildmay, Silius Titus and James Harrington. King Charles, as usual, tried to maintain a positive outlook, but he was suspicious that any plans he made to escape would probably be passed on to Hammond by someone in his current household.

James, Duke of Hamilton, leader of the Scottish 'Engagers', who actively supported the King.

Some effort was made to provide him with a diversion by the building of a bowling alley. Also he was not denied all contact with the outside world – visitors were admitted and he received printed news-sheets from London. One visitor, a former Army Chaplain, Mr Obadiah Sedgwick, came to discourse with him about his spiritual concerns and '. . . to present . . . a book he had lately writ . . . His Majesty, after he had read some part thereof, returned it with this short admonition and judgment; That by what he had read in that book, he believed the composer stood in some need of sleep. The King's advice being taken in the best sense, the minister departed with seeming satisfaction.'[7] The poor King seems to have been besieged by those who were determined to dispute theological matters with him. Several were turned away but were thanked for their good intentions. One can almost imagine the royal sighs of resignation tinged with exasperation as these earnest men appeared. His Majesty was permitted to write letters to Parliament and to members of his family. He was also allowed to worship alone without the presence of ministers of religion whom he refused to accept, although he is said to have enjoyed evening disputations with the governor's young Presbyterian chaplain.

In the meantime, the situation in Ireland developed, and there were demands for support from those who still adhered to the King. Consequently, Ormond planned to return there to assume his former responsibilities. In England there was a growing swell of Royalist feeling, while in Scotland the Engagers were busily recruiting an

The Revd Obadiah Sedgwick, who visited the King at Carisbrooke Castle and gave him his book to read.

James, Duke of York, who
escaped to France in disguise.

army on his behalf. One matter which delighted the King was news
that James, Duke of York had escaped from Syon House, dressed in
women's clothes, and was now safe in France.

Matters came to a head in March when, after exchanges recorded
between the King and Parliament were published, followed by other
tracts in support of the King, there was a Royalist resurgence of
action. It began in Wales when Pembroke and its castle declared for
the King, and soon about 8,000 men rallied to the cause in the
principality. Cromwell, accompanied by five regiments, embarked on
a successful campaign in the west to reduce the Royalist forces in

North and East Wales. This was achieved by early June but Pembroke Castle and its garrison held out until July 1648.

Other risings occurred in the south of England, mainly in Norfolk, Kent and Essex. In the north a group of eighty Royalist horsemen, with others riding pillion, surprised and took Pontefract Castle. Sir Marmaduke Langdale recruited a force which captured Berwick and Carlisle. He then paused, awaiting the arrival of Hamilton with the promised army of 40,000 Scots. In the event Hamilton failed to recruit to that number and eventually was able to field only 10,000 soldiers. Even so, with Langdale's Royalists this army in the north, although split by internal dissension, presented a serious danger to the Parliamentary troops who opposed it.

Henry Rich, Earl of Holland, Royalist leader captured during the Second Civil War.

The New Model Army responses to these attacks are well documented. The defeat of the uprising of the Kent Royalists; the siege and capture of Colchester, with its consequent firing-squad execution of two prominent Royalists, Sir Charles Lucas and Sir George Lisle; the reduction of Pembroke and finally, Cromwell's defeat of the Scottish and Royalist northern forces at Preston, Lancashire, between 17 and 19 August, all occupied the Army's close attention.

There was a great deal of Parliamentary and Army concern when, in May, some ships of the Navy mutinied off the Downs and declared for the King. It was feared that they might land seamen to free him from Carisbrooke Castle while the Army was engaged elsewhere. However, when the Prince of Wales joined the ships they cruised along the south-east coast and up the Thames, merely taking some merchantmen as prizes. The Prince tried by a letter to change the allegiance of the Earl of Warwick, who was in high naval command again, but he replied that perhaps the Prince would like to change sides and join him! Then, after a bloodless confrontation with a larger, heavier Parliamentary squadron, the Prince withdrew his ships to Holland.

Many senior Royalists fell into the hands of the New Model Army at the conclusion of the fighting, which was called the Second English Civil War even though the action in the north involved an army from another nation, Scotland. Among those captured were the Duke of Hamilton, the Earl of Holland, the Earl of Norwich and Arthur, Lord Capel, who was taken at Colchester. They were lodged in the Tower of London, but Hamilton was later held in Windsor Castle.

It was probably a matter of satisfaction and self-congratulation for those Independents who had suspected that the King had been

Arthur, Lord Capel, Royalist general captured at Colchester in 1648.

Free Grammar School, Newport, Isle of Wight, scene of the Newport Treaty negotiations.

planning an alliance with the Scots. Their distrust of His Majesty would have been increased by the recollection that among his prominent visitors at Hampton Court had been Lauderdale the Scottish Commissioner, Ormond, Langdale and Lord Capel, all of whom had been involved in the subsequent uprisings. The circumstantial evidence that the King had plotted with them would have aroused great suspicions.

While the Army had faced these new threats, the Parliamentary majority, the Presbyterians, sought further negotiations with the King, despite the objections voiced by Cromwell. His Majesty proposed that the treaty, or negotiations, should be held in the grammar school at Newport on the Isle of Wight. Subsequently, in August, having repealed the Act which forbade further discussions with the King the majority in the Commons approved the holding of further talks. Independents in London were opposed to this and a twenty-seven-point petition was sent to Parliament in September that included two submissions underlining the prevailing mood among them. These were: 'That they would have done Justice upon the Capital Authors and Promoters of the former or late Wars'; and,

'That they would have laid to Heart the Abundance of Innocent Blood that hath been spilt, and the infinite Spoil and Havoc that hath been made of peaceable, harmless People, by express commission from the King; and seriously to have considered, whether the Justice of God be likely to be satisfied, or is his yet continuing Wrath appeased by an Act of Oblivion.'[8] This clear indictment of the King with his Royalist and Scottish supporters, whose guilt could not be washed away by an act of Parliamentary forgiveness, was reflected in the attitude of the Army, which had been further incensed by the deaths of comrades in the Second Civil War.

The Treaty at Newport began on 18 September in the grammar school, when fifteen Parliamentary Commissioners, five from the Lords and ten from the Commons, met the King. His Majesty was supported by advisers, but they were not allowed into the room where the discussions were being held. They were in another room, curtained-off so that they could hear the proceedings and be able to counsel the King when he withdrew to seek their advice.

Those who had not seen the King for some time were startled by his appearance. His hair was long as he had refused to have it cut since his servants had been removed from him almost a year before. It was now grey. His clothes were old as he had again refused to have new ones since the departure of his attendants, 'so that his aspect was very different from what it had used to be: otherwise his health was good, and he was much more cheerful in his discourses towards all men than could have been imagined, after such mortification of all kinds'.[9]

In the discussions King Charles made some further concessions, including increasing the period during which Parliament could name high officials to ten years; that Parliament could control the militia for twenty years; that Presbyterianism could be the exclusive religion for three years, during which time the authority of bishops would be suspended but not abolished, although the rest of the Church hierarchy might be abolished. During this time the Assembly of Divines would consider the long-term form of Church government for agreement between King and Parliament. The Court of Wards could also be abolished, with the Crown compensated for its loss by £100,000 a year. Other points of agreement concerned the withholding of pardon for Irish rebels and the identification of categories of Royalist who could compound for their part in the wars. As for King Charles himself he still refused the take the Covenant, or

The Treaty at Newport. A
Victorian interpretation.

to impose it on others. Nor would he agree to the sale of bishops'
lands or to repudiating Ormond's activities in Ireland.

As usual Charles played for time, he asked for more information
and the talks dragged on to fill the time originally allotted. They
were then extended in the hope of reaching a good conclusion.
Although the King had added to the concessions he had previously
offered, Parliament still had not obtained all that it wanted,
especially agreement on the Covenant and on the sale of the bishops'
lands, both of which were crucial in the relationship with their
Scottish allies. The first was needed to keep their side of the
agreement with Scotland about the enforcement of Presbyterianism
in England and Wales; the second to raise money to pay the Scots
Army its final instalments for withdrawing from England.

On balance the Commissioners returned to London fairly satisfied.
They believed that they and the Army were now in a good position

to negotiate a final settlement with the King. This was a view shared by Fairfax and many moderate Members of Parliament. Others thought differently, however.

While the Newport talks were taking place, the Army presented a Remonstrance to Parliament on 20 November, demanding as the first item 'that the King be brought to Justice, as the capital Cause of all the Evils in the Kingdom, and of so much Blood being shed'. This charge is reminiscent of the story of the crocodile's defence when it was accused of killing people. The insulted reptile claimed that he killed no one. All he did was to take them under the water. It was the water that killed them.[10]

The Army's Remonstrance went on to demand the return of the King's two eldest sons to stand trial and that their failure to return would bar them from government. The capital 'Causers' or 'Actors' in the war were to be tried, with mercy for others who sought it. The soldiers were to have their arrears. Public debts were to be repaid by fines imposed on 'delinquents' (i.e., Royalists) and the estates of those excluded from pardon. The present Parliament was to conclude at a date to be fixed and future Parliaments were to be guaranteed and to last for one or two years. Parliaments were to be supreme in government and, among other provisions, no monarch should be allowed to ascend the throne until they had sworn to uphold these conditions.

These proposals aimed to subordinate the monarchy to Parliament at a time when the majority in Parliament considered that the concessions which the King had made at Newport, even if he had offered little of permanent importance in terms of religious policy, could form the basis of a settlement that would recognise the principle of King and Parliament working together in a partnership.

Charles realised that he had been forced to make substantial concessions, even if these contained time limits. On 29 November, after the last Commissioners had left Newport, he wrote to his eldest son, '. . . you may see how long we have laboured in search of peace . . . Censure us not, for having parted with too much of our own right; the price was great; the commodity was security to us, peace to our people. And we are confident another Parliament would remember how useful a King's power is to a people's liberty.'[11] The tone of this letter gives the strong impression that the King truly believed that the negotiations at Newport had, at last, provided a sound basis for peace.

In order to attend the talks the King had given Hammond his word that he would not attempt to escape during them, or until he had withdrawn his word. Some of his supporters urged him to take the opportunity provided by the talks to escape to safety, as it was seriously believed that his life was threatened. He refused. It was Hammond who left the island, recalled and arrested by the Army as it was thought that he was 'too much the courtier' to remain completely loyal to the Army and its aims.

The debate about a settlement with the King, founded on the negotiations at Newport, was about to begin in Westminster as the Army prepared to march to London from its headquarters at Windsor to seek satisfaction from a dilatory Parliament.

CHAPTER SIX

A Bleak December

Which sense may reach and apprehend
Else a great Prince in Prison lies.

John Donne, 'The Extasy'

On the morning of 30 November Lieutenant-Colonel Ralph Cobbett of Fortescue's regiment and a large body of men arrived at Newport, where the King had been quartered during the treaty, to take Charles away. His Majesty, as was his practice, had asked to see Cobbett's authority, but he refused to show it. It was assumed by some that the orders had been issued by Fairfax. Thomas Herbert, who was with the King, recorded, 'But that he had orders, or secret instructions for this bold act, is not to be doubted; for though there was but one General, yet things were at that time so much out of frame, both in the Commons House and Army, as there were many commanders.'[1]

Cobbett also refused to reveal where he intended to take His Majesty. All he would say was that no harm or violence would be done to him. The King and his advisers who had been at the negotiations were surprised and apprehensive at this turn of events. The King '. . . at other times cheerful, at his parting from his friends showed sorrow in his heart, by the sadness of his countenance; a real sympathy'.[2] The uncertain prospects now looming must have been a blow to him. The King had seemed fairly confident in his letter to his son the previous day that matters were nearly settled. This surprise, mysterious, move must have worried him, but obviously not enough to make him forget his personal dignity.

When the King had entered the coach that was to take him away, Cobbett made to enter it uninvited. His Majesty put his foot up 'to oppose him', as Herbert observed. Cobbett, 'made sensible of his rudeness, . . . with some shame mounted his horse and followed . . ., the coachman driving as he directed'.

Some seventeenth-century
coaches.

King Charles and his servants were taken to Yarmouth and from
there embarked on a three-hour sail across the Solent to Hurst Castle,
which stood on a long spit of land which jutted out into the sea south
of Milford on Sea, in Hampshire. This small, cramped, stone fort had
been built during King Henry VIII's reign and its surroundings on
that dull winter day promised less than joy. The atmosphere was
made even gloomier at the sight of Hammond's replacement as
Governor of the Isle of Wight, Lieutenant-Colonel Isaac Ewer.
Herbert, who mistook him for the Governor of Hurst Castle, later
reported that 'The Captain of this wretched place was not unsuitable;
for at the King's going ashore, he stood ready to receive him with
small observance: his look was stern, his hair and large beard were
black and bushy; he held a partizan in his hand, and (Switz-like) had a
great basket hilt sword by his side; hardly could one see a man of
more grim aspect, and no less robust and rude in his behaviour.'[3]

Ewer, as Herbert remarked, was puffed up with self-importance as
he viewed the royal prisoner. He acted in such an overbearing, severe
and threatening manner that he frightened some of the royal
servants, until Cobbett spoke very sharply to him and reduced him
to the level of an obsequious attendant. Cobbett himself was
courteous and respectful to the King and to his few companions. He
was very tolerant of the people who came from the surrounding area
to see His Majesty and to pray for him.

Hurst Castle, Hampshire, the King's prison after his departure from the Isle of Wight.

The King's accommodation was spartan. The rooms were small, stone-walled and not warm, with such tiny windows that candles had to be lit at midday so that the occupants could read. The surroundings were also unattractive. The air was 'equally noxious by reason of the marshy ground around' and 'the unwholesome vapours arising from the sargassos and weeds'. However, the King walked for 2 miles as often as the weather allowed along the narrow spit of land towards the shore, accompanied by the governor or Captain Reynolds, another officer on duty at the fort, and with either Thomas Herbert or James Harrington in attendance. These walks, which were always conversational, were a trial to the King because the deep gravel over which they walked was 'very offensive to his feet'. On these occasions features from which he derived pleasure were the views of the Isle of Wight and the mainland, and particularly 'the sight of ships of all sizes daily under sail'.[4]

Herbert records that James Harrington was expelled from the fort. His only apparent crime had been to praise the King's wisdom in the

Sir James Harrington, political
theorist, dismissed from
attendance on the King.

recent discussions at Newport and also to extol his skill in debates
with various Presbyterian divines. The governor and the officers to
whom he had spoken took exception to this praise and took drastic
action. The King regretted the departure of Harrington, who was
also a most able political theorist, but commented on the need for
caution in conversation with men who were 'very little obliging to
his Majesty'. Herbert may have got the timing and reason for
Harrington's expulsion wrong. It may have occurred later, and have
been because Harrington refused to reveal the names of the men who
plotted the King's escape *en route* to Windsor, although he had sworn
he had not been personally involved in any such plans.

During the King's stay at Hurst Castle events in London were
gathering pace. On 30 November the House of Commons, by a
majority of ninety, had deferred consideration of the Army's
Remonstrance presented to them on 20 November. On 1 December
Sir Thomas Fairfax wrote to the City of London to inform its leaders

that the Army was about to march to the capital because Parliament continued to ignore its grievances, particularly the arrears of pay. He assured the City authorities that the soldiers were not coming to plunder or offer violence to the inhabitants, nor would the people of London be required to provide free quarters for them. In spite of these assurances, Fairfax was not averse to a little gentle extortion, for he added that to ensure there would be no violence, the sum of £40,000 should be provided by the evening of the following day as an advance towards the outstanding arrears of pay. Parliament objected to the Army's proposed advance from Windsor, but agreed that the City should send the required money to the Army. The Speaker of the Commons sent a letter to Fairfax forbidding the Army to come nearer, but before it was received, or perhaps even after it arrived, the vanguard was already at Kensington and within 2 miles of the Parliament building.

The morning after the Army's arrival, Fairfax deployed his regiments in the heart of Westminster. Making his headquarters in Whitehall, he ordered Colonel John Hewson and his regiment to occupy the royal Palace of Whitehall and Thomas Pride with his troops to go to St James's Palace. Other regiments were sent to The Mews (now Trafalgar Square), Suffolk House and other positions in the area.[5] Fairfax vindicated the Army's actions, as he saw them. In a letter to the Speaker of 3 December he wrote, 'We do not insist upon the things declared or propounded as for our own will or judgment, but the reason or righteousness that is in them, and as they are for the public interest and the safety of the nation.'[6] Such a statement could be adopted as the pattern of justification for every subsequent action taken, 'for the common good'.

A caricature of the one-eyed Colonel John Hewson.

The arrival of the Army, although it caused Parliament apprehension, did not interrupt its planned business of the day, which was consideration of the King's concessions at Newport. No conclusion was reached during that Saturday sitting and the House adjourned until the following Monday. At that session news arrived of the King's removal from Newport to Hurst Castle and the House, before resuming its deliberations, expressed its displeasure that this should have taken place without its advice and consent. The sitting went on into the night, lasting until 5 a.m., when the main proposal, 'That his Majesty's Concessions to the Propositions of Parliament upon the Treaty were sufficient Grounds for settling the Peace of the Kingdom', was agreed by 129 votes to 83. Immediately after this vote the House, concerned about its poor relationship with the Army, appointed a small committee to confer with Fairfax the following day to resolve their differences. At that time it would have appeared that peace was about to be agreed between the King and Parliament as well as between Parliament and the Army. That was not the case, for other interests were at work.

On the night of 5 December six men met in Whitehall to form a plan. Henry Ireton and Edmund Ludlow were certainly present and it is very likely that the other four were Lord Grey of Groby, Henry Marten, Sir Hardress Waller and Colonel Thomas Pride. They planned that troops should take over the Parliament and exclude all Members who did not support the Army's views. Members of Parliament, their political and religious affiliations and their likely reactions were discussed. Finally, a list was drawn up of all who were to be prevented from entering Parliament the following day. Ireton told his fellow conspirators that he would inform Fairfax of the plan.

The following morning, while Fairfax was engaged meeting the Parliamentary Committee in an attempt to resolve their differences, the Army took action. Colonel Nathaniel Rich's Regiment of Horse occupied New Palace Yard, the area outside the Parliament House, and three foot regiments, Pride's, Hewson's and Hardress Waller's, expelled the City of London Trained Bands troops who had been guarding Parliament. They then took charge of the Parliament building and the areas around it. Pride, equipped with the list of

Colonel Edmund Ludlow, who helped plan the *coup d'état*.

Pride's Purge. A Victorian impression.

names and advised by Lord Grey of Groby, who stood at the entrance lobby with him, then prevented the selected members from entering the chamber. About 140 members were excluded and 41 of them were arrested and confined in a nearby building called 'Hell'. The officer who was put in charge of them there was, so it was claimed, called Devill. The imprisoned Members, no doubt in varying states of deep anxiety about their personal safety, were kept there overnight and then, on 7 December, moved to two taverns in the Strand.

Fairfax asserts, believably as a man of honour, that he was completely unaware of the Army's intention to take control of Parliament. He later wrote, '. . . I never had any knowledge . . . till it was done. The reason why it was so secretly carried that I should have no notice of it was because I always prevented those designs when I knew them.'[7] That the Lord General was not involved was confirmed by the Parliamentarian Bulstrode Whitelocke as well as by the Royalist Clarendon. Fairfax deeply deplored what had happened, later expressing his views in writing, 'And unto such failings all Authority may fall. As sometimes Kingly Authority may abuse to their, and the Kingdom's prejudice; sometimes under a Parliamentary Authority, much injury hath been done; so here, hath a General's Power been broken and crumbled into a Levelling Faction, to the great unsettlement of the nation.'[8]

The other senior general of the Army, Lieutenant-General Oliver Cromwell, was, at this time, still in the north and did not return to London until 7 December. His absence does not, however, exonerate him from influence on, if not direct implication in, this *coup d'état*. Ireton, who had married Bridget Cromwell in June 1646, was his protegé and is unlikely to have acted without the approval of his father-in-law. Cromwell told Edmund Ludlow on his return that '. . . he had not been acquainted with this design; yet, since it was done, he was glad of it, and would endeavour to maintain it'.[9]

The leadership he was to assume clearly demonstrated his wholehearted support. Fairfax tried to keep out of politics, concentrating instead on administering and commanding the Army in the tasks necessary to ensure control and also to acquire the money which Parliament had agreed towards the arrears. He was careful to ensure strict discipline and quartered his troops mainly in large empty buildings to avoid antagonising the bulk of the population. The City was slow to produce the money and so on 8 December two regiments of foot and some troops of horse marched to the Goldsmiths' Hall and the Weavers' Hall to confiscate what parliamentary money might be contained there. They reportedly came away with £35,000.

The political leadership of the Army presented a paper to the remaining Members of Parliament to justify their conduct. This was probably quite unnecessary as the remaining Members, who became known as 'The Rump', were in support of the Army's action, especially as they were benefiting from it. The paper accused the excluded members and Major-General Richard Browne, the Sheriff of London, of all sorts of treason ranging from bringing a Scots army into England to treacherously reversing parliamentary decisions, particularly the decision to hold no further negotiations with the King, while their opponents were engaged elsewhere. This purely political tirade, prepared by Edward Whalley among others, was aimed at influencing the population as a whole rather than just Members of Parliament.

Major-General Richard Browne, Sheriff of the City of London, arrested during Pride's Purge.

The Independents, now in the main the only Members of Parliament, were paradoxically no longer independent. They clearly held their positions by courtesy of the Army and, in the unlikely event of their failing to satisfy the demands made on them, they could be removed. They were, of course, unlikely to do much to antagonise the military in these early days, although the excluded Members allegedly published a protest, which both Houses declared to be false, scandalous and seditious. It is probably not surprising that a fundamental change such as the one brought about by the *coup d'état* had a disorientating effect. It changed the rules of the political game completely. What had previously been an acceptable belief, Presbyterianism, was now regarded as an anathema to the new rulers. Similar experiences must have befallen the minor capitalists when the whole ethos of society was changed by the Communists in Russia, China and elsewhere.

Not that the Army escaped serious criticism. The Presbyterian ministers in London began to preach against them and refused to allow one of the Army's religious champions, Hugh Peters, to use their pulpits to preach in its defence. Peters therefore, on 13 December, preached to a large crowd from a position on the eastern side of the Banqueting House in Whitehall, a traditional location for sermons before the King. Certainly a militant man of religion, Peters was reported to have told the arrested Members of Parliament who queried the authority on which they had been arrested by Pride that they had been 'arrested by the power of the sword', and that when he uttered that pomposity he was himself armed with 'a great sword by his side'.

A satirical representation of the Revd Hugh Peters, the self-appointed religious champion of the Army.

The Army Council of Officers now made the political running. Their aim was the destruction of the monarchy, the bishops and Presbyterianism. They were also determined to try the King. On this latter issue there was increasing support in the form of petitions from regiments, garrisons and even one from what had previously been a very Royalist county, Somerset, calling for the trial of His Majesty and others who were to be charged with bringing disaster on the country. Somerset, however, had known much loyal Parliamentary support in the towns of Wellington and Taunton, the county town.

Attendance at the reduced House of Commons was by no means dedicated. Some Members, although thought to be allies of the

Army, resented the continued detention of MPs and registered mild protest by staying away. This made it even easier for the Army to obtain the passage of Bills which aided their policy. The vote for a settlement based on the Newport Treaty was annulled and fines were imposed on prominent Royalists who had taken part in the Second Civil War. Yet the Commons was not totally subservient to the military because, despite pressure, it ignored calls for it to dissolve itself to allow new elections.

Although much involved in day-to-day politics, the Army's Council of Officers had not forgotten the King. On 15 December they ordered that he should be brought from Hurst Castle and the following day Thomas Harrison, he of 'the clutch of preaching officers and troopers', left to effect the move. On the night of 16 December the King, who 'could not choose but have some melancholy apprehensions', was woken at about midnight by the sound of the fort's drawbridge being lowered. In the morning he was alarmed to hear that the visitor was Harrison, but could not find out the reason for the visit. When questioned about his increasing nervousness after learning that Harrison was in the fort, Charles told Thomas Herbert, '. . . do you not know that this was the man who intended to assassinate me, as by letter I was informed, during the late Treaty . . . this is a fit place for such a purpose'.[10]

The King's mind was subsequently put at rest when he was told the real purpose of Harrison's visit, to convey him to Windsor Castle

Colonel Thomas Harrison, the extreme Independent, who first called the King, 'This man of blood'.

Windsor Castle, another place where the King was held prisoner.

within three days. The King was cheered by the news that he was to go to Windsor, which was one of his favourite places. Some Royalists believed that he had been put into Hurst Castle so that the 'nauseous, pestilential Air' might kill off His Majesty,[11] just as they claimed that Cromwell and Whalley had conspired to allow King Charles to escape from Hampton Court so that he would flee the country. These thoughts may be fanciful, or they may contain grains of truth. One has only to see the motives attributed in modern politics to see that in conflict antagonists will use any assertion to discredit their opponents. At least the second accusation was more charitable than the first, since it did not aim to cause the death of the King.

Harrison stayed two nights at Hurst Castle and left without seeing the King, or speaking to any of his attendants. The day following Harrison's departure, Lieutenant-Colonel Cobbett came to inform King Charles of his destination, for which, this time, His Majesty, not without a touch of irony, thanked him. When he had been taken from Newport, His Majesty was kept in a worrying ignorance about where he was being taken.

The King's small escort arrived on the mainland near Milford, where it was joined by a larger party of horse. They rode to Ringwood, then to Romsey and on to Winchester, where the King was greeted with all respect and ceremony by the mayor, the aldermen and the clergy. People flocked in great numbers to see him in the city and along the road, many of them kissing his hand and praying for his happiness. Through Alresford and on to Alton the people came out to see him 'with joyous acclamations' and 'prayers for his preservation'. Between Alton and Farnham they passed a 'troop of cavalry drawn up in good order' – this was the rearguard waiting to escort the King.

Its commander was 'gallantly mounted and armed', a velvet round cap on his head, 'a new buff coat upon his back, and a crimson silk scarf about his waist richly fringed; who as the King passed with an easy pace (. . . as delighted to see men well horsed and armed) . . . gave the King a bow with his head, all a Soldade [in military fashion], which His Majesty requited'. The King asked Herbert who the officer was and on being told it was Thomas Harrison, 'viewed him more narrowly . . . the King said, "He looked like a soldier, and that his aspect was good, and found him not such a one as was represented . . ."'. He went on to claim some experience of judging men by their faces and if he had seen Harrison previously he would not have had such a bad opinion of him; 'For oft times the spirit and disposition may be discerned by the countenance.' In relating this incident Herbert finished with the seventeenth-century equivalent of 'how wrong can one be' when he wrote, 'yet in that one may be deceived'.[12]

That night was spent at Farnham in a private house. Before their meal the King spoke with Harrison for about half an hour or more. Harrison assured the King that what he had heard about the plan to assassinate him was untrue, but when the discussion became political and he then told the King that the law applied to great and small and that justice was no respecter of persons, His Majesty soon ended their talk.

Plans had been made for the King to escape during the halt for a midday meal at Lord Newburgh's house at Bagshot the next day, but on arriving there they learnt that the horse prepared for his escape, supposedly 'the most notorious for fleetness that was in England',[13] could not be used as it had been lamed by a kick from another horse. This plan had involved a relay of horses along an escape route through Windsor Forest to allow the King, familiar as he was with the forest and its bridleways, to outpace pursuit. The laming of the fast horse and the fact that the King was so closely guarded by 'a hundred horse, the officers all exceedingly well horsed, and every man, officer and soldier, having a pistol ready . . . in one hand, [ensured] that he resolved not to pursue that design'.[14] The King had complained about the horse he had been riding and Harrison had promised to provide a better one. A watchful and suspicious guard, he is unlikely to have agreed to the King being mounted on a fast, unknown horse that might aid any escape attempt.

Later that day, 23 December, the journey continued through part of the forest and ended at Windsor Castle, where the King was met by the Duke of Hamilton, now imprisoned there. The Duke, on his knees, kissed the King's hand and had time only to utter the briefest of loyal words as the royal embraced him before he was hurried away by his guards and not allowed near His Majesty again. Shortly after the arrival at the castle there was a disturbance in the town when people agitated against the Army's treatment of the King. The ensuing riot resulted in the death of some of the townsfolk at the hands of the soldiers who quelled this demonstration of loyalty. This evidence, despite the resulting fatalities, and the reception the King had received along the route from Hurst Castle, through Hampshire and Surrey into Berkshire must have warmed him after the cold, detached atmosphere of that low stone fort and the impersonal antipathy of his escorting guards and their commander.

Such examples of steadfast loyalty and affection from some of his subjects could have caused the King to misjudge the dangers which faced him. Always the optimist, his return to Windsor, a place he always liked, may have encouraged him to think that his circumstances were improving. Although the frequent suggestions and plans offered by close supporters for escape may have been attractive, his reluctance to make a determined attempt could suggest the confidence he had in his ability to arrive at an acceptable settlement with his enemies. It certainly did not demonstrate any lack of personal courage; the King had that in abundance, possibly too much for caution. The courtesy he received at Windsor could also have dulled any acute awareness of danger. The King was not a fool. He was an intelligent man, although possibly blinded to reality by the strength of his personal convictions on the rights of kings and religious issues, as well as his belief in his own invulnerability as the anointed of God.

At Windsor Herbert implies that all the ceremonial practices of the King's Court were continued, even though the Army Council of Officers had forbidden them. His servants knelt when attending to his needs; the governor was courteous and as considerate as his gaoler duties allowed; and the companies of soldiers guarding him were well behaved towards him and his attendants. His life was as normal as it could be without his family, freedom or the day-to-day affairs of state. He spent most of each morning in prayer along with other acts of piety and religious study. The afternoons, when weather permitted, were spent in healthy exercise, usually walking the very long but favourite North Terrace, which overlooked the meadows flanking the River Thames, Eton College and the countryside of Buckinghamshire beyond. Initially he was accompanied on the walks by the Parliamentary Commissioners who had awaited his arrival at the castle but when they had returned to London the governor, Colonel Whitchcote, joined him as companion and, of course, close supervisor.

Herbert recorded that 'None of the nobility, nor few of the gentry, were suffered to come into the Castle to see the King, save on Sundays to sermon in St George's Chapel, where the Chaplain to the Governor and garrison preached.'[15] That the King listened to a sermon, despite his previous refusals to do so, was probably intended as a practical demonstration of his intent to adhere to the concessions

A prosperous leader of the City of London.

he had made on religion at the Newport negotiations. Herbert believed that His Majesty was happier at Windsor than at any other time since his stay at Hampton Court, where he had been able to see his children, a pleasure denied him at Windsor.

The King's time at Windsor Castle was spent uneventfully, apart from two incidents recorded by Herbert. The King, who always wore the insignia of the Order of the Garter with its 'George' (a locket which was a part of the Order's regalia), lost his personal diamond seal which had hung from a gold chain around his neck. This caused Herbert to spend a day engaged on a fruitless and secretive search – as it was not thought wise to let the garrison know of the loss. It was eventually found by the King, who saw it glinting in the candle- and fire-light of the royal bedchamber. The other episode Herbert made a note of concerned a fire in a little room next to the King's bedchamber. Herbert slept there and was awakened when a spark from his fire ignited two baskets of charcoal kept there for the King's fire. The resulting panic caused commotion but no real damage. Herbert and other servants put out the blaze, although they woke the King who praised their sense of duty. The fact that these two minor incidents seemed worthy of mention to Herbert indicates the even, possibly mundane, routine nature of the King's life at Windsor.

Herbert knew that King Charles was aware of 'how preposterously things went in both Houses of Parliament, wherein he was concerned; and how that Army officers had then published a Remonstrance,[16] designing thereby an alteration of the Government, and trial of his person by some way that was extraordinary and unprecedented'.[17] With this in mind, when Colonel Whitchcote told the King in mid-January that he was shortly to be taken to Whitehall, His Majesty '. . . immediately retired to his Bedchamber, and was a good while private in his addresses to God, ever having recourse to Him by prayer and meditation, in what condition soever he was, as being the surest way to find comfort'.[18] Herbert's description of this incident would seem to indicate that no matter how calm and controlled His Majesty might outwardly seem, his innermost thoughts were probably in a state of great turmoil as a result of the unprecedented nature of what now faced him.

CHAPTER SEVEN

The Coup d'Etat

The greater the power, the more dangerous the abuse.
Edmund Burke, Middlesex Election Speech, 1771

It was Sir Jacob Astley who uttered the memorable prayer just before the start of the Battle at Edgehill in 1642: 'O Lord! thou knowest how busy I must be today: if I forget thee, do not thou forget me.'[1] He also made a most prophetic statement after his surrender to the New Model Army soldiers at Stow-on-the-Wold in March 1646 when he said, 'You have done your work, boys. You may go play, unless you fall out among yourselves.'

As has been seen, the Parliamentarians did fall out among themselves. The Army had expelled the Presbyterians from Parliament but there were schisms within the Army. The Council of Officers, led by Henry Ireton, was involving itself even more deeply in the political affairs of the country, while Sir Thomas Fairfax, much more a soldier than a politician, worked largely to administer and maintain discipline in the Army. He was not alone. He was supported in these responsibilities by Philip Skippon, John Lambert, Robert Overton and by Cromwell's brother-in-law, John Desborough (or Disbrowe). Further, not all the New Model Army Members of Parliament supported the Independents. Sir Robert Pye and Edward Harley, two of its colonels, were arrested during the coup. The Army's Council of Officers had three main aims. First they wished to produce plans for a revision of secular and religious government; second to consider the fate of the King and other senior Royalists; and, finally, to secure the balance of the enormous arrears of pay owed to the officers and soldiers.

Invariably, during the breakdown of an established order, all kinds of ideas are suggested for change, and there were some important differences among the Independent sects that clearly divided them. However, the Independents were now almost the sole Members of

Sir Jacob, Lord Astley, Royalist general defeated at Stow-on-the-Wold, Gloucestershire.

A caricature of Presbyterian ministers.

A true blew Prieſt a Lincey Woolſey Brother —
One Legg a Pulpitt holds a Tubb the other
. In Orthodox, grave, moderate, Preſtbyterian —
Half Surplice, Cloake half Prieſt half Puritan,
Made up of all theſe halfes hee cannot Paſs,
For any thing intirely, but an Aſs

the Parliament. At one sitting, shortly after Pride's Purge, there were fewer that forty Members of the Commons present, below the number needed to form a legal quorum under the rules of the House. In the Lords, there were even fewer – four!

Many Independents still absented themselves from the Commons as a protest against the continued imprisonment of the members who were arrested by Pride on 6 December. As if to demonstrate their independence from the Army, in the following days there were several addresses to Fairfax from these absent members calling for the release of

Colonel John Lambert, who avoided politics between 1648 and '49.

those who were still held. The imprisoned members were eventually freed on a parole that they would never try to return to the House. That parole did not apply to those eleven Presbyterians whose previous expulsion had been demanded by both the Army and the Independents. Three of them, Denzil Holles, John Clotworthy and Edward Massey, along with Richard Browne and Lionel Copley who had been arrested later, continued to be held on charges of plotting the Duke of Hamilton's Scottish invasion. Massey was later to escape to France, but the others remained captive. Cromwell himself had even ridden to Windsor on 14 December in an attempt to obtain evidence against these men from Hamilton, but the Duke refused to incriminate them. They were not tried, but remained imprisoned illegally for several years.

Major-General Philip Skippon, the popular leader of the New Model Army Foot regiments.

The Independents shared the basic aims of the politically committed officers and men in the Army, even if a few of the ideas put forward by some of the men were considered far too radical. Issues such as the proposal for universal male suffrage, for example, were regarded as far too revolutionary in a society whose foundations still rested heavily on the ownership of land and property.

Lieutenant-Colonel John Lilburne and a committee of sixteen, including four Army officers, had drawn up a new 'Agreement of the People' as a basis for a new constitution. Lilburne had understood Ireton to mean that this document would be accepted without discussion, but was incensed when it had to be considered by the Council of Officers before it could be adopted. Discussions began on 11 December 1648 with wrangling about, among other things, those matters that would be exempt from parliamentary control, the main issue being religion.

The eventual resolution of this dispute was the acceptance that Parliament should be paramount in all things secular, but in religious matters it would not be allowed to interfere in the worship of peaceful sects. However, there were marked exceptions to this: the papists and the prelates, the hierachical priesthood, the archbishops, bishops and their priests in the Church of England. Another matter of difference in the interpretation of the points of the Agreement was in the power of Parliament to punish outside the law. Lilburne and his committee proposed that as the supreme authority in the land, Parliament should have this right. Ireton and others disagreed, not wanting an uncontrollable Parliament to be supreme. A compromise allowed the Parliament merely to punish public officers who failed to do their duty.

On the issue of what should be done about the King and senior Royalists, who, it was claimed, were completely responsible for the blood that had been spilt and the destruction caused in the two recent wars, opinions varied. All the Army, the Independents and even some Presbyterians believed that the King and others should be tried. The differences emerged over the penalty to be imposed. The Presbyterian London Authorities presented their own 'Agreement of the People'. This proposed that after the King's trial and his restoration to the throne it should be enacted that if any King thereafter should challenge the power of Parliament, or refuse the Royal Assent to laws passed to him for approval by Parliament, 'after consultation with the Lords . . . he may be deposed . . . and that any subject assisting him therein was to be treated as guilty of high treason'.[2]

Colonel John Desborough, Cromwell's brother-in-law.

That was one possible way of dealing with the problem of the King. Ireton had a different idea, namely that after trial the King should be imprisoned until such time as he agreed to 'abandon his negative voice on Church lands' and 'to abjure the Scots'. Cromwell, however, considered that the King's trial should be postponed until after the trials of the defeated leaders of the most recent war, Hamilton, the Earls of Norwich and of Holland, as well as Arthur, Lord Capel, who had been taken at Colchester.

There were those who advocated the King's death since they believed that there could be no settlement of the kingdom's difficulties while he lived. Clarendon wrote of three methods of removing the King that were canvassed among the extremists who held this view, namely, that he might be poisoned 'which would make the least noise', that he might be assassinated, 'for which there were hands ready enough to be employed', or that he should be brought to trial and executed 'as a malefactor; which would be most for the honour of the Parliament, and {would} teach all kings to know that they were accountable and punishable for the wickedness of their lives'.[3]

There were further arguments in favour of the death of the King. If he were to be imprisoned he would continue to be an embarrassment and a focus for the continued loyalty of the Royalists. He would have to be closely confined since his supporters would without doubt instigate plots for his escape. In addition, his prolonged imprisonment would most certainly generate sympathy for him even from people who were not currently extremely Royalist in opinion. The recent reception given to him on the way to Windsor and the demonstration in Windsor itself were indications of that.

In about mid-December a proposal that apparently advocated the death of the King was defeated in the Council of Officers by a majority of merely five votes. One of the arguments against killing the King was the realisation that his successor, as the future King Charles II, would

Lieutenant-Colonel John Lilburne, the Leveller 'Freeborn John'.

not be in their hands as his father was. The new King had powerful allies in the foreign monarchies and would be sickened by the execution – therefore he could and would be a great danger to the country.

It is significant that in the discussion of all these options there seemed to be no recognition of the fact that King Charles I could be acquitted of the crimes with which he might be charged. The Army and the Independents seemed, at this stage, more concerned with the public proclamation of guilt than with the process of true justice.

There were some voices that questioned whether the Parliament, or the Army, had any legal right to place the King on trial. It was the issue of the legality of bringing the King to trial which exercised many, including Cromwell. He and Richard Deane met and consulted with three moderate men, who would find any threat of violence against the King totally repugnant. These were Bulstrode Whitelocke, Sir Thomas Widdrington, both lawyers and Commissioners for the custody of the Great Seal (without the imprint of which Acts of Parliament had no legal standing), and the cautious but courageous Speaker of the House of Commons, William Lenthall. These men had three meetings with Cromwell, during one of which he lay on a royal bed, and tried to encourage the Army to abandon any thought of a trial for the King. It would appear that Cromwell and others at this time, about 21 December, wished to preserve the King's life, even if they wanted to see him pronounced guilty in a public trial.[4]

Bulstrode Whitelocke, MP, one of the prominent lawyers consulted by Cromwell.

Cromwell consults the lawyers about the trial of the King. A Victorian interpretation.

In the much depleted House of Lords, where the highest attendance since Pride's activities had been seven, there was deep concern about the extremist proposals for the King's future. Four peers, Pembroke, Salisbury, Denbigh and North, visited Fairfax to discuss another attempt to get the King to make further concessions on the remaining issues. It appears that Cromwell endorsed the aim behind this approach to the King, urging that the King's life be spared if he were completely to accept the propositions that were still under dispute. The Lieutenant-General spoke to this purpose at the Council of Officers.

On 23 December the House of Commons had appointed a committee to consider the future of the King. It was possible that this committee was formed with the additional aim of exerting further pressure on the King to make further concessions.[5] Although the Commons had in effect restored the Ordinance that forbade any further negotiation with the King, the Earl of Denbigh went to Windsor, ostensibly to see his brother-in-law, the imprisoned Duke of Hamilton, but in reality hoping to discuss matters with the King and to seek his agreement to the outstanding issues. His Majesty, who would hardly have been unaware of the purpose of the visit, did not invite Denbigh to meet him. Denbigh's visit was meant to be a secret but in practice was widely known about, so the King's failure to meet him became common knowledge and was seen as the final royal rejection of the offered settlement. This injected a greater urgency into consideration of the King's future. His action was seen as further proof of his stubborn refusal to compromise and therefore the uselessness of further negotiation.

The King's behaviour and the interpretations placed on it did much to weaken the resolve of his more moderate opponents. There had been those in the Army and even some among the Independents who had spoken against extreme action before Denbigh's rebuff. Now they were less sure of their grounds for opposition. Fairfax was still unhappy about the prospects of the drastic action that the King's trial would represent. Other Independents, concerned about the integrity of Parliament, disapproved of the Army's usurpation of responsibility. However, after the King had ignored the approach by Denbigh, Cromwell, who had opposed any policy of death for the King, now stopped speaking against it.

On 27 December the Commons voted that all Court ceremonial would be banned at Windsor and that the King's servants should be replaced by fewer and less exalted attendants. Having borne the

William Lenthall, the Speaker of the House of Commons, who was consulted by Cromwell about the King's trial.

discomfort and inconvenience of Hurst Castle, Charles was unlikely to have been more than mildly irritated. Spiteful though it was, the action was more a blow at kingship than at the King himself, since by removing ceremony it sought to remove any semblance of awesome formality from any service to the Lord's anointed.

The following day the Committee appointed to consider the future of the King presented an Ordinance to the House of Commons for its First Reading. On its arrival, Henry Elsing, the Clerk to the House of Commons, expressed his firm opposition by immediately resigning his position. The Ordinance accused the King of subverting the ancient and fundamental laws of the country and of waging war against Parliament and the kingdom. It went on to appoint 3 judges and 150 Commissioners to try the King on these grievous charges. Among the Commissioners were to be Members of the Houses of Lords and Commons; officers of the Army; aldermen and other commanders of the City, with some gentlemen from the counties.

During the debate and before the Ordinance was sent to the House of Lords, Oliver Cromwell spoke in the Commons. He said, 'If any man whatsoever hath carried on the design of deposing the King, and disinheriting his posterity; or, if any man had yet any such a design, he should be the greatest traitor and rebel in the world; but, since the Providence of God hath cast this upon us, I cannot but submit to Providence, though I am not yet provided to give you advice.'[6] Although this statement lacks directness, its intent is clear. Cromwell, whose influence was extremely powerful, was justifying the trial and the removal of the King from his throne as being the responsibility of 'the Providence of God'. He gave the Members the chance to shed responsibility and to deny any guilt that might attach to the actions. Although he claimed that he could not give advice on the matter, he gave those who wished to take it a way to excuse treason and rebellion. It was as if the crocodile was once more defending itself.

Cromwell was not one to believe in the inevitability of divine providence any more than he believed in the predestination doctrine of the Calvinistic Presbyterians. He believed in freedom of worship and therefore in Free Will, man's God-given gift to make choices. In this speech to the Commons he gave Members the opportunity of making their own decisions and the backing of God's Providence to make a decision that would suit him. His words showed his awareness that the trial of the King would amount to rebellion and treason and that there was nothing in England's laws to justify it, but he considered it to be necessary. Apart from any outcome, the threat of a trial and retribution might possibly help to bring the King to his senses and to an acceptance of the changed situation in his kingdom.

After its Second and Third Readings on 29 December 1648 and 1 January 1649 the Ordinance was sent to the House of Lords, where the following day it immediately encountered opposition from the fifteen peers present, as well as from the three men who were nominated to be the King's judges. They were Lord Chief Justice Henry Rolle, the Lord Chief Justice of the King's Bench; Lord Justice Oliver St John, Lord Chief Justice of the Court of Common Pleas; and Lord Justice Baron John Wilde. The Earl of Manchester contended that to declare the King a traitor contradicted the fundamental principles of the law. Algernon Percy, the Earl of Northumberland, claimed that fewer than one in twenty of the people in the country knew whether the King or Parliament had first waged war. He also considered it to be unreasonable to declare the King's treason before it was proved, particularly as there was no existing law under which the charge could be tried. While Philip, the Earl of Pembroke, took a neutral stance, Basil Feilding, the Earl of Denbigh, the acting Speaker of the Lords, asserted that he would rather be torn to pieces than sit as a commissioner at the King's trial. The three judges also spoke against the Ordinance, refusing to be involved with it because of its complete illegality.

The Lords rejected the Ordinance and adjourned for a week in the belief that the Commons would be unable to proceed without their agreement and that a delay might enable their views to prevail. They completely misjudged the determination of the Commons, who gave themselves the power to act. They removed the names of the six lords in the original Ordinance, replacing them with six others, among whom was John Bradshaw, a Serjeant-at-law (a junior judge). Incensed by the House of Lords' attempt to foil their wishes, the Commons then voted unanimously:

1. That the People under God are the Original of all just Powers.
2. That the Commons of England assembled in Parliament, being chosen by, and representing the People, have the Supreme Authority of this Nation.
3. That whatsoever is enacted and declared Law by the Commons of England assembled in Parliament, hath the Force of Law, and all

the People of this Nation are included thereby, although the Consent and Concurrence of the King and House of Peers be not had thereunto.[7]

This near-republican declaration by the much-truncated Parliament may have suggested to the Members that they were now the supreme body in the land. They were not. The politically active leaders of the Army were the people who called the tune. 'The Rump' more or less just sat and followed where the Army directed, going on to pass the Ordinance in an amended form. In essence it now read:

Whereas it is notorious, That Charles Stuart, the now King of England, not content with those many Encroachments which his Predecessors had made upon the People in their Rights and Freedoms, hath had a wicked design totally to subvert the ancient and fundamental Laws and Liberties of this Nation, and in their Trade to introduce an Arbitrary and Tyrannical Government; and that besides all other evil Ways amd Means to bring this Design to pass, he hath prosecuted it with Fire and Sword, levied and maintained a cruel War in the Land against the Parliament and Kingdom, whereby the Country hath been miserably wasted, the public Treasure exhausted, Trade decayed, Thousands of people murdered, and infinite other Mischiefs committed; for all which high and treasonable Offences the said Charles Stuart might long since justly have been brought to exemplary and condign punishment . . .

The text went on to say that there had been hopes that when the King was in the hands of Parliament that this 'would have quieted the Distempers of the Kingdom', but he and his 'Complices' had raised new troubles, rebellions and invasions. In order to prevent such events being repeated, and that

No chief Officer or Magistrate whatsoever may hereafter presume traitorously and maliciously to imagine or contrive the enslaving or destroying of the English Nation, and to expect Impunity for so doing:
    Be it ordained and enacted by the Commons in Parliament, and it is hereby ordained and enacted by the Authority thereof, that Thomas Lord Fairfax, Oliver Cromwell, Henry Ireton, Esquires,

Sir Hardress Waller, Knight, Philip Skippon, (and a Hundred and Forty-five others) shall be, and are hereby appointed and required to be Commissioners and Judges for the Hearing, Trying and Adjudging of the said Charles Stuart, &c.[8]

Apart from the imaginative rewriting of early history, where the King's predecessors had stolen liberties that their subjects never had, the objective of this Ordinance is clear. The King was accused of being personally responsible for all the ills of his reign, especially those during the previous years of bloodshed and destruction.

The stage was being set for the trial of the King, but before that event was to occur there would be much shifting of position, searching of conscience, shuffling of feet, evasion of responsibility and changing of minds.

CHAPTER EIGHT

To Try the King

. . . Give dreadful note of preparation
Shakespeare, *King Henry V*

While the Army and the Independents carried on with their plans for his trial, the King was still at Windsor, now attended by fewer servants and in more austere circumstances. His Christmas had been sombre and although now provided with a large quantity of new clothes to replace those he had stubbornly worn for the previous months, he could not reflect on the festive season with any sense of pleasure.

The Independents placed no particular significance on Christmas Day, which that year fell on a Monday. In Parliament it was a normal working day. For this, and of course other reasons, King Charles was denied the solace of an Anglican clergyman to conduct the religious service and so he dressed in his best clothes to read to those around him the service appointed for the day in the *Book of Common Prayer*, a further minor act of defiance. The King now dined in his own room, but the Christmas Day meal was as sparse as his other meals had now become and, as *Perfect Occurrences* of the time recorded, he was disappointed by the cook, who provided neither 'minc'd pye', nor 'plum porridge', a forerunner of plum pudding.[1]

As time wore on the King spent more time reading. The Bible, with Shakespeare's plays and those of Ben Jonson, took most of his attention. Just as he missed his family, so they missed him. The Queen, still in Paris, wrote to Parliament seeking permission to visit her husband, but her request was refused. It might have given the Independents and the Army the opportunity to place her under arrest, if only as a hostage to extort further concessions from the King. Some of the Parliamentarians must have remembered that he signed the death warrant for the Earl of Strafford because he was fearful for the safety of his wife and family. It is probable that such a plan would have occurred to the more unprincipled of the King's enemies. It is possible that adverse foreign reaction might have deterred them, but it is most likely that they were no longer concerned about obtaining concessions from the King. They had decided that his trial and deposition were the only solution to his stubbornness.

In January, after its disregard of the views of the House of Lords and following its virtual declaration of republican status, the Commons pressed on with the arrangements, somewhat thwarted by the lack of a precedent. On 6 January they considered their Ordinance for the trial yet again, reaffirming its contents with a vote of twenty-nine for and twenty-six against, surprisingly close when compared with the unanimity of their votes towards republicanism. They reduced the number of Commissioners to 135, eliminating the Members of the House of Lords and others who would certainly refuse to become involved.

This document was now no longer referred to as a Parliamentary Ordinance, but as an Act. This change might appear minor, but legally it had a constitutional significance. During the Civil War, when the King would certainly not give the Royal Assent to Parliamentary decisions, these could not be called 'Acts', being known as 'Ordinances'. There were, after all, many lawyers with minds that demanded legal accuracy sitting as Members in the Long Parliament. This new change of title was made in a farcical effort to proclaim to all that the decisions of this tiny Parliamentary body now had the authority, weight and, dare one say it, the majesty of acceptable constitutional law. Other than this the practical planning of the trial was advanced no further. The Commons set neither time nor place for the momentous event. The Commissioners who were to try the King were left to make those decisions at their meetings.

Parliament occupied itself with discussion about the procedure to be adopted during the forthcoming trial and how the charge should be framed. In whose name was the King to be arraigned? His Majesty could not be charged in his own name, neither could he be called to account in the name of the constitutional Parliament, as the Commons had effectively decreed that the House of Lords no longer wielded any power.

After much discursive debate on these matters, they made a decision: these points were to be referred to a committee. This body was '. . . to draw up an Expedient, and report to the House with speed'.[2]

Another matter called for their attention: the Scottish Commissioners in London had written to Parliament stressing the need for consultation and joint action over the matter of the King. The Covenant required it and, after all, Charles was also King of the Scots. This interjection was undoubtedly a nuisance, interrupting their deliberations to remind them that there were other subjects of the King who had a vital interest in his future. The 'Army Parliament', as it was sometimes called by opponents, resented this reminder and, mindful of the recent Scottish invasion under the Duke of Hamilton, took another decision. It deferred consideration of the Scottish letter.

Monday 8 January 1649

The 135 Commissioners nominated to try the King were to attend a meeting at the 400-year-old Painted Chamber in the Palace of Westminster to decide on the points referred to them by Parliament. These matters comprised the date, time and place of the trial; the procedure to be followed in this 'High Court of Justice'; and the precise wording of the charges against the King.

When the meeting assembled at 8 a.m. there were only fifty-four Commissioners listed as being present. Fairfax attended, but having seen for himself the intentions and mood of that assembly, he did not sign the proclamation that the Commissioners had drawn up for public announcement. Although his was not the only missing signature – sixteen other names were absent – Fairfax alone, of those who attended this first meeting, decided to have nothing further to do with the enterprise. He made no objection at the time, but just did not attend any subsequent meetings of the Commissioners or of the High Court of Justice. He was later to write of the Council of Officers in his *Short Memorials* that, '. . . I never gave my free consent to anything they did: but (being then undischarged of my place) they set my hand, by way of course, to all their Papers; whether I consented or not'.[3]

The Commissioners established their terms of reference and began the appointment of officials to serve the needs of the High Court of Justice. As Clerk to the Court, they named Henry Elsing's successor, the new Clerk to the House of Commons, John Phelps. The second Clerk, Greaves, was also nominated. Then they chose the lawyers who were to conduct the prosecution of King Charles, naming four in all. They were William Steele of Gray's Inn, the Attorney-General, who was to be the chief prosecutor; Doctor Isaac Dorislaus, a lawyer of Dutch birth, who had been appointed a Judge of the Court of Admiralty in the previous April; John Aske, of whom little is known, although Markham claims that one of Fairfax's cousins, Richard Aske, was one of the prosecuting counsel;[4] the final man chosen was John Cook, also of Gray's Inn, who is reported as having had a chequered career in London, Ireland and elsewhere. He was to be the Solicitor.

Another appointment made was that of Sergeant-at-Arms, a post to be occupied by one Edward Dendy, whose first duty ordered by the Commissioners was to proclaim the existence of the High Court of Justice. He was to do this at Westminster Hall, a carefully chosen place, in and around which several of the English High Courts of Justice sat.

Tuesday 9 January 1649

Accordingly, at 10 a.m. Dendy, on horseback, carried his mace into the centre of Westminster Hall. He was accompanied by six trumpeters. It has been suggested that his escort of two troops of horse also rode into the Hall. It is most unlikely that there would have been 207 horses within that space, with all the consequent crowding, noise and equine deposits. The escort probably remained outside where drums beat loudly to attract the crowds.

Inside the Hall the six trumpeters blew their fanfare silencing the proceedings of the Court of Chancery which was then in session. Dendy, still mounted, then proclaimed his message:

Buildings on the south of New Palace Yard, showing the entrance to Westminster Hall.

By virtue of an Act of the Commons of England assembled in Parliament for erecting of an high court of Justice, for the trying and judging of Charles Stuart, King of England, we, whose names are hereunder written being Commissioners (amongst others) nominated in the said Act do hereby appoint that the High Court of Justice mentioned in the said Act shall be held in the Painted Chamber in the Palace of Westminster, on Wednesday the tenth day of this instant January by one of the clock in the afternoon. And this we appoint to be notified by public proclaiming hereof in the great Hall at Westminster tomorrow being the ninth day of this instant January betwixt the hours of Nine and Eleven in the forenoon. In testimony whereof we have hereunto set our hands and seals the eighth day of January Anno Domini 1649.

The Commons were so pleased with this display and ceremony that Dendy was ordered to repeat the proclamation with drums, escort and, this time, 'tenn' trumpeters at the Old Exchange and in Cheapside in the City of London. The crowds who came to watch and hear at midday, when these additional performances occurred, offered Dendy neither insult nor injury.[5]

Later that day the House of Commons, still unsure about the form of the charge, voted that the present Great Seal of England should be broken up and that a new one should be made immediately. With their usual regard for the legal niceties, they also voted that until the new Seal was made, all their actions and decisions would have the force of law, although they would still be under the imprint of the old Seal.

The design of the new Seal was then considered and ordered to incorporate the Arms of England, the Harp and the Arms of Ireland engraved on one side, with the inscription, 'The Great Seal of England'. The other side was to bear 'the Sculpture or Map of the Parliament' and the words, 'In the first year of freedom by God's blessing restored, 1649.' As the previous Great Seal had depicted the enthroned King Charles on one side and a mounted charging knight on the other, this radically different design was to be a further indication of the imminent abolition of royal power, at the very least.

The Great Seal of Charles I.

Wednesday 10 January 1649

The second formal meeting of the Commissioners at the Painted Hall, so spectacularly announced by Dendy, was attended by only forty-six of those nominated, only about one-third of the original number.

Some may have had duties and responsibilities which would have kept them away. Others, like Fairfax, had made the decision never to take part. Greaves, who, with John Phelps, was to have acted as Clerk to the High Court of Justice, had asked to be relieved of the duty because of the '[unspecified] great and important employment . . . in behalf of the Common Wealth, from which he cannot be spared without prejudice to the public'.[6] The Commissioneers agreed to his release, nominating Andrew Broughton in his place. They then allocated some minor posts, appointing the ushers for the Court, Edward Walford and another man whose name was Vowell. They also added another messenger, Litchman, to the Court Staff and appointed John King to be the Court Crier.

There was, however, a far more significant appointment made, for on this day the Commissioners elected the man who was to be President of their High Court of Justice. It is hardly surprising that in elections to very unpopular or hazardous official appointments, the lot frequently falls upon someone who is not present. It is interesting to speculate that this may have happened in the choice of man for this post.

The man chosen as President was John Bradshaw, who was absent from the meeting, away in Cheshire where he was the Chief Justice. He was a judge in Wales and had been a judge of the Sheriff's Court in London for some years. It is likely, however, that there had been discussion concerning his new appointment beforehand. His selection would have been canvassed in advance among the Commissioners. A summons was sent to recall him in time for the next meeting and for the rest of that session, William Say, another lawyer, acted as the President.

Conscious of their lack of experience in bringing kings to trial, a fact that became very obvious in the following days, the Commissioners nominated two committees to begin work on essential preparatory details. The first of these was composed of the four lawyers who were to prepare and present the charge against the King according to the Act of Parliament, copies of which were given to them. The other committee was 'to consider of all circumstances in matters of order and method for the carrying on and managing the King's trial . . .'.[7] This body's members were Nicholas Love, John Lisle, Gilbert Millington, Augustine Garland, Henry Marten, Thomas Chaloner, Sir John Danvers and Sir Henry Mildmay, and it could function in the presence of any two of them. They were to liaise with the prosecuting counsel and to make a report at the next meeting.

John Bradshaw, the Lord
President of the High Court of
Justice set up to try the King.

After these transactions had been completed, the doors were
opened and the public were admitted. The crier proclaimed the
Court's sitting three times and then, after the roll of Commissioners
was called, orders were given for summonses to be sent out to the
eighty-nine missing members.

The nomination and election of Bradshaw to the cardinal position
in this High Court of Justice has an element of 'Hobson's Choice'
about it. Thomas Hobson of Cambridge had hired out horses; he
always let them strictly in their turn, irrespective of their quality. If a
person refused the horse that Hobson offered, he had to go without.
It was that horse, or none. Hobson, who had died in 1631, was

apparently notorious for this practice and some of the Commissioners, particularly those from East Anglia (the area around Cambridge), would have either known him or at least known of him. The parallel might not have been lost on them.

In their search for a President, the Army and Independent leaders were hard pressed to find a lawyer of eminence who was prepared to serve. Three Lord Chief Justices had declared the Court to be illegal and they were certainly not going to involve themselves in any illegality. The two well-respected lawyers who had been consulted by Cromwell about the trial, Bulstrode Whitelock and Sir Thomas Widdrington, had spoken against it and had advised moderation in dealings with the King. Even if, against their better judgment, they had considered serving as President, they were very probably not acceptable to either the Army or the Independents. Most of the lawyers who sat in the House of Commons had been expelled by Colonel Pride, and, therefore, the choice was very limited. The appointment of someone else to the Presidential seat was likely to have produced a collective sigh of relief from the other lawyers who might have been nominated.

Sir Henry Marten, the republican who played a prominent part in bringing the King to trial.

Bradshaw was not a Member of Parliament, but had been added to the list of Commissioners as one of the replacements for the peers and others who were deleted from the original list. He was, however, a Serjeant-at-law and, although only a junior judge, probably the most senior lawyer in the list of Commissioners likely to give faithful attendance at the Court. It is said that he came to the notice of the Independents when in June 1647 in Chester he made a fiery speech against the King, attacking him as a tyrant who was 'worse than Nero'.[8] The appointment was significant, the nominee less so. Like the character Malvolio, the house steward who aspired to higher things in Shakespeare's *Twelfth Night*, it might easily be written about Bradshaw that 'Some men are born great, some achieve greatness and some have greatness thrust upon them.'[9] At his appointment Bradshaw was certainly a man in the third category.

The business of the day on 10 January completed, the Court adjourned until the following Friday.

Friday 12 January 1649

At this meeting Bradshaw was present as ordered and made 'an earnest apology for himself to be excused' the position of President. This was refused. It was then voted that his title should be that of

'Lord President' inside and outside the courtroom while the trial lasted. Bradshaw again demurred, but was again overruled by the other thirty-four Commissioners recorded as being present.

The clandestine Royalist news-sheets, as can be imagined, found a new target in this aggrandised 'Lord President'. He was reviled as one who delighted in the position he now held, particularly the title. His newly found prominence and that of the Court might also have been threatened with actual physical violence from several possible quarters. Apart from possible Royalist attack, some of the more extreme Scots Presbyterians might have presented a possible threat. Resentment from excluded Members of Parliament might have triggered a violent reaction and there was always the danger of attempts on the lives of the President or any of the Commissioners by disaffected individuals such as John Felton, who had murdered the first Duke of Buckingham.

Security before, and especially during, the trial was of the utmost importance. The Commissioners were so aware of the potential risks that they deputed Sir Hardress Waller and Thomas Harrison to gain Fairfax's approval for the provision of sufficient soldiers to attend and guard the Court during its present and future sittings. The Lord General, despite his objections to the trial, complied with the request.

A third committee was set up, composed of Colonels Robert Tichborne and Owen Roe, with Messrs John Blackston and John Fry, to 'make preparations for the trial of the King, that it may be performed in a solemn manner'. They were given the responsibility for ensuring that the facilities and layout of the Court met this requirement. There had, at this time, been no formal decision about the exact location of the trial, another committee was considering that, but the Commissioners, being a close-knit group, would know what the likely outcome was, although this would require formal approval.

Nicholas Love reported that he and his colleagues, in consultation with the lawyers, recommended that during the open Court proceedings no one should be allowed to speak except the Lord President and the four Counsel. The Commissioners should be allowed to examine witnesses, but not directly. Questions should be passed to the Lord President who would then relay them. The four Counsel were instructed to present the charge to the Commissioners for consideration the next Monday morning, 15 January.

Love's group was required to draw up the necessary rules and instructions for the procedure in consultation with Bradshaw and the lawyers. Then the Lord President and the Counsel would be instructed to manage the business in accordance with those established rules. Oliver Cromwell, Hardress Waller, Edward Whalley, Thomas Scott, Robert Tichborne, Thomas Harrison and Richard Deane were instructed to join Love's committee at a meeting the following morning at 9 a.m. to consider the actual venue for the trial. The Court then adjourned, to re-convene at 2 p.m. the following day.

Colonel Richard Deane, who was greatly involved in preparations for the trial.

Saturday 13 January 1649

Thirty-eight Commissioners attended the meeting at which the Sergeant-at-Arms was ordered to take soldiers to search and secure the vaults under the Painted Chamber where they regularly sat. The need for greater security was becoming a prominent issue in the minds of the Commissioners. After all, the Gunpowder Plot orchestrated by Robert Catesby, Guido Fawkes and their accomplices had occurred within living memory.

Augustine Garland gave the report of the committee that had been considering the location for the trial, after which the Court ruled that it should be held in Westminster Hall. Inside the Hall, the High Court should be sited at the southern end of the building where the Courts of the King's Bench and Chancery normally sat. To enlarge the space the partitions that divided these two Courts from one another were to be removed and the committee responsible for the practical preparations was to take the necessary action to effect this. The meeting was then adjourned until the following Monday.

Initial considerations for the location of the trial had centred either on Windsor or London. As this was to be what would now be termed 'a show trial', a location in London was far preferable to one at Windsor, which was by no means the focus of political attention. There were also practical considerations. It would be tedious for 150 Commissioners to travel to Windsor and to stay there for the duration of the Court. It was not clear how long it would take to deal with the charges against the King. A hurried, hasty judicial hearing would not allow enough time for the King to be exposed to public gaze as 'the Man of Blood'. Also, apart from the castle, which was scarcely public, Windsor had no venue large enough to accommodate an event of such size and political magnitude.

Whatever the final sentence might be, it was essential that King Charles should be discredited in the eyes of the people. It would be more convenient and politically more significant if the trial were to

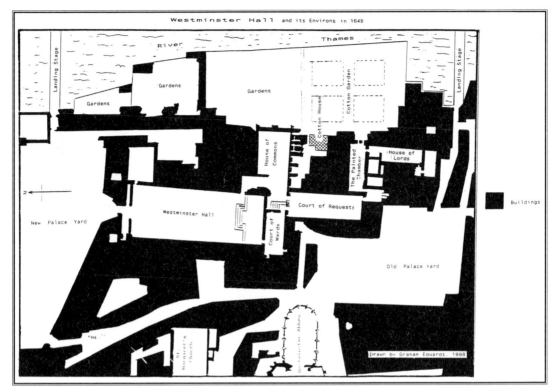

Westminster Hall and its Environs in 1649

River Thames

Landing Stage

Landing Stage

Gardens

Gardens

Gardens

Cotton Garden

Cotton House

Cotton House

House of Commons

The Painted Chamber

House of Lords

Buildings

Court of Requests

Westminster Hall

Court of Wards

New Palace Yard

Old Palace Yard

St. Margaret's Church

Westminster Abbey

Drawn by Graham Edwards. 1998

Plan of the Palace of Westminster.

be held in the more highly populated London, where the Army had established its control. The memory of the riot at Windsor in sympathy with the King's plight may also have helped to confirm London as the more suitable location.

Charles, the Prince of Wales, was well aware of the imminent dangers facing his father. He was doing his best to obtain support from the Continent. As the Commissioners sat in the Painted Chamber on Saturday 13 January, the young Prince was in The Hague, which had become the country of his sister Mary following her marriage to the Prince of Orange. There he attended a meeting of the States of the United Provinces, the Parliament of the Netherlands, which Sir William Boswell, the diplomatist, addressed in French on his behalf. The Prince thanked them for the courtesy he had been accorded since his arrival there and, knowing full well that he was in a republic, told them that not only was there a threat to the life of his father, the King, but that the Army in England had 'marched into London and imprisoned the members of Parliament and such other persons of the City whom they found most inclined to peace'.

He emphasised the dangers this action posed to other states and pointed out that the increase in the numbers of religious sects, '. . . exposes the Protestant religion to the invasion of more heresies and schisms than have in any age infested the Church of Christ'.[10]

The address did not end with a specific request for practical assistance, but in a call upon the States' conscience and 'the great estimation and regard they have always professed to such an ally'.

Six days later, still in The Hague, Prince Charles wrote two letters to France, seeking assistance to save his father. In one to his aunt by marriage, the Queen Regent, Anne of Austria, he asked her to help because the threat to his father's life and crown set '. . . a dangerous example to all other princes'. He sought her influence to ask her son to use 'his authority' to intervene and preserve King Charles's life and crown. Her son, King Louis XIV, was not yet ten years old and the Queen Regent ruled France, aided by her chief minister, Cardinal Mazarin, to whom Prince Charles addressed the second letter seeking support.[11]

Charles, Prince of Wales.

The French were, however, beset by their own difficulties in Paris with the movement known as the *Fronde*. This was reacting to the arrest of two members of the assembly called the *Parlement*, which had protested against several arbitrary laws the Queen Regent and her chief minister had introduced. The *Parlement* had drawn up Twenty-seven Articles, corresponding to the English Parliament's Grand Remonstrance of December 1641, as a basis for a National Constitution. The quarrel between the French monarchy and its subjects turned to violence when Parisians took to the streets and erected barricades. They were confronted by the victorious general, the Prince de Condé, whose brother, the Prince de Condi, commanded the forces of the *Fronde*. The royal family, fearing violence, fled from Paris. Therefore, Prince Charles's appeals to the French brought no practical results and his father's enemies simply carried on with their plans.

Monday 15 January 1649

In London fifty-seven Commissioners of the High Court of Justice met again in the Painted Chamber and at 2 p.m. the Court's lawyers, William Steele, John Aske, Isaac Dorislaus and John Cook, presented their prepared draft of the charges against the King in a closed session. When the document was read it was thought to be too long, not political enough and probably too legal in its phrasing.

Therefore, another committee was formed consisting of Henry Ireton, Gilbert Millington, Henry Martin, Edmund Harvey, Thomas Chaloner, Thomas Harrison, Miles Corbet, Thomas Scott, Nicholas Love, John Lisle and William Say. Any three of them would form a quorum to provide advice to the Counsellors in case of any difficulty and also, with the lawyers, 'to compare the charge against him with the evidence'.[12]

If further example were needed of the Army's intentions, this marshalling of evidence to fit predetermined charges, rather than the charges emerging from the evidence, provides clear confirmation of the fears expressed by Prince Charles for his father's safety. The more mundane arrangements for the trial were then ordered to be considered by another committee, which was instructed to plan the arrangements for keeping and lodging the King during the trial, how he was to be brought to the Court and to consider the detailed security of the Court during its sittings and the deployment of guards to meet all these requirements.

This group of Commissioners was to be any three of the following: Edmund Ludlow, William Purefoy, John Hutchinson, Adrian Scroope, Richard Deane, Edward Whalley, John Hewson, Thomas Pride (recorded as Price in the document), Sir Hardress Waller and Sir William Constable, all of whom had had considerable military experience. They were to work with the committee already appointed to make the remaining preparations for the trial. They were ordered to meet in the inner Star Chamber the following day at 8 a.m.

Colonel John Hutchinson, an active Parliamentarian.

It was brought to the notice of the Commissioners that as the trial was to take place in Westminster Hall it would be necessary for Parliament to adjourn the Courts of Justice that usually sat there and in other buildings close by. It was considered that a period of fourteen days would be sufficient. The High Court of Justice then adjourned itself until the following Wednesday at 8 a.m.

The Scots Parliament, whose earlier urgent request for close co-operation over the King's future had not been acted upon, wrote to the English Parliament expressing its unanimous 'dissent from the proceedings of the Parliament of England' in the toleration of religion as being opposed to the Covenant, in the intention to try the King and in the alteration of the form of government. In two of these issues the Scots had certain rights. They and the English Parliament had signed the Solemn League and Covenant by which the English Parliament had undertaken to introduce the Presbyterian religion throughout the country. Now, the body that claimed to be the

English Parliament had declared that there should be freedom of peaceful worship, with the exception of the Papists and the Episcopalians. As King Charles was also King of Scotland the Scots had an understandable concern for his future, especially if they were to be denied the right to have any say in it. The Scots' objection to the alteration in the form of English government was possibly less sustainable, except in the sense that a Parliament might express concern about the fate of a similar body taken over by military force; just such a concern was advanced in Sir William Boswell's speech to the States of the United Provinces mentioned earlier.

The Commissioners had now deliberated, fairly ineffectually, for a week with little or no practical outcome. Worries about adverse and hostile reaction from people nearer than the Scots led to the injection of a sense of urgency into their efforts.

The Presbyterian clergy in London were now taking a more positive stand against events. Forty-seven ministers, including Stephen Marshall, who had tried to convert the King to Presbyterianism, and Obadiah Sedgwick, who had presented His Majesty with a copy of his latest book at Carisbrooke, prepared a letter which they sent to Fairfax on 17 January. A copy was also sent to Lady Fairfax.

The letter set down the ministers' complaints about the Army's actions and about the Army's efforts to meet with them to enlist their aid. They had refused the meeting, not wishing to be associated with, or tainted by, the Army's actions in its imprisonment of Members of Parliament and seizure of the King. They reminded Fairfax of the Parliamentary resolutions of 1641, which forbade the arrest of MPs, and they urged him to order the Army to return to its proper duty. The Lord General took no definite action. The ministers arranged for the publication of their letter, which appeared in Royalist newspapers on 20 January, just before those publications were suppressed by an order published in Fairfax's name.

The politically active Army leaders, exercised as they were with the trial preparations, had been ignoring the activities of the ministers, leaving their response mainly in the hands of their militant Independent minister, Hugh Peters. He received active support from Cromwell and Ireton for his verbal replies to the Presbyterian strictures. Peters had tried to frighten the Presbyterians by visiting the house of one of them, Mr Cawley, accompanied by a party of musketeers. Cawley, who was discussing matters with other ministers, was told that he was to be taken to Fairfax for questioning.

This he refused to believe and while Peters engaged in argument with the others, slipped away to see Fairfax, to be told by the Lord General that Peters had no such orders and that he (Peters) was a knave.[13]

Wednesday 17 January 1649

This meeting of the High Court furthered the aims of the Army Parliament more than any other gathering. After the initial formalities, the irritation of the fifty-three Commissioners present showed in their peremptory decision to order all those others who had never appeared at any meetings, 'to be summoned by warrant . . . to give their personal attendance at this Court to perform the service to which they are by Act of the Commons of England . . . appointed and required'. The Sergeant-at-Arms, or his Deputy, was also ordered to summon forthwith all the absent Commissioners who lived within 20 miles of London.[14] As well as calls to obey Parliament, these orders reveal more than a trace of the desire and need to spread the responsibility for unpopular actions as widely as possible.

Proposals from the committee that had considered the practical aspects of the trial were presented by Colonel John Hutchinson and after discussion it was decided that during his trial the King would be accommodated at the house of Sir Robert Cotton, which was close to Westminster Hall, across Old Palace Yard. The Cotton House was to have accommodation built in the garden close to the River Thames as quarters for a royal guard of 200 foot soldiers. Ten companies of foot, about 1,000 men, would be constantly on duty to secure the Court, its surroundings, the King's person and his accommodation. They would be deployed in the Court of Requests, the Painted Chamber and 'other necessary places . . .'. The passage from Old Palace Yard into Westminster Hall was to be 'made up' – got ready for use. The stairs that led to the door at the Court of Wards were to be barred to enforce limited access.

Within Westminster Hall two rails were to be erected across the body of the hall, 40 ft from its southern area where the Court would sit. In the northern section of the hall there would be rails running from the two cross-rails towards the main entrance from New Palace Yard to separate the people into two enclosures, which would be surrounded by the soldiers on guard in the hall. Certain sections of the floor were to be raised to allow the guards a better view of the people standing on the floor of the hall. These alterations were to be

The Cotton House, where the
King was held during the trial.

put in hand by the committee responsible for the procedure at the
trial. Also within the hall there would be guards at all entrances and
exits, along paths leading to the hall and at all windows. The Lord
General, Fairfax, was to be asked to supply mounted guards from
time to time. The officers of the Ordnance at the Tower of London
would be required to supply weapons to arm the guards inside the
hall. These weapons were to be either 200 halberds or partisans,
shafted spears about 6 or 7 ft in length. The halberd had an axe-head

as well as a point, while the partisan had two crescent-shaped cutting edges below its spear-point. During the trial other external precautions included the sealing up of all back doors from 'the house called Hell' that led into the area adjacent to Old Palace Yard.

Accommodation for the Lord President during the trial would be arranged at Sir Abraham Williams's house in New Palace Yard, where twenty officers and other gentlemen would attend him there and during the journeys to and from the Court. Sir Henry Mildmay, Mr Cornelius Holland and Mr Humphrey Edwards would be responsible for making the arrangements for the provisions and necessaries required by the Lord President, as well as for the King during the time he was at the Cotton House. As a matter of security as well as ceremonial, the Court would foregather in the Exchequer Chamber before each session. The group would then walk in state to the Court, the Lord President leading, preceded by the Sergeant-at-Arms bearing the Mace and by the Sword of State carried by Colonel John Humphries. The matter of dress for the Court and its servants was delegated to the committee responsible for the procedure of bringing the King to trial, which was to seek the advice of the College of Heralds on this matter.

Those issues having been considered, the Court adjourned until 3 p.m. Then, in private sitting, the further draft of the charge against the King was assessed. It was still not completely acceptable and was again referred back to the group that had presented it. Oliver Cromwell was also added to the membership of that particular body. The revised charge was to be presented again at 2 p.m. the following day. One reason for the addition of Cromwell appears to have been that he was to be given the responsibility of actually escorting the King from Windsor to London for trial at an appropriate time. This committee was to meet at 8 a.m. the following day to discuss when His Majesty should be moved. After these decisions were made, the Court adjourned.

Thursday 18 January 1649

When the committee convened the following day, there were just thirty-nine Commissioners present. It sat in private and considered only one topic.

Colonel Robert Tichborne reported that he had visited William Steele, the Court's Attoney-General, and found him in bed 'very sick' and therefore unlikely to be able to continue to carry out his duties.

Steele had stressed, and asked the Colonel to repeat to the Court, that he was not absent 'out of any disaffection to it, but professed himself to be so clear in the business that if it should please God to restore him, he should manifest his good affection to the said cause'.[15] Following this, the Court ended its meeting and ordered its members to meet again the next day.

Meanwhile, the House of Commons countered an attempt by the House of Lords to prevent the planned fourteen-day adjournment of the Courts of Justice and therefore to hinder the trial of the King by preventing the use of Westminster Hall, the largest building in London. The Lords claimed that there could be no such adjournment without their approval. This gave the Commons another opportunity to declare that the supreme power in England was vested in the people and their chosen representatives. All committees that had previously comprised members of the Lords and Commons were empowered to act, even in the absence of any Member of the House of Lords.

On Thursday evening Major-General Edward Massey, who had been imprisoned at Pride's Purge on 6 December, escaped from St James's Palace where he had been held captive.

Friday 19 January 1649

Forty-eight Commissioners attended the private sitting of the High Court of Justice in the Painted Chamber at 2 p.m. Oliver Cromwell was not present. Before they considered the draft of the charges against the King once more, Colonel John Hutchinson reported that the committee that had considered dress for the Court officers had recommended that three ushers should be provided with gowns and that the three messengers on duty should wear cloaks.

Gilbert Millington told the Court that the draft of the charge against the King was now complete. When it was read, three times, it was still not wholly acceptable to the committee and was referred back for minor amendments, even though the trial was due to begin the following day. There was also discussion about the draft of the statement with which William Steele the Attorney-General, or in his absence, John Cook, the Solicitor, would introduce and read the charges against the King. After some amendment the following was agreed: 'My Lord, According to an order of this high court to me directed for that purpose, I do in the name and in the behalf of the People of England exhibit and bring to this Court a charge of High

Treason and other high crimes whereof I do accuse Charles Stuart, King of England, here present. And I do, in the name and in the behalf aforesaid desire the said charge may be received accordingly and due proceedings be had thereupon.'

Before adjourning until the next day, the Court instructed Henry Ireton, Thomas Harrison, Sir Hardress Waller, or any two of them, to appoint those who were to attend the King and the Lord President of the Court. Instructions were also given to the Sergeant-at-Arms to ensure that a gallery in Westminster Hall was made secure. There were many entrances to the galleries of the hall from the houses which had been built against its western wall.

That afternoon, Friday 19 January 1649, King Charles I was brought from Windsor Castle under the control of Colonel Matthew Thomlinson. His Majesty, heavily guarded, travelled in a six-horse coach. This was preceded on horseback by the Reverend Hugh Peters, who acted 'like bishop almoner, triumphing'.[16] Hugh Peters's attitude was not purely idiosyncratic – in addition to stimulating hatred of the King by his sermons, he also reflected the views held by many soldiers and others who had suffered privation and faced acute danger during the two Civil Wars. They had no reason to love a King they blamed for all the hardships that had been imposed on them and on their families. This attitude was evident when it was reported that on the road to London a Mr Proctor, astride his horse watching the royal coach pass, doffed his hat. His Majesty graciously acknowledged the greeting, but this exchange so angered some of the escorting soldiers that they flung the offending Mr Proctor into the ditch, horse and all.

On arrival in London, the beleaguered King was taken to St James's Palace, where he was kept in close and watchful confinement for the night.

CHAPTER NINE

The Commissioners Prepare

To that high Capital, where kingly death
Keeps his pale court in beauty and decay, He came.

Percy Bysshe Shelley, *Adonais*

Saturday 20 January 1649

At 9 a.m. the High Court of Justice met in the Painted Chamber to prepare for the trial, which was to begin that afternoon. However, the Commissioners had time only to complete one item of business before they were interrupted. They had first ordered one of their number, Sir Henry Mildmay, the temporary keeper of the Sword of State, to deliver it to Colonel John Humphries, when a Sergeant-at-Arms from the House of Commons came to summon Members of Parliament to the House.

The Members' presence was required because Lieutenant-General Thomas Hammond, the Lieutenant-General of Ordnance of the New Model Army, accompanied by many senior Army officers, had arrived at the Commons to present an important petition, drawn up by the General Council of the Army. This document, known as 'The Third or Officers' Agreement of the People'[1] set out the Army's proposals for the settlement of affairs in the kingdom, proposals that the Council of Officers was determined to see implemented.

Among its clauses were provisions for: the dissolution of the present Parliament by the end of April 1649; a redrawing of constituency boundaries to produce a more equitable representation by the 400 Members of Parliament; elections every two years; and the exclusion of Royalists for a period of seven years; the franchise to be extended to include 'natives or denizens of England, not persons receiving alms but such as are assessed [i.e., taxed] ordinarily towards the relief of the poor, not servants to or receiving wages from any particular person. And in all elections (except for the Universities), they shall be men of 21 years old or upwards and house-keepers [householders] dwelling within the division for which the election is provided'.

The executive responsibility for government was to be vested in a Council of State appointed by Parliament for a period of two years. No member of a Council of State or any officer of any salary forces in Army or garrison, or any treasurer or receiver of public moneys (while such) was to be elected to Parliament and any lawyer elected must cease the practice of law. The 'Agreement' then described the areas of responsibility, powers and the limits of influence of the Council of State. Additionally, in matters of religion, there was to be promotion of religious education to refute 'heresy, error, and whatsoever is contrary to sound doctrine'; an end to religious persecution, but those in error to be 'won by sound doctrine and the example of a good conversation'; toleration of religious freedom to worship, within limits, for all except 'Popery and Prelacy'.

This long, detailed document was presented to the Commons at a time when it had other pressing matters to consider and it could not be debated immediately. However, it was read in its entirety and the Commons, having given its obsequious thanks to the officers who delivered it and to the General Council of the Army 'for all their unwearied and gallant service to this nation', ordered that the document be printed and published, 'that the kingdom may take notice of the union and affection between the Parliament and the Army. And the Agreement should be taken into speedy and serious consideration.'[2]

The Commons then adjourned and the High Court reassembled in private session in the Painted Chamber at noon. There they rehearsed the 'form and methods' of procedure for the start of the trial that afternoon, including the reading of the commission by which they sat; the summoning and the bringing of the prisoner to the bar of the Court; informing the prisoner of why he was there; the receiving and reading of the charge; and the prisoner's response.

The Commissioners, having never tried a sovereign before, were understandably very apprehensive, particularly at the prospect of the King's responses to the charge. They gave the Lord President, Bradshaw, discretion to respond to the King's reaction. If the King

The trial scene.

were to be insolent, outrageous, or contemptuous to the Court in language or posture, it was to be left to Bradshaw to admonish him, or even to order him to be removed from the hall. The Lord President was also to have the authority to withdraw or adjourn the Court. It was proposed that the King, as a mark of respect to the Court, should remove his hat, but after discussion it was decided 'not to insist upon it for this day'. When the question arose about the King's right to answer the charge, it was agreed that the Lord President should allow him time to do so.

Conscious of the demands likely to be made on him, Bradshaw asked that John Lisle and William Say, both lawyers, should be his assistants and be seated close to him. This was agreed. The Solicitor, John Cook, then presented the charge against the King which had been 'engrossed' (written in legal form) on parchment. When it had been read, it was signed by Cook, inspected and returned for him to read in open court in the King's presence.

There was undoubtedly an acute nervousness and tension among many of the Commissioners, including the Lord President. The discussion about whether the King should remove his hat and Bradshaw's request for two assistants demonstrate this. Some, very probably Cromwell, Ireton, Harrison and others who had witnessed much of the fighting and carnage of the Civil Wars, may not have been as uneasy as others and may even have welcomed this day, if not with pleasure, certainly with determination.

Algernon Sidney, who after two meetings had decided to disassociate himself from the proceedings, recorded evidence of this determination in a letter written to his father, the Earl of Leicester. Describing an exchange of views he had had, the dedicated republican wrote,

Algernon Sidney, the republican who opposed the King's death.

> I did positively oppose Cromwell, Bradshaw, and others who would have the trial to go on, and drew my reasons from these two points. First the King could not be tried by no court [*sic*], secondly that no man could be tried by that court. This being alleged in vain, and Cromwell using these formal words, 'I tell you we will cut off his head with the crown on it,' I replied, 'You may take your own course, I cannot stop you, but I will keep myself clear from having any hand in this business', immediately went out of the room, and never returned.[3]

While the High Court of Justice prepared itself for the first session of the trial, the King was being brought from St James's Palace to Whitehall. On arrival there, to avoid crowds that might be waiting to cause a disturbance in his favour, he was to embark on a barge and travel a short way up the Thames to a landing place close to Sir Robert Cotton's house, where the King was to be quartered during the trial. The well-guarded rear approach to the hall would enable his captors to bring the King to the bar of the Court without having to pass through any crowds waiting at the main entrance. It would also limit any access to the King by the unprivileged spectators within the hall, cordoned off as they were at its northern end. The location of the Court and its prisoner at the southern end of the hall would make it more difficult for spectators within the building clearly to see and hear all the transactions. This enabled the King's accusers to hold a public trial in form if not in reality.

The first part of the journey from St James's Palace was made with the King enclosed in a sedan chair, heavily guarded and closely surrounded by troops under the command of Colonel Matthew Thomlinson, who had accompanied the King from Windsor. He was now the colonel of the New Model Army regiment formerly commanded by Sir Robert Pye and had been at Holdenby House, where he had tried without success to prevent Joyce carrying the King away. Now he and his men were extremely watchful, fearing a possible Royalist attempt to free the King on the march to the Palace of Whitehall, where they were to embark the King. Royalist sympathisers had been ordered to leave London and were forbidden to re-enter, but such an order was likely to be more honoured in the breach than the observance.

People had heard that the King was to travel a short way up the river by barge and so, when he appeared still under a strong guard and took his seat under the canopy of the vessel, he was cheered by spectators who were waiting in boats on the water. The barge, rowed by a waterman, was preceded by another large vessel carrying musketeers and followed by a second guard-boat containing men armed with partisans. The small convoy, under the command of Colonel Francis Hacker, travelled the short distance to the landing stage near the Cotton House, where the King disembarked and was taken inside.

The arrangements for the King's stay at the house had been decided by the Commissioners three days earlier. They had ruled that the King's bedchamber should be next to the study and that 'the great chamber before the said lodging chamber be for the King's dining room and that a guard of thirty officers or other choice men do always attend the King. Who are to attend him at his lodging above stairs, and that two of the said thirty do always attend him in his bedchamber.'[4]

While the King was being settled, briefly, in the house, where responsibility for his safekeeping lay with Colonel Hacker and Colonel Hercules Huncks, the Commissioners of the High Court of Justice prepared for their progress from the Painted Chamber into Westminster Hall. First came Colonel Fox leading twenty soldiers armed with halberds. Then came the messengers in their capes, the ushers and the Court Crier, all bareheaded. Colonel John Humphries bearing the Sword of State marched ahead of Sergeant-at-Arms Edward Dendy, who bore the Mace. The Lord President, John Bradshaw, dressed in 'a black tufted [lawyer's] gown', came immediately behind the Mace, his sign of authority. He was followed by the other sixty-seven Commissioners in attendance. William Steele, the selected Attorney-General, was absent, still unwell.

The Commissioners took their places in the hall, having been joined by others who had not been at the Painted Chamber. When all were assembled, there were sixty-eight Commissioners present, but of the other sixty-seven men who had been nominated to act there was no sign.

The Lord President, Bradshaw, was seated on a scarlet velvet chair on a small raised platform, flanked by Lisle and Say, his two assistants. Before him, as he faced the northern end of the hall, was a small desk bearing a scarlet tasselled cushion. Bradshaw, Lisle and Say all wore their black barristers' gowns and, as with all the Commissioners, their black, high-crowned, broad-brimmed hats. Bradshaw's headgear differed from the others in that it was, in effect, an iron-plate, hat-shaped, felt-covered helmet, which he had had made for protection in case he was attacked.

The remaining Commissioners were ranged on five tiers of wooden benches, the seats of which were covered with red baize. Behind the Commissioners, on the south wall, beneath the large window, hung the impaled arms of England and Ireland. For a short distance along each wall flanking the Court there were two-tiered galleries that accommodated privileged spectators, who would undoubtedly have been carefully identified before being allowed to take their seats.

Just in front of the Presidential dais, in the body of the hall, a table, covered with a brilliant red and blue patterned Turkey carpet, had been provided for the two Clerks of the Court, John Phelps and Andrew Broughton. When the Court was in session this table also held the Mace and the Sword of State, symbolically displayed with the Sword crossed over the Mace. Beyond this table, facing the Court, was the Bar, a dock-like structure containing a chair covered in red velvet on which the King would be seated. He would have his back to the members of the general populace, who were enclosed in two large pens, divided by an aisle. These pens were further enclosed by a rank of soldiers, musketeers and halberdiers, who stood with their backs to the crowd, carefully observing the people in the opposite enclosure. Also present were soldiers, dressed in their red coats, and officers, in similar but more ceremonial uniforms, positioned at all the strategic points in the hall. They added splashes of colour to an otherwise sombre scene of black and old-wood brown. These soldiers, of Colonel John Hewson's regiment, were commanded by Lieutenant-Colonel Daniel Axtell, as Hewson himself was sitting in the Court as a Commissioner.

When all were settled and the buzz of public conversation resumed, the Court Crier called for silence and made the traditional announcement requiring all who had business with the Court to attend. The Commons Act commissioning the Court to try the King was then read, each person named as a Commissioner being required to stand and answer to his name. The first name called was that of Sir Thomas, Lord Fairfax. At this there was an interruption from a gallery holding privileged visitors when a masked woman, identified later as Lady Fairfax, the Lord General's wife, called out. There is some dispute about her words: Clarendon wrote that she shouted when her husband's name was called, '. . . he had more wit than to be here'; Rushworth recorded that she interrupted the proceedings 'by

Anne, Lady Fairfax, who interrupted the trial.

The King during his trial.

speaking aloud to the Court . . . that her husband . . . was not there in person, nor ever would sit among them, and therefore they did wrong to name him as a sitting commissioner'.[5] From what one has read of the lady, the daughter of Sir Horace, Lord Vere, a most famous soldier, the Clarendon version has the pithiness one might expect of a woman who was the daughter of one soldier and the wife of another. She was not to be silenced and was later to cause another interruption to the proceedings.

The roll-call continued and it would not have been lost on the spectators that only one half of the nominated Commissioners had acknowledged their presence. When it was completed, Dendy, the Sergeant-at-Arms, was ordered to summon the King to the Court. A quarter of an hour later, Colonel Thomlinson, still in charge of the King, brought him into the hall escorted by Colonel Hacker and thirty-two officers armed with partisans. The King was also attended by his own servants.

King Charles was dressed in black, wearing around his neck a white lace collar and on a blue ribbon the jewelled 'George' of the Order of the Garter, the silver star of which emblazoned his black cloak. In his hand he carried a white stick with a silver top. His complexion was pale, his long hair and his beard now grey. On his head he wore a tall-crowned hat with a broad brim. His expression was impassive and he showed neither recognition of anyone nor any curiosity.

On being conducted to the bar of the Court by Dendy, he took his seat, neither removing his hat nor glancing to right or left. At his right stood a small table with writing materials, should he wish to make notes. The small enclosure to the King's right, within about an arm's length, was then occupied by the three lawyers who were to undertake the prosecution, Cook, Aske and Dorislaus.

When order had been called and the spectators had quietened, the momentous trial of King Charles I began.

The dress of a puritan noblewoman in the 1640s.

CHAPTER TEN

The Trial Begins

Obtruding false rules, pranked in reason's garb.

John Milton, *Comus*

Saturday afternoon, 20 January 1649

The names of the Commissioners who sat in judgment on the King on that first day were:

John Bradshaw, Serjeant-at-Law, Lord President

Oliver Cromwell	John Hutchinson	James Chaloner
Henry Ireton	Sir Michael Livesey	Humphrey Edwards
Sir Hardress Waller	Robert Tichborne	Gregory Clement
Valentin Wauton	Owen Roe	John Fry
[or Walton]	Robert Lilburne	Sir Gregory Norton
Thomas Harrison	Adrian Scroope	Edmund Harvey
Edward Whalley	Richard Deane	John Venn
Thomas Pride	John Okey	Thomas Scott
Isaac Ewer	John Hewson	William Cawley
Lord Grey of Groby	Daniel Blagrave	Anthony Stapley
Wm, Lord Mounson	William Goffe	John Downes
Sir John Danvers	Cornelius Holland	Thomas Horton
Sir Thos. Maulverer	John Carey	Thomas Hammond
Sir John Bouchier	John Jones	John Lisle
Isaac Pennington,	Thomas Lister	Nicholas Love
an Alderman of London	Peregrine Pelham	Vincent Potter
Henry Martin	Francis Allen	Augustine Garland
William Purefoy	Thomas Chaloner	John Dixwell
John Barkestead	John Moore	Simon Mayne
John Blackston	William Say	James Temple
Gilbert Millington	John Aldred	Peter Temple

| Sir Wm Constable | Francis Lassells | John Browne |
| Edmund Ludlow | Henry Smith | Thomas Wogan[1] |

Before the formal proceedings started, the King, having sat down, stood up again and turned around and looked at the soldiers and the people packed into the enclosures behind him. The royal servants took their place to the left of the King's position. When the King had turned to face the Court and seated himself, the Court Crier called for silence and the Lord President, John Bradshaw, addressed the prisoner, saying:

> Charles Stuart, King of England, the Commons in England assembled in Parliament, being sensible of the evils and calamities that have been brought upon this nation and of the innocent blood that hath been shed in it, have resolved to make inquisition for this blood, and according to the debt they owe to God, to Justice, the kingdom and themselves, and according to that fundamental power that is vested, and trust resposed in them by the People (other means failing through your default) have resolved to bring you to trial and judgment, and have therefore constituted this high court of justice, before which you are now brought. Where you are to hear your charge, upon which the court will proceed according to justice.[2]

As he finished speaking, John Cook, the acting Attorney-General, unrolled the parchment containing the charge and prepared to exhibit it to the Court and the spectators.

The King spoke, calling on Cook to 'Hold!', but the lawyer made to continue. With that the King extended the cane he carried and tapped Cook on the shoulder several times to engage his attention. With that the silver head of the cane came off and fell to the floor. The King retrieved it himself and put it in his pocket. In those religious, but also deeply superstitious times, some who witnessed this incident regarded it as a bad omen. Sir Philip Warwick, the King's secretary, believed that the King himself regarded it as such.

Bradshaw ordered Cook to continue, but the King intervened again, seeking the chance to comment. Bradshaw, no doubt with nervous irritation, pronounced: 'The Court commands the charge shall be read: if you have anything to say, after, the court will hear you.'[3] Cook then exhibited the charge, of 'High Treason and other High Crimes . . .' for and on behalf of the people of England against

Charles Stuart, King of England, passing it to the Clerk of the Court to be read. At this point, Clarendon claims there was a further interruption by Lady Fairfax, who is said to have called out at the claim that the trial was in the name of the people of England, 'No, nor a hundredth part of them.' The indomitable lady was then required to withdraw from the hall.[4]

It was subsequently claimed that at the same time as Lady Fairfax's outburst Lady Anna De Lille, who was also in the gallery, called out that it was not the people of England who charged the King, but 'rebels and traitors'. She, it was said, was then seized and branded on her shoulder and her head by Colonel John Hewson, 'to the horror of the King'. His Majesty 'then seeing her flesh smoke and her hair all of a fire for him by their hot irons, much commiserated her . . .'. However, this report, written in 1665, may have inconsistencies. At the time of the incident, Hewson was a sitting member of the Court and not directly responsible for the security of the proceedings. It may be that another senior officer ordered the alleged branding, but it seems strange that there should be branding irons so close to hand that an immediate punishment could be inflicted. If the penalty had not been instant, the King would not have been able to see the event, as was claimed. It is possible that Lady De Lille did join in the protest by Lady Fairfax, but, although this later account appears to be heavily embroidered, she may have suffered the brandings at a later date, since their existence on her body appears to be well documented.[5]

In summary, the charges claimed that the King had attempted '. . . to erect and uphold in himself an unlimited and tyrannical power, to rule according to his will and to overthrow the rights and liberties of the people . . . and hath traitorously and maliciously levied war against the present Parliament and the people therein represented'. The charge then listed many battles and engagements of the First Civil War that caused the deaths of many thousands. Charles was also accused of causing the Second Civil War in 1648 in which, '. . . much innocent blood of the free people of this nation hath been spilt, many families have been undone, the public treasure wasted and exhausted, trade destructed and miserably decayed, vast expense to the nation incurred and many parts of the land spoiled, some of them even to desolation'.

The Clerk ended by stating that John Cook, on behalf of the people of England, impeached '. . . the said Charles Stuart as a tyrant, traitor, murderer and a public and implacable enemy to the commonwealth of England and pray that the said Charles Stuart, King of England, may put to answer all and every the premises and that such proceedings, examinations, trials, sentences and judgments may be thereupon had, as shall be agreeable to justice'.[6]

While the charges were read out, the King gazed expressionlessly around him at the Commissioners, at the spectators in the galleries and even stood again to look at the guards and the people behind him. He betrayed none of his inner feelings until he was accused of being a tyrant and a traitor, when, once again seated, he laughed in the face of the Court.[7] It is perhaps worthy of note that none of the charges concerned any matters of religion, presumably because of the complex problems of framing accusations that could involve Anglicanism, Presbyterianism and the many emerging sects covered by the label 'Independent'. It was probably better to keep the charges simple, even if their basis was questionable.

After the reading of the charges, Bradshaw addressed the King, 'Sir, you have now heard your charge read containing such matters as appear in it. You find that in the close of it, it is prayed to the court, in behalf of the Commons of England, that you be put to answer to your charge. The court expects your answer and are willing to hear it.'

At this point events are disputed among the contemporary reporters. One incomplete report claims that as the King replied the doors to the hall were opened and people streamed in, drowning His Majesty's words. Other accounts indicate that the general public were already in the hall to hear the charges as well as the King's response. His Majesty is reported to have said in answer to the Lord President:

First I must know by what power I am called hither before I will give answer. I was not long ago in the Isle of Wight. How I came here is a longer story than I think is fit at this time for me to speak of. But there I entered into a treaty with both Houses of Parliament with as much public faith as it's possible to be had of any people in the world. I treated there with a number of honourable lords and gentlemen, and treated honestly and uprightly; I cannot say but that they did very nobly with me. We were upon a conclusion of the treaty. Now, I would know by what authority, I mean lawful, there are many unlawful authorities in the world – thieves and robbers by the highways – but I would know by what authority I was brought from thence and carried from place to place, and I know not what. And when I know what lawful authority, I shall answer. Remember I am your King – your lawful King – and what sins you bring upon your heads and the judgment of God upon this land, think well upon it – I say think well upon it – before you go further from one sin to a greater. Therefore let me know by what lawful authority I am seated here and I shall not be unwilling to answer. In the meantime, I shall not betray my trust. I have a trust committed to me by God, by old and lawful descent [i.e., by hereditary right]. I will not betray it to answer to a new unlawful authority. Therefore resolve me that, and you shall hear more of me.

An exterior view of the Painted Chamber.

This was just the royal answer which had perplexed the Commissioners during their noontime meeting in the Painted Chamber that day. This is known because a Royalist, Sir Purbeck Temple, had bribed the Keeper of that Chamber to secrete him in a hole in the wall behind a tapestry where he could observe and hear what went on. During the trial of Henry Marten in 1660 after the Restoration of King Charles II, Temple said that when news came to the Commissioners that the King was landing (from the Thames) at Sir Robert Cotton's house,

> Cromwell ran to the window, looking on the King as he came up the garden. He turned as white as the wall . . . then turning to the board, said thus: 'My masters, he is come, he is come, and now we are doing that great work that the nation will be full of. Therefore I desire you to let us resolve here what answer we shall give the King when he comes before us, for the first question he will ask us will be by what authority and commission do we try him.' To which none answered presently. Then, after a little space, Henry Marten . . . rose up and said, 'In the name of the Commons in Parliament assembled and all the good people in England.' To which none contradicted. When they came to the court in Westminster Hall, I heard the King ask them the very same question that Cromwell had said to them.[8]

Bradshaw's answer to the King's question was almost the same as the one agreed upon at the noon meeting, but delivered with the testiness of an adult scolding a small child. He said, 'If you had been pleased to have observed, what was hinted to you by the court at your first coming hither, you would have known by what authority.

Which authority requires you – in the name of the people of England, of which you are elected King – to answer them.'⁹

The King's denial brought forth the statement that the Court would proceed anyway, but Bradshaw's mistaken reference to him being elected brought the King's correction about the hereditary nature of the Crown, even if he was himself wrong in claiming that method of succession for 'near these thousand years'. The last elected King of England, and under fairly dubious circumstances, had been Harold Godwinson in 1066. King Charles went on to assert that he stood more for the liberty of his subjects than 'any here that come to be my pretended judges'. He again insisted on being told the authority on which he was being tried.

By this time, the King's persistence on this one demand was beginning to unsettle Bradshaw. He said sarcastically that the way in which the King had managed his trust, the care of the liberty of his people, was well known, but the King's way of answering the charges was to interrogate the Court and he had already been told of the authority for his trial 'twice or thrice'. The King was not to be browbeaten. He challenged the Court's right to take him there by force and stated that he was not prepared to be there in a submissive role. He was prepared to protect the privileges of the House of Commons, 'rightly understood, as any man here . . .', but he saw no presence from the House of Lords, which would be necessary to form a Parliament, especially a Parliament that constitutionally also required the willing presence of the King.

King Charles's determination to stand on the legal constitutional position and his persistence in adhering to that stand was beginning to exasperate Bradshaw and his colleagues. They were fully aware of the legal situation, as their earlier meeting in the Painted Chamber made clear. The only answer they could make in response to the King's telling central question was weakly to evade the legal reality, include the use of high-sounding but legally meaningless phrases that relied on a heavily reduced Rump House of Commons, which in itself was not unanimous (only twenty-six Members voted for the trial while twenty opposed it) and the uncertain clarion call that invoked, spuriously, the name of the people of England.

The King's continued intransigence forced Bradshaw to employ the only sanction left to him. He pronounced that as the King would not answer, the Court would decide what was to be done. In the meantime he was to be taken away by those who brought him to the hall. Still the King would not be silenced. He warned them that 'it is not a slight thing you are doing' and that if they acted with usurped authority it would not last long. He again demanded to know the legal authority by which they sat – without it he could not betray his trust and the liberties of the people. 'Satisfy me in that, and I will answer . . . For I do avow that it is as great a sin to withstand lawful authority as it is to submit to a tyrannical or otherwise unlawful authority. Therefore satisfy God and me and all the world in that, and you shall receive my answer.' Defeated by this defiance, Bradshaw repeated the Court's demand for a final answer, but was forced to consider an adjournment unless the King answered to the charges. He said that the Court was satisfied that it had the authority and that 'it is upon God's authority and the kingdom's'.

The King repeated his demand to be shown the legal authority, since that which they claimed 'satisfies no reasonable man', only to be told by Bradshaw, weakly and with obvious truculence, 'That's in your apprehension. We think it reasonable that are your judges.' This almost farcical exchange led to the King's parting shot, 'It is not my apprehension, nor yours either, that ought to decide it.' Bradshaw, supported by his colleagues and all the soldiers, had the last frustrated and retreating word when he closed the session with, 'The court hath heard you, and you are to be disposed of as they have commanded.'[10] As the King left Westminster Hall, he is reported as having pointed his cane at the sword which lay on the Clerks' table, saying, 'I do not fear that.' As he went down the stairs, some people in the hall cried 'God Save the King!', while others called out for 'Justice!'. The Court Crier uttered his traditional cry of 'Oyez' and the Court adjourned until 9 a.m. on Monday 22 January in the Painted Chamber and from there to Westminster Hall.

It would have been evident to an impartial observer that the King had won the oral exchanges in the first session of the Court. Even so, his situation was not hopeful. It is clear that His Majesty's attitude was based not only on constitutional legality, but also on his personal determination not to concede anything further to his enemies. His reference to the treaty at Newport was significant for three reasons. First it emphasised that he had arrived at an agreement with a properly constituted, if rebel, Parliament which was represented by Members of both Houses. Secondly, they had dealt fairly with one another and, by implication, both sides had made concessions. Lastly, he was conscious of the concessions he had made there and had excused them in his letter to the Prince of Wales, mentioned earlier. At this stage he was not prepared to grant any further concessions to this illegal gathering, whose members had even deposed the rebel Parliament that he had previously refused to recognise.

Charles's repeated challenge to the legality of the 'Pretended High Court of Justice', as its opponents called it, had unsettled the Commissioners. The King, despite his tendency to slow speech, had acquitted himself well and demonstrated again that his inborn wit was fairly sound, now that once more he had no advisers. Bradshaw seems to have been somewhat at a loss when faced with the King's determination and the transcripts of the proceedings indicate a growing irritation that weakened his effectiveness, despite having been warned of the King's tactic.

Monday 22 January 1649 – the Second Day

It is of interest to note that those who had been dedicated to bringing the King to trial were careful, when they were unable to attend, to stress that they were not changing their minds. When the sixty-two Commissioners met at the Painted Chamber at 9 a.m. Edmund Harvey presented the apologies for absence from Mr John Corbet, who had only been present at one Commissioners' meeting, on 10 January. Corbet wished all to know that he was away on state business and not absent 'from any disaffection'. He did not attend any of the Court's subsequent sessions.

Having considered the first session, the Commissioners expressed approval that the trend of events had followed the sense and direction of their thoughts. They made no comment about the effectiveness of those thoughts and resolved that as the King was intent to destroy the authority of the Court, he should not be allowed to question its legality. If he should try the same tactic again, he was to be told that he must accept that the Court was commissioned by the Commons of England assembled in Parliament. Then if he still refused to plead, he should be informed that his action would be regarded as patent insubordination and a wilful refusal to obey a legal authority. This would be recorded as such and he would be ordered to answer to the charges. If he were still to refuse, the Lord President was to command the Clerk to demand a reply in the name of the Court in the following words: 'Charles Stuart, King of England, you are accused in the behalf of the people of England of divers high crimes and treasons, which charge hath been read to you. The court requires you to give a positive answer whether you confess or deny the charge, having determined that you ought to answer the same.'[11] The sixty-two Commissioners then adjourned to Westminster Hall.

When the Court assembled at the hall, eight more Commissioners joined them, then, after silence had been ordered on pain of imprisonment and the nominal roll taken, the King was brought to face his judges. As he appeared in the hall, a shout of support was heard and the Captain of the Guard was ordered to arrest anyone who made a disturbance.

The proceedings were opened by John Cook, who addressed the Lord President. He went through the charade of explaining to the Court, as though it was an impartial and deaf body, that the King had made no answer to the charges and had challenged the legality of the Court. He then requested that, '. . . the Prisoner may be directed to make a positive answer either by way of confession or negation, which if he shall refuse to do, that the matter of charge be taken as confessed and the court may proceed according to justice'.[12] This new tactic, in which silence was to be taken as a confirmation of guilt, was in direct contravention of contemporary principles of English Common Law, where silence could not be interpreted as guilt.

Bradshaw spoke to the King, telling him that the Court was satisfied with its authority, which he was not to challenge again. If he were to deny the charge, the Court would undertake to prove it. 'And therefore you are to lose no more time, but give positive answer thereunto.' This development posed a difficult problem for the King. If he pleaded to the charge, he acknowledged the legality of the Court. If he kept silent, his guilt would be assumed.

In Doctor Samuel Johnson's words, 'Depend upon it, Sir, when a man knows he is to be hanged in a fortnight, it concentrates his mind wonderfully.'[13] The King obviously concentrated. It is possible, even likely, that he would have expected that such a tactic might be employed. If, however, it was sprung on him as a surprise, his reaction showed a far keener wit and understanding than he has been given credit for. He quickly changed the direction of his challenge while still questioning the Court's legality as his main premise.

He began to justify his stance, which widened the argument. He said that he questioned the Court's legality not only on his own behalf, as 'a King cannot be tried by any superior jurisdiction on earth', but on behalf of the people of England and their liberty. Significantly he added, '. . . for if power without law can make laws, may alter the fundamental laws of the kingdom, I do not know what subject . . . in England . . . can be sure of his life or anything that he calls his own'.

When the King began to elaborate his reasons still further by referring to his duty to God and his people, Bradshaw interrupted him, claiming that what he was saying was not acceptable to the Court, 'before whom you are a prisoner and are charged as a high delinquent . . . You are to submit unto it. You are to give in a punctual and direct answer whether you will answer your charge or no, and what your answer is.'

The King's response was, 'Sir, by your favour, I do not know the forms of the law; I do know law and reason, though. I am no lawyer professed, but I know as much about the law as any gentleman in England, and therefore I do plead for the liberties of the people of England more than you do.' As he went on to affirm that reason would not allow him to yield to their demand, Bradshaw interrupted him again to claim that reason and law were against him; that the vote of the Commons in Parliament was the reason of the kingdom and that the Commons had given the kingdom the law, within which he, the King, should have ruled.

Charles queried the statement that a King could be a delinquent and also claimed that by any known law even a delinquent had the right to question the legality of any proceedings. As in many arguments that end with 'because I say so', this argument was drawing towards an abrupt conclusion. The King persisted in demanding his right to give his reasons for refusing to acknowledge the Court and also for refusing to plead. He said, 'If you deny that, you deny reason.'

The Lord President appeared by this time to be losing what calm he had when he again denied the King's right to challenge the Court's legality, for he said, 'They sit here by the authority of the Commons of England'. Then he made an error when he continued, 'and all your predecessors and you are responsible to them———'. Immediately the King broke in with, 'I deny that. Show me one precedent!'

Bradshaw could only rebuke the King, saying 'Sir, you ought not to interrupt while the court is speaking to you', adding, after recovering from his error and the King's riposte, 'This point is not to be debated by you, neither will the court permit you to do it. . . . they have considered of their jurisdiction. They do affirm their own jurisdiction.' The King then denied that the Commons of England had ever been a court of trial law and asked how they had come to be so. Bradshaw repeated that the King was not allowed to go on in this fashion.

At Bradshaw's instructions, the Clerk of the Court then read the short statement of the charges agreed that day at the earlier meeting in the Painted Chamber, ending with, 'The court have determined that you ought to answer the same.' The King's answer was a repetition of his previous statements, 'I will answer the same as soon as I know by what authority you do this.' The exasperated Bradshaw could then only say, 'If this be all that you will say, then, gentlemen, you that brought the prisoner hither, take charge of him back again.'

King Charles would not allow so peremptory a dismissal, saying, 'I do require that I may give my reasons why I do not answer. And give me time for that.' To which Bradshaw retorted, 'Sir, 'tis not for prisoners to require!' The exchange between them continued with the King bridling, 'Prisoners? Sir, I am no ordinary prisoner!' To which Bradshaw could only repeat, 'The court hath . . . already affirmed their jurisdiction. If you will not answer, we shall give orders to record your default.' The King refused to be silenced. 'You have never heard my reasons yet.' This drew the reply, 'Sir, Your reasons are not to be heard against the highest jurisdiction.' The King answered, 'Show me that jusridiction where reason is not to be heard.' Bradshaw continued on the same tack, 'Sir, we show it to you here, the Commons of England. The next time you are brought you will know more of the pleasure of the court, and their final determination.' The King still refused to be silenced: 'Show me where ever the House of Commons was a court of judicature of that kind.' Bradshaw's response was to order the Sergeant-at-Arms to take away the prisoner.

King Charles, determined to have the last word if he could, then announced, most probably for the benefit of all the spectators within earshot, 'Well, sir, remember that the King is not suffered to give his reasons for the liberty and freedom of all his subjects.' Bradshaw, taking the chance to gain some form of verbal revenge, replied, 'Sir, you are not to have liberty to use this language. How great a friend you have been to the laws and liberties of the people, let all England and the world judge.' To which the King answered, defensively, 'Sir, under favour, it was the liberty, freedom and laws of the subject that ever I took, defended myself with arms. I never took up arms against the people, but for the laws.' Bradshaw then announced, 'The command of the court must be obeyed. No answer will be given to the charge.' To which the King responded in agreement, 'Well, sir.'

The King's refusal to reply was then entered in the Court record and he was taken under guard back to Sir Robert Cotton's house. The Court ajourned until midday, Tuesday 23 January in the Painted Chamber, from which they intended to move to Westminster Hall for the next session.

The King had drafted a speech in which he had proposed to address the Court outlining his reasons for refusing to recognise its legality and his steadfast refusal to plead to the charges. As has been seen, he was denied the opportunity to do this, even though he did indicate the line of his thoughts and reasons before he was constantly interrupted by the Lord President.

In the text of this speech, subsequently annotated by the King and published, he set out to demonstrate that this Court was illegal and he repeated his concern that the illegality of the trial did not threaten him alone. If the Court were to sit unchallenged, its actions would be a threat to the legal rights of all in the kingdom. He therefore wished to speak on behalf of the people as well as on his own account.

No proceedings against any man could be justified if they were not governed by the laws of God, or by 'the municipal laws of the country where he lives'. The King drew on the Old Testament (Ecclesiastes 8:4), 'Where the word of a king is, there is power: and who may say unto him, What doest thou?', to support his unshakeable belief in the Divine Right of Kings. He claimed that in the law of the land, 'I am no less confident that no learned lawyer will affirm that the impeachment can lie against a King, they all going in his name. And one of their maxims is that the King can do no wrong.' This challenge that the King could not be impeached in his own name was to provoke an immediate response, not only in the Court, but in Parliament, as will be seen.

The King then attacked the claim that the House of Commons could 'erect a court of judicature which was never one itself (as is well known to all lawyers)' and it was just as strange that they should pretend (i.e., claim) to make laws without the King or the House of Lords. Further, the claim of the Commons, as they now were, to represent the people of England could not be maintained, as they had 'never asked the question of the tenth man in the kingdom'. Their authority was therefore non-existent without the formal consent of those who elected the Parliament.

Charles had planned to speak of the violated privileges of Parliament and the events which destroyed public faith in that

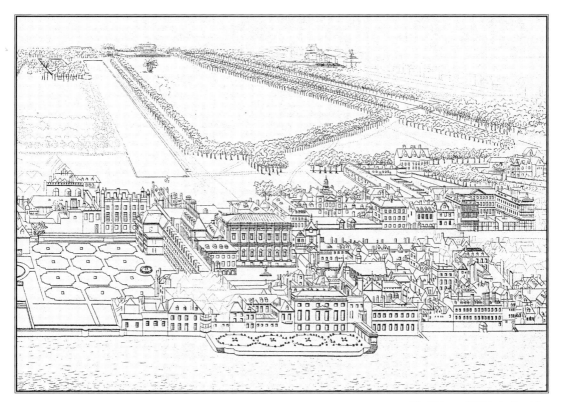

The Palace of Whitehall, with
St James's Park and Palace to
the distant right and
Buckingham House to the
distant left.

institution. The previous Parliament had agreed a treaty with him at
Newport but it was dislocated by the subsequent events, which also
affected Parliament itself. He was made a prisoner and the House of
Lords was totally excluded from government. The majority of the
House of Commons was either 'detained or deterred from sitting'. So,
even if he had no other cause to protest, that fact in itself would be
sufficient grounds for challenging the legitimacy of this Court.

The King stressed that there could be no hope of a settlement, of
peace, 'so long as power reigns without rule or law, changing the
whole frame of that government under which this kingdom hath
flourished for many hundred years'. He then forecast that the people
of England would not thank them for this change, which would only
bring unhappiness. He made the claim that he only took up arms to
defend the fundamental laws of the kingdom against those who
supposed that his power had transformed the ancient government.

These, he would have said, had he been allowed to deliver the
speech, were the reasons why he could not submit to the Court's
claimed authority without violating the trust he had from God to

maintain the welfare and liberty of his people. Finally, he would have challenged the Court to show him that he was in error '(and then truly I will answer), or that you will withdraw your proceedings'.

It is hardly surprising that the Court refused to allow the King to speak. For a man who is 'no lawyer professed' he would have shown that he had a firm grasp of the implications of the law. Whether his view of past events, particularly those he had initiated, was just as accurate is questionable. He was perhaps, on matters such as forced loans or fines to avoid the responsibilities of knighthood, 'remembering with advantages'.

The Court refused to hear him because, without any defence from him, or even allowing witnesses in his support, they had already decided on his guilt. Their attitude was almost a precursor of the statement traditionally attributed to Judge Jeffreys at the Bloody Assizes at Taunton Castle almost forty years later, 'Bring forth the next prisoner. Let us see his rascally face.' Then to the man in the dock, he is supposed to have said, 'Don't waste the court's time by pleading your innocence. You would not be here if you were not guilty!'[14]

The eventual publication of the King's forbidden speech gives a good insight into the workings of his mind. He was an intelligent man, whose powers of argument made his adversaries very apprehensive. They, for that reason and to prevent a resurgence of support for him, denied him the opportunity of publicly exposing the legal, constitutional and moral weaknesses of their own position. They, on the other hand, believed that all the recent ills which had befallen the kingdom could be laid firmly at the King's door.

CHAPTER ELEVEN

The Trial Continues

Our torments may in length of time, Become our elements
                                    John Milton, *Paradise Lost*

Tuesday 23 January 1649 – the Third Day

The King's determined interventions and his challenges to the legality of the Court had probably hastened a legal discussion in the Parliament.

On 23 January the Commons, sensitive about the legal weaknesses in their assumption of power, considered an Ordinance, 'for settling of the courts of justice and in what way writs should be issued for the future'. They ruled that writs out of Chancery should go in the name of the Chancellor or Keepers of the Seal, also in other courts in the name of the judge or judges. Of particular significance in view of the King's trial, it was decided that, '. . . whereas it had formerly charged upon malefactors that they have acted "contrary to the Peace of our Sovereign Lord the King, his Crown and Dignity", it is now to be thus, "against the Peace, Justice and Council of England"'.

When the sixty-three Commissioners of the High Court reconvened privately in the Painted Chamber at noon they fully approved of what the Lord President had done in the previous open session in the face of the King's challenges. It was, no doubt, pleasing to Bradshaw to receive the endorsement of his fellow Commissioners, many of whom were more notable than he. However, he must also have been a little apprehensive that after each session of the Court his performance was formally to be reviewed.

The Commissioners decided that despite the King's attitude, he should be given one more chance to plead to the charges. The Clerk to the Court was to read the following to him, 'Charles Stuart, King of England, you are accused on the behalf of the people of England of

Doctrina
Libertinorum
et
Quakeorum
de
Regno
Millenario

Pietas
et
Paupertas
Simulata

John Cook, Solicitor and
acting Attorney at the trial.

divers high crimes and treasons, which charge hath been read unto
you. The court now requires you to give your final and positive
answer by way of confession or denial of the charge.' Should the King
again refuse, the Lord President was to tell him that the Court would
'proceed to judgment for his former contumacy [stubborn refusal]
and failure to answer'. If he were to answer and request a copy of the
charge, it was to be given to him and he would be required to answer
to the charge 'the next day at 1 of the clock in the afternoon'. The
meeting then adjourned to Westminster Hall for the opening of the
next session of the trial at which seventy-three Commissioners were
present.

After the formalities, John Cook addressed the Lord President
saying that this was the third time the prisoner had been brought to
the Bar and still there had been no progress with the trial. Cook

again enlarged on the charge listing the crimes that the King was alleged to have committed, to which he stubbornly had refused to plead, and further that he continued to challenge the legality of the Court. The Solicitor, still acting as the Attorney-General, then came to the main point, his request that if the prisoner still refused to plead, 'whereby he may [therefore] come to a fair trial, that as by an implicit confession it may be taken as confessed, as it hath been done to those who have deserved more favour than the Prisoner at the Bar has done'.

In a final impassioned, emotional plea, recorded by the Clerks of the Court, Cook ended with:

The House of Commons, the supreme authority and jurisdiction of the kingdom, they have declared that it is notorious that the matter of the charge is true, as it is in truth, my lord, as clear as crystal and as the sun that shines at noonday, which if your lordship and the court be not satisfied in, I have notwithstanding on the people of England's behalf several witnesses to produce. And therefore I do humbly pray, and yet, I must confess, it is not so much I as the innocent blood that hath been shed, the cry whereof is very great for justice and judgment, and therefore I do humbly pray that speedy judgment be performed against the Prisoner at the Bar.

Bradshaw then addressed the King, giving him the ultimatum decided upon earlier. In reply the King again asked if he would be allowed to speak 'for the liberties of the people of England'. Bradshaw's reply was the same as all his others, but he offered the King a chance to defend himself against the charge if he were to plead. To this Charles replied, 'For the charge, I value it not a rush. It is the liberty of the people of England that I stand for. For me to acknowledge a new court that I have never heard of before . . . indeed I do not know how to do it.' He went on again to challenge the legality of the proceedings and repeated his view that they were a threat to the traditional laws of the kingdom. His request for time to present his detailed reasons was again rejected, and the Clerk was instructed to read out the demand for the King to plead.

The King still refused to acknowledge the Court's legality. When Bradshaw ordered him to be taken away, he tried to say again that he took his stand not for himself but for the liberties of the people. The Lord President interrupted him, saying, 'Sir, you have heard the pleasure of the court, and you are, notwithstanding you will not understand it, to find that you are before a court of justice.' One wonders if his use of 'court of justice' rather than 'court of law' might indicate some misgivings in Bradshaw's own mind.

When the King had been taken away, the Court adjourned to the Painted Chamber. They reconvened to rule that no Commissioner should leave the Court without specific permission and that, despite the King's continued refusal to plead, his silence should be regarded as a confession and that the examination of witnesses should begin.

The ruling against the unauthorised absence of Commissioners would seem to indicate a concern that some members of the Court might be losing their resolve. This decison to start the examination of witnesses might appear to be over-emphasising the state of affairs. The Court had just ruled that as the King had refused to plead he was to be deemed guilty. If he were guilty, there was no legal need for witnesses, since a plea of guilty normally led directly to a sentence. The need for witness testimony was clearly for public consumption only and confirmed yet again that what Molière said of Paris, 'Here . . . they hang a man first and try him afterwards', was equally true of London in 1649. The Commissioners were recorded as requiring the confirmation of witnesses '. . . for the further and clearer satisfaction of their own judgments and consciences'. Orders were issued for the summoning of the witnesses, but consideration of the way in which they were to be examined was deferred to the following day in the Painted Chamber at 9 a.m.

While the Court was sitting in the Painted Chamber, the Reverend Hugh Peters appeared with a request from the King that he might be allowed to speak privately with his own chaplains. As the House of Commons had already ruled against this, the Court considered that it was 'not proper for them to intermeddle therein'.

Wednesday 24 January 1649

The House of Commons met, adjourned immediately and forty-seven Commissioners assembled in the Painted Chamber as directed. There, they appointed a committee to examine the witnesses. Its members were Colonels Thomas Horton, Richard Deane, John Okey, John Hewson, Owen Roe, Robert Tichborne, Edward Whalley, Matthew Thomlinson, William Goffe, Isaac Ewer, Adrian Scroope, with Messrs Nicholas Love, Thomas Scott, Thomas Chaloner, Gilbert Millington and Sir John Danvers; any three of them forming a quorum. Millington and Chaloner were sent to John Browne, the Clerk of the House of Lords, to bring any relevant papers and records, Browne being ordered to release them.

Thirty witnesses had been summoned and when they had been sworn, the High Court of Justice adjourned, leaving its Clerks with the committee for the examination of witnesses. When the examination began, an usher was sent to Westminster Hall to tell the people there that the Court would not sit in the hall that day as they were engaged in the Painted Chamber. All who had been required to attend were told to appear again when summoned.

John Okey, Colonel of the New Model Army Regiment of Dragoons and a Commissioner of the High Court.

Thursday 25 January 1649

The House of Commons met, only to adjourn immediately. The High Court of Justice, with thirty-two Commissioners present, met in open session in the Painted Chamber at 9 a.m. Their first business was to call for the attendance of Mr Holder, a prisoner at Whitehall, to testify against the King. While Holder was being brought by a marshal, the Court ordered that the Dean's House in Westminster Abbey should be provided and furnished for the lodging of the Lord President, his servants, guards and attendants. A committee was formed to see to this. Bradshaw was being moved from his previous lodging in New Palace Yard, now regarded as insecure because of a suspected plot against him and the Court. Major Fox, a member of the Lord President's guard, had been arrested and committed to Ludgate Prison. Three other men, Messrs John Hall, Nelson and Evans, were subsequently arrested as accomplices.

When Holder arrived he begged to be excused from testifying against the King lest he incriminate himself. As he was already a prisoner, the Court agreed to his request. The depositions made by the witnesses before the committee of examination the previous day were then read out in Court and the men affirmed the truth of their evidence.

In brief, the incidents these men recounted covered the presence and actions of the King at many events of the First Civil War, from Nottingham and Edgehill in 1642 to Naseby and afterwards. Typical of the evidence was that given by George Seeley of London, a cordwainer (shoemaker). On oath, he swore that he had seen the King at the head of a brigade of horse at the siege of Gloucester in 1643 and that he had also seen the King with his troops at both Battles of Newbury in 1643 and 1644, when there were many slain on both sides. The other evidence was of a similar nature. This process lasted the whole morning and after the Court had adjourned for an hour, it reconvened in the afternoon, during the first part of which it heard further witness statements and then evidence from royal letters and documents which were produced for inspection. It is important to note that, against any accepted legal procedure, the King was not present to crossexamine when the witnesses either made or confirmed their earlier depositions.

After this the Court sat in private, with forty-five Commissioners present, finally and formally to determine the fate of the King. They resolved that the decision on the sentence would not mean the conclusion of the Court and 'that the court will proceed to sentence of condemnation against Charles Stuart, King of England; that the condemnation of the King shall be for a tyrant, traitor and murderer; that the condemnation of the King shall be likewise for being a public enemy to the commonwealth of England; that this condemnation shall extend to death'.

The meeting considered the deposition and deprivation (the depriving of a person from office and/or honours) of the King, but deferred discussion of his execution to another time. Thomas Scott, Henry Marten, Thomas Harrison, John Lisle, William Say, Henry Ireton and Nicholas Love, or any three of them, were ordered to prepare the written draft of the sentence, 'with a blank for the manner of his death'. The Court then adjourned until 1 p.m. the following day and warrants were sent out for all members in and around London to attend.

Friday 26 January 1649

In the House of Commons the Speaker announced that ambassadors from the States-General of Holland had arrived at Greenwich, wishing to wait on the House. The Master of Ceremonies was sent to conduct them to London, with all civil respects.

Mr Lisle reported that the Act for settling courts had been read twice. It was ordered to be prepared for publication. Preparation of the new Great Seal was reported to be in hand and that Thomas Simon should have the sum of £200 for the work. Simon was the most noted medallist and seal-engraver of his day. As the Chief Engraver of the Mint, he not only cut the Great Seals for the Commonwealth in 1649 and 1651, but also that of King Charles II in 1661. He was also to engrave Cromwell's portrait for the medal

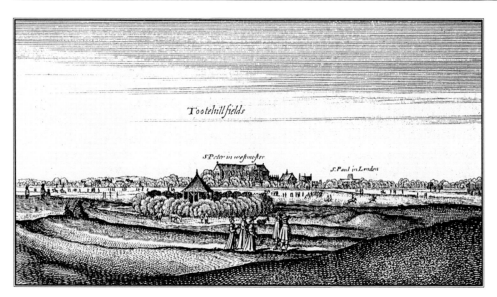

A distant prospect of Westminster in 1640s.

struck after the Battle of Dunbar in 1650, as well as the dies for Cromwell's coinage of 1656 and 1658. Simon died of the plague in 1665. Finally, in the Commons the committee for considering the letters and papers from the Scottish Commissioners was instructed to examine whether they had been printed and by whom. This reflected the Commons' concern lest Scottish views adverse to their present policy should receive wide publicity.

The High Court of Justice convened in the Painted Chamber, in private, at 1 p.m. The draft of the sentence on the King was considered and, after 'several readings, debates, and amendments by the court', it was resolved that the sentence as it now read be agreed; that it be engrossed (prepared for publication on parchment) and that the King be brought to Westminster Hall the next day to receive his sentence. With that, the Court adjourned until 10 a.m. the following day, when it would first meet in the Painted Chamber before convening in Westminster Hall.

CHAPTER TWELVE

The Sentence

Saturday 27 January 1649

Sixty-eight Commissioners gathered in the Painted Chamber at 10 a.m., where they read the previously agreed sentence on the King once more before its publication in Westminster Hall later that morning. Discussion again centred on the way in which Bradshaw should handle the proceedings and, as usual, within limits, the matter was left to his discretion, advised by his assistants John Lisle and William Say. There was still concern that the King would continue to deny the legality of the court, but should he decide to accept its jurisdiction and request a copy of the charge, proceedings would be suspended and they would withdraw to consult. The same was to happen should the King 'move anything else worth the court's consideration'. There was, therefore, still uncertainty in the Commissioners' minds, even though the outcome seemed fixed.

If the King would still not submit, the Court would remain and the Lord President would command the sentence to be read. If the King wished to say anything before sentence, he should be allowed to do so, but he should be allowed to say nothing after the sentence was pronounced. It was agreed that the Lord President should address the prisoner before sentence, as was the usual practice, making as many observations relevant to the case that 'he should conceive most seasonal and suitable to the occasion'. It was unlikely that Bradshaw would neglect such an opportunity, as will be seen. It was ruled that after the sentence, the Lord President was to announce that this was the unanimous verdict and resolution of the whole Court at which all the Commissioners should stand to demonstrate this.

The Court then adjourned to Westminster Hall where the Lord President Bradshaw, now resplendent in a scarlet gown, matching the dress of the soldiers, ordered the formal proclamation to be made announcing that the Court was now in session. As the King was brought to the Bar, silence was called for and again the Captain of the Guard was ordered to arrest anyone making a disturbance. When Bradshaw stood to address the spectators, the King indicated that he would wish to speak before sentence was pronounced. He was assured that he would be allowed to do so, but that he should wait until the Court had spoken.

Bradshaw's speech to the spectators reviewed the course of the trial, stressing that the King was being tried in the name of the people of England; that his refusal to accept the legitimacy of the Court or to enter a plea against the charges was contumacy and that his refusal to plead legally amounted to a confession of guilt. Other evidence had been considered and now sentence was ready to be pronounced. As the prisoner had made it known that he wished to be heard further, he would be allowed to address the Court, which was 'ready to hear him as to anything material which he would offer to their consideration, before sentence was given, relating to the defence of himself concerning the matter charged'.[1]

A second version of these events[2] claims to give a verbatim account of the exchanges between Bradshaw and the King and also mentions an interruption by a lady when the Lord President mentioned that the King was charged on behalf of the people of England. She is said to have cried out, 'not half the people!'. This could have been a second outburst from Lady Fairfax, or the intervention of Lady De Lille mentioned earlier.

When the King spoke he claimed again that he wished to defend the peace of England and the liberty of the people, but as that was not to be allowed he would not speak of it. He said that if he valued his own life above the peace of the kingdom and the liberty of the people he would have been able to mount a strong defence against the charge and so delay 'the ugly sentence which I believe will pass upon me'. He continued, that 'an hasty sentence once passed may sooner be repented of than recalled' and to request that his defence might be heard in the Painted Chamber before the Lords and Commons. Such a delay would not be prejudicial to this Court. He offered to withdraw from the hall while the Court considered this suggestion, but he could not resist adding, 'But if I cannot get this liberty [to defend himself before the Lord and Commons], I do protest that these fair shows of liberty and peace are pure shows, and that you will not hear your King.'

Charles was once again challenging the legality of the Court in asking to speak to another body, which would judge him. This, as well as his last remark about 'pure shows', was hardly likely to encourage this assembly of his enemies to grant his request. His emphasis on the peace of the kingdom related to the Newport treaty, which the Parliament before the Purge had considered to be a good basis for a settlement. It was surely a vain hope that the Commissioners would agree to revive the emasculated House of Lords and restore the expelled Members of the Commons to provide the King with that forum for his statement of defence.

Bradshaw, of course, refused the King's request, accusing him of persisting in his challenge to the legitimacy of the Court and of attempting to delay the proceedings once again. He reasserted the Court's legality as bestowed by the Commons of England, but as the King declared that he was not 'declining' the legality of this Court by making this request, even though he could not acknowledge its jurisdiction, Bradshaw decided to withdraw the Commissioners to the Court of Wards in the adjacent building to consider this.

John Nalson, the Royalist chronicler, in his version of these events claims that the Commissioners withdrew for half an hour to mask a disturbance by one of its members, Colonel John Downes, who wanted the Court to agree to King Charles's proposal. While the Court deliberated and, according to Nalson, chided Downes in the nearby building, the King was removed from Westminster Hall.

On their return and the re-entry of the King, Bradshaw rejected the royal request, claiming that the suggestion was only put forward to delay matters further. He then decided to quote the Magna Carta at the King, saying 'They are good words in the Great Old Charter of England, "To no one will we refuse, to no one will we sell, to no one will we delay justice."' He went on to say that there must be no more delay, the King had held up proceedings for long enough. They were resolved 'to proceed to sentence and to judgment' – this was another interesting reversal of sequence, where in normal courts judgment usually came before the sentence.

The King protested that he was not being allowed to state his case to the Lords and Commons, which was followed by warm exchanges with Bradshaw, after which the King, resignedly, said, 'I have nothing more to say. But I shall desire that this may be entered what I have said.' Bradshaw tartly replied, 'The court then, sir, hath something to say unto you, which although I know it will be very unacceptable, yet notwithstanding they are willing and resolved to discharge their duty.' His 'something to say' was a long harangue in which he justified the Court's proceedings with classical, legal and historical examples, many, according to Nalson, tenuous and misinterpreted. He concluded that the King was a tyrant, a traitor, a murderer and a public enemy to the commonwealth of England.

After this the King, who had listened patiently for over half an hour, tried to speak 'concerning those great imputations that you have laid to my charge'. Bradshaw refused him permission, but the King persisted. Bradshaw berated him because of his denial of the Court's legitimacy, adding that it was clear that he regarded them 'as a sort of people brought together' without any authority. He continued, referring to the clandestine Royalist news-sheets, 'And we know what language we receive from your party.' The King said, 'I know nothing of that.'

Bradshaw continued his tirade against the King's refusal to recognise the Court. He claimed that the Court was not there to create the law but (merely) to clarify it, and quoted scripture (Proverbs 17:15) to substantiate his argument, 'for to acquit the guilty is of equal abomination as to condemn the innocent'. He then ordered the Crier to call for silence and the Clerk of the Court to read the sentence which was, after a long catalogue of crimes, attributed to the King: 'For all which treasons and crimes, this court doth adjudge that he, Charles Stuart, as a tyrant, traitor, murderer and public enemy to the good people of this nation, shall be put to death by the severing of his head from his body.'

When the sentence had been read, the Lord President stood and said, 'The sentence now read and published is the act, sentence, judgment and resolution of the whole court.' All the Commissioners then stood to acknowledge that fact.

The King asked permission to be allowed to speak, but Bradshaw told him he was not to be heard after the pronouncement of the sentence. The King, still protesting his right to speak, was taken out of the Court and as he left, called out, 'I am not suffered to speak. Expect what Justice other people will have.'

Many reports of the King's behaviour after being taken from the Court record his calmness and dignity in the face of some ill-mannered and personally offensive behaviour, including being spat at by a few of the soldiers, urged, it was claimed, by Lieutenant-Colonel Axtel. Some called out 'Justice' and 'Execution' as he left to be carried to the Whitehall Palace from Sir Robert Cotton's house in a sedan chair. The King is said to have commented that they would have shouted the same things for the execution of their commanders, provided they were paid to do it. Not all the military were hostile. One soldier is said to have called out to the King, 'God bless you, Sir!', only to be beaten with a cane by his officer. The King was reported to have scolded the officer because the punishment he had inflicted was too severe for the offence.

Some people, observing from shops and stalls along the route, protested because the King was being carried in a common sedan chair, 'as they carry such as have the plague'. The two porters who carried him had removed their headgear out of respect for their passenger, but were beaten by some of the soldiers and made to put their caps back on. Other bystanders who made adverse comments to the soldiers were also beaten. Sir Purbeck Temple, who had witnessed these events and recalled them during the trial of the Regicides in 1660, said that he had followed the King's sedan chair from the Court to the middle of King Street, but was forced to retire because of 'the injuries and hurts I had received in my person from the soldiers under Axtel's command, they carrying him through the streets shouting in triumph'.[3] Other reports, however, notably Herbert's, speak of both sides of King Street being lined with 'a guard of Footsoldiers, who were silent as his Majesty passed'.

In his memoirs, Thomas Herbert, who was in close and continuous attendance on His Majesty, wrote that the King's state of mind was such that 'Nothing of the fear of death, or indignities offered seemed a terror, or provoked him into impatience, nor uttered he a reproachful word reflecting upon any of his judges . . . or against any Member of the House, or officer of the Army; so wonderful was his patience, though his spirit was great, and might otherwise have expressed his resentments upon several occasions'. Herbert also judged that the King was 'bidding farewell to the world', 'his whole business', as he put it, 'was a serious preparation for death'.[4]

After Charles had been taken from Whitehall to St James's Palace, he ordered Herbert to allow no one to visit him, except his children. The King knew that his nephew, Prince Charles Louis, the Elector Palatine, brother to the Princes Rupert and Maurice, would wish to see him, as would some of his most loyal subjects. When the Elector arrived, accompanied by the Duke of Richmond, the Marquess of Hertford and the Earls of Southampton and Lindsey, Herbert explained the King's wishes, which they obeyed, presenting their humble duty to His Majesty with their prayers. 'They returned full of sorrow, as appeared by their faces.'

Not all those concerned accepted the inevitable. The appeal made by the Prince of Wales to the States-General of Holland had brought their ambassadors to London to appeal to Parliament and to the Army to spare the King's life, or at least to obtain a deferment of his execution. The Presbyterians too were concerned for his spiritual welfare, as was evident when some of the London ministers, including Caryl, Calamy, Vines and Dell, came to the King to pray with him and make other offers of service. Charles thanked them kindly for their thoughts for his soul, but said that Parliament had agreed to allow Dr William Juxon, until lately the Bishop of London, to be with him and to help him to prepare for eternity. He asked them, however, to remember him in their prayers. Herbert also relates how his kinsman, Philip Herbert, Earl of Pembroke sent a gold alarm watch to the King in the care of a very senior Army officer. It never reached His Majesty, who, when he heard of this, is said to have remarked that had the officer known it was for the King he would have delivered it, aware that it would be enjoyed for only a short time.

The Revd Edmund Calamy, who with other ministers, visited King Charles after the trial.

That evening, Saturday, an attendant of the Prince of Wales arrived from The Hague with a letter that the Prince had written six days earlier. The courtier, Mr Seymour, was much distressed to see the King in his present state, having only previously seen him in regal spendour. King Charles read the letter and sent a message in return to his eldest son with Seymour, who left to return to Holland. The King then went to his devotions where Dr Juxon prayed with him and read some selected chapters from the Scriptures.

Later that night the King sent Herbert, with an emerald and diamond ring, to visit a lady living in Channel Row, behind King Street, Westminster. This lady, wife of Sir W. Wheeler, was the King's laundress. Herbert was to give her the ring and say nothing. Having received permission to leave St James's Palace from Colonel Thomlinson, Herbert made his way past the sentries, but not without some difficulty because of a typically officious corporal of the guard. The night was very dark but eventually he was able to present the ring to Lady Wheeler as ordered. In return he was given a little cabinet, its door secured by three seals, two of them the King's Arms, the third the figure of a Roman. On Herbert's return to the palace, the King said that he would see the cabinet opened in the morning.

Dr William Juxon, the former Bishop of London, on whom the King relied in spiritual and other matters.

The prospect of a good night's sleep for the King was not only blighted by the situation facing him, but also by the rigid attention to duty of Colonel Francis Hacker, who now commanded the guard immediately around him. Hacker insisted that two musketeers should be present in the King's bedchamber throughout the night. When King Charles heard this, as Herbert observed, '. . . he made no reply, only gave a sigh'. Bishop Juxon and Herbert were not prepared to accept Hacker's ruling, '. . . apprehending the horror of it, and the disturbance it would give the King in his meditations and preparation for his departure out of this uncomfortable world; . . . representing the barbarousness of such an act, they never left the Colonel until he reversed his order by withdrawing these men'.[5]

Then, undisturbed, the King continued reading and praying for a further two hours.

As the King was being removed to Whitehall, the High Court of Justice had adjourned to the Painted Chamber. Here the Commissioners appointed Commissary-General Henry Ireton, Sir Hardress Waller, Colonel Thomas Harrison, Colonel Richard Deane and Colonel John Okey to be a committee '. . . to consider the time and place for the execution of the sentence against the King'.[6] The Court then adjourned until 'Monday morning at eight of the clock to this place'.

In the House of Commons a committee had been named to draw up a declaration that should anyone attempt to proclaim the Prince of Wales as King after the death of his father, that person would be guilty of High Treason and that anyone who spoke or preached against the present proceedings of the Commons of England assembled in Parliament would be liable to punishment. A member of the Army had earlier told some MPs that in the event of a sentence of death being passed on him, the King had two requests, both of which the Parliament granted. He had asked if he might see his children before his execution and further, that he might have the comfort of the presence of Dr Juxon.

Before it was adjourned on Saturday, the Members of Parliament were warned to be at their places by 8 a.m. on Monday 29 January 1649, 'There being much business that would be offered to the House that day.'

On Sunday 28 January the Bishop arrived early from his lodgings near the palace and, after prayers, the King broke the seals of the cabinet and showed Juxon and Herbert its contents. They were diamonds and jewels, mostly from broken insignia of the Order of the Garter, 'Georges', and damaged jewel-encrusted Garters, which he had wanted in his hands to give to his two children, Princess Elizabeth and Prince Henry. He remarked ruefully to his companions that now they were able to see all the wealth that was currently in his power to give his children.

Much of the King's day was spent in prayer and devotions, but two chroniclers, Sir William Dugdale and Sir Roger Manley, recorded that he was visited by some of 'the prime leaders' of the Army, who came to offer him his life if he were to agree to certain proposals they had. One of these was that there should be a standing Army of 40,000 men under the command of those they would nominate; that the Council of Officers would have the power to recruit and to nominate new officers and men as they thought fit; that they should have the power to raise taxes to provide the pay for the Army and that they should themselves levy those taxes. The King refused to sanction these proposals, saying that he would rather become a sacrifice for his people than betray their laws, liberties, lives and estates with the Church, Commonwealth and Honour of the Crown to so intolerable a bondage of armed faction. If the accounts of Dugdale and Manley are correct, it would seem that despite the formality of the trial and the sentencing, the decision to kill the King was still not irrevocable. It may have been an elaborate charade to pressure His Majesty into an agreement with the Army. This, however, is fairly unlikely, since the Army grandees, particularly Cromwell, Ireton and Harrison, appeared to be determined that King Charles should die.

The dress of a minister in the 1640s.

The Presbyterian ministers in London ignored the order from Parliament that no one should speak against the proceedings which had been taken and were about to be undertaken against the King. That Sunday the Presbyterian pulpits rang with condemnation of these acts, but it appears that no one was prepared to report these ministers, nor yet provocatively to publish what they said in print.

Hugh Peters, the almost self-appointed religious champion of the Army and the Independents, also preached that day, taking as his text the 149th Psalm, verses six to nine: 'Let the high praises of God be in their mouth and a two-edged sword in their hands, to execute vengeance upon the heathen and punishments upon the people. To bind their kings in chains and their nobles with fetters of iron. To execute upon them the judgments written, this honour have all the Saints. Praise ye the Lord!' Although this sermon gives a flavour of the intensity of some of the emotion that was driving the King's enemies, the coldly implacable nature of the determination to punish the King for his part in the death and destruction of the wars is probably better expressed in Cromwell's earlier comment to Algernon Sidney that they would have the King's head with the crown upon it.

CHAPTER THIRTEEN
_____

The King's Last Day

For now I see Peace to corrupt no less than war to waste.

John Milton, *Paradise Lost*

Monday 29 January 1649

When the Commons met at 8 a.m. an unnamed Member who had been excluded on 6 December attended the House. The Rump, determined to keep its Independent majority, then ruled that anyone who had previously voted on 5 December to accept the King's terms offered at Newport as a basis of settlement should not be readmitted, and should also be barred from sitting as an MP in the future.

This reaffirmation of the Army's actions in December was followed by the arrival of the Dutch ambassadors, who read their instructions and Letters of Credence in French, the accepted language of diplomacy at the time. They appealed for the King's life, since his death might destroy 'a fair correspondency between this nation and the States of Holland'. There was no English translation of the appeal available, although one was promised for the following morning. As the ambassadors were not prepared to leave the original papers, this gave the King's implacable enemies the chance to sideline the Dutch request and vote that '. . . the House at that time could not proceed with the debate thereof'.[1] This allowed them the time they needed to arrange the King's death without seeming to ignore the Dutch approach completely.

The Members then went on to make alterations to the preambles to offical legal, fiscal and other documents, changing the name, style and title from that of the King to one which gave their illegal *coup d'état* at least the veneer of legitimacy, namely, 'Guardians of the Liberty of England by the Authority of Parliament'.

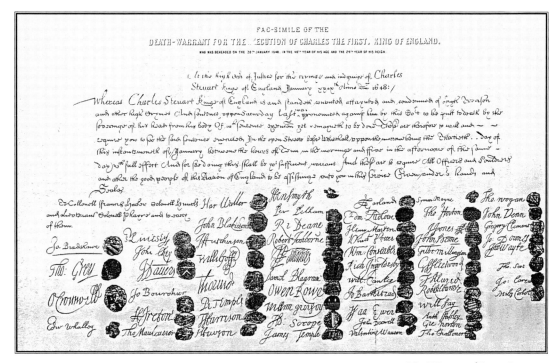

The Warrant of Execution,
with seals and signatures.

Meanwhile, at the Painted Chamber, forty-eight Commissioners of the High Court of Justice met to consider the report of the Committee that had been nominated to study the time and place of the King's execution. The basis of the report's conclusion was '. . . the open street before Whitehall is a fit place and that the said committee consider it fit that the King be there executed the morrow, the King having already notice thereof'. The Court approved of the proposal and 'ordered a warrant to be drawn for that purpose. Which warrant was accordingly signed and agreed to and ordered to be engrossed.' The minutes of the meeting as recorded in *Bradshawe's Journal* are very sparse, misleading and give little indication of the hectic activity and actions surrounding the signing of this warrant, which read as follows:

At the High Court of Justice for the trying and judging of Charles Stuart King of England Jan 29 1648[9]

Whereas Charles Stuart, King of England, is and standeth convicted attainted and condemned of High Treason and other

High Crimes. And sentence upon Saturday last was pronounced against him by this Court, to be put to death by the severing of his head from his body. Of which sentence Execution yet remains to be done. These are therefore to will and require you to see the said sentence executed in the open street before Whitehall upon the morrow, being the thirtieth day of this instant month of January between the hours of ten in the morning and five in the afternoon of the same day with full effect. And for so doing this shall be your sufficient warrant. And these are to require all officers and soldiers and other the good people of this nation to be assisting unto you in this service. Given under our hands and seals.

To Col. Francis Hacker, Col. Huncks and Lieutenant Col. Phray [*sic*] and to every of them.

Sealed and subscribed by

John Bradshaw	Vincent Potter
Tho. Gray	Will. Constable
Oliver Cromwell	Rich. Ingolsby
Edmund Whaley	Will Cawley
M. Livesley	J. Barkstead
Jo. Okey	Isack Ewer
J. Davers	John Dixwell
Jo. Bourcher	Valentine Wauton
H. Ireton	Simon Meyne
Tho. Mallevery	Tho. Horton
John Blackiston	John Jones
J. Hutchinson	John Moore
Will. Goffe	Har. Waller
Tho. Pride	Gilbert Millington
Peter Temple	G. Fleetwood
Tho. Harrison	Jo. Alured
J. Hughson	Robt. Lilburne
Hen. Smith	Will Say
Per. Pelham	Anth. Stapley
Rich. Deane	Gre. Norton
Robert Tichborne	Tho. Chaloner
Houmfrey Edwards	Tho. Wogan
Daniell Blagrave	Jo. Venn
Owen Rowe	Gre. Clement
Will Purefoy	John Downes
Ad. Scroope	Tho. Waite

James Temple	Tho. Scott
A. Garland	Jo. Carew
Ed. Ludlow	Miles Corbet
Hen. Martin[2]	

These fifty-nine names, reproduced as they were written on the original document which still exists in the House of Lords, were not all added to the warrant on 29 January. Some had been written before that date and Gregory Clement's signature was added over one that had been erased. Some of the fifty Commissioners present on 29 January did not sign, and fifteen of the men who did sign were not present on 29 January. It is possible also that the warrant would have originally been directed to Fairfax, since the names of the addressees, Hacker, Huncks and Phray (Phayre) are also written over wording that has been deleted.

A comparison of the Court records for both days indicates that some of the signatures would have been obtained on the day on which the King was sentenced, as those who signed and were absent on the Monday were present on the previous Saturday. This would have been before Ireton and his colleagues had decided when and where the King should die. It is possible that a prepared death warrant could have had spaces left blank in order that the time and place could be inserted. The deleted names raise some questions. It is possible that some who signed an incomplete death warrant on 27 January might have changed their minds, or that, possibly, some names had been added in anticipation of a signature later denied. There are various queries about the validity of the methods employed to prepare the document as a whole. These discrepancies did not materially affect the immediate outcome, although they lead one to treat the official accounts with at least a little scepticism.

It was not as easy to obtain as many as 59 signatures on the warrant as the 'official' records of the Court implied, even though there were 135 Commissioners named. Analysis shows that only 82 attended more than 2 sessions of the Court. Fairfax and three others attended only once. Clarendon related, with relish, how Richard Ingoldsby was forced to sign by Cromwell and others who, laughing, possibly with nervous tension or hysteria, held him and forcibly guided his hand to add his name.[3] Colonel Isaac Ewer confirmed the almost prankish nature of this fateful exercise. He reported that during the signings in the Painted Chamber Cromwell and Henry Marten larked about, marking each other's faces with ink from the pens they held.

At their trials after the Restoration other Regicides claimed that they had been threatened if they did not sign. Downes who, on the Saturday, had pleaded for the King to be allowed to address the Lords and Commons said, 'I was threatened with my very life. By the threats of one who hath since received his reward I was induced to do it.' It is not clear whether he meant Cromwell, Ireton or Thomas Harrison. Henry Smith claimed that he had signed because '. . . there were those then in authority whom he dared not disobey'. Others also signed under duress: Waite told how, 'On Monday I went to the House; they were labouring to get hands [signatures] for his execution. Saith Cromwell "Those that are gone in shall set their hands. I will have their hands now."'

Despite this evidence, some steadfastly refused to sign, although they had participated in the trial. Edmund Harvey objected to the sentence and refused, as did Alderman Isaac Pennington and William Heveningham. One must consider some of these statements with caution, however, as in 1660 the Regicides were in the hands of a vengeful son and were on trial for their lives. In such cases it is truly vital to have a most 'helpful' memory.

After the signing was complete, the Court ordered the officers of the ordnance in the Tower of London '. . . in whose hands or custody the bright execution axe for the executing malefactors is, do forthwith deliver unto Edward Dendy Esq., Sergeant-at-Arms attending this Court or his deputy or deputies, the said axe and for their or either of their so doing this shall be their warrant'.

Whilst these preparations were made, it must have been a day of ineffable sadness for the King when his two children, Princess Elizabeth who was fourteen and the nine-year-old Prince Henry, came from Syon House to St James's Palace for a short visit to see their father for the last time. Both children were deeply affected, the Princess weeping bitterly and her brother, more bewildered, joining her in tears.[4] Having raised both children from their knees, the King blessed them and told his daughter to remember that when she saw her brother James, the Duke of York, she was to tell him that it was her father's last wish that he should 'no more look upon Charles as his elder brother only, but to be obedient to him as his sovereign . . .'. When her father suggested that she would forget this, the Princess replied that she would never forget it as long as she lived, promising to write it down.

The King, taking Prince Henry on his knee, said,
'Sweetheart, now they will cut off thy father's head.' Upon which words the child looked very steadfastly upon him. 'Mark, child, what I say, they will cut off my head and perhaps make thee a king. But mark what I say; you must not be a king so long as your brothers Charles and James do live. For they will cut off your brothers' heads, when they can catch them, and cut off thy head too, at the last.' At which the child sighing said, 'I will be torn to pieces first.' Which falling unexpectedly from one so young it made the King rejoice exceedingly.[5]

The Princess also later recorded that the King, realising that he would not be allowed to write to her and that their time together was to be short, wanted her to read and learn the fundamental principles of the Protestant religion, '. . . to ground her against popery', and to send messages to the rest of the family. She wrote:

He wished me not to grieve and torment myself for him, for that would be a glorious death he should die, it being for the Laws and liberties of this land and for maintaining the true Protestant religion. He told me that he had forgiven all his enemies and hoped God would forgive them also, and commanded us and all the rest of my brothers and sisters to forgive them. He bid me tell my mother that his thoughts had never strayed from her and that his love would be the same to the last. With all he commanded me and my brother to be obedient to her. And bid me send his blessing to the rest of my brothers and sisters, with commendation to all his friends . . .[6]

The King gave his two children the jewels that Herbert had collected from Lady Wheeler, retaining only the 'George' he wore. Herbert described the final parting:

The King, . . . again kissing his children, had such pretty and pertinent answers from them both, as drew tears of joy and love from his eyes; and then praying God Almighty to bless 'em, he turned about, expressing a tender and fatherly affection. Most sorrowful was this parting, the young Princess shedding tears and crying lamentably, so as moved others to pity, that were formerly hard hearted; and at opening the bedchamber door, the King turned hastily from the window and kissed 'em and blessed 'em; so parted. This demonstration of pious affection exceedingly comforted the King in his affliction; so that in a grateful return he went immediately to prayer, the good Bishop and Mr Herbert being only present.[7]

The conversation with his children demonstrates that the King truly believed in his defence of the laws and liberties of his peoples and especially his wish to preserve the Protestant religion as he saw it. His efforts during the trial to speak in support of these beliefs were not just a legal tactic, even though he did alter the emphasis of his argument once he had seen the immediate futility of challenging the legal basis of the Court and its proceedings. It was this single-mindedness that had delayed the possibility of reaching several earlier settlements, weakening the position of his more moderate opponents and resulting in their being undermined by those holding more extreme views.

The King had previously written a long letter to his eldest son advising him about the difficulties of kingship, including the need for toleration. He also wrote a final letter to his wife. There is some uncertainty about the way in which both these letters were to be delivered. It has been claimed that both communications were taken by Herbert to Seymour after he had left the King to avoid their confiscation had Seymour been searched on leaving the King's quarters. This is probable, but it has also been suggested that Herbert took the Queen's letter to Seymour, leaving the one for the Prince in the hands of the Bishop for final delivery. The former hypothesis would seem more probable, as it was unlikely that Seymour, bound for The Hague, had only been given the letter to the Queen in Paris and not the one to the Prince, whose attendant Seymour was. The Bishop might also have found it very difficult to arrange the delivery of the Prince's letter.

Seymour had brought with him two blank sheets of paper signed by the Prince of Wales. These were to give the King's enemies freedom to fill in any conditions they wished over the Prince's signature in return for the King's life and his release. One was delivered to Parliament and ignored. Seymour gave the other to the King, who, with an appreciative smile at his son's efforts on his behalf, burnt it, determined to make no further concessions to his enemies even to save his own life. The King also arranged the burning of all his papers and 'his several clavises [cyphers] to his private letters'. This action appears to have given him and the Bishop much satisfaction.

Through Herbert, who was able to move around reasonably freely, the King received messages of goodwill from his supporters who were praying for him. He himself spent much of the rest of the day in prayer and meditation, as well as hearing a sermon from the Bishop, the text of which was taken from Romans 2:16, 'At that day when God shall judge the secrets of men by Jesus Christ, etc'. Throughout the day he ate and drank very sparingly and it was some time after nightfall before the Bishop took his leave, having again spent many hours in shared devotions with the King. As the Bishop was leaving, the King asked him to return early the following morning.

Archbishop Laud, who appeared in Herbert's dream. He was executed by Parliament in 1645.

King Charles continued in reading and prayer for more than two hours after the Bishop's departure. When he finally retired to his bedchamber, he asked Herbert to lie on a pallet beside the royal bed, where for about four hours the King slept soundly. Herbert spent an unquiet night, but was asleep when, two hours before dawn, the King opened the curtains of his bed and woke him, having seen by the burning nightlight that his attendant was restless. He asked Herbert why he had had such a disturbed night. The attendant told him of a vivid dream he had had that the King had been visited by the ghost of Archbishop Laud, who had been central to the introduction and implementation of the King's religious policy and who had also been executed by Parliament in 1645.

The King's last night on earth had been spent in St James's Palace, rather than in the Whitehall Palace, because the building of the scaffold and barrier railings outside the Banqueting House went on all night and the noise of the workmen would have been disturbing. This is a remarkable example of consideration by enemies for the thoughts, feelings and comfort of the man they intended to behead the next day.

The exact location of the scaffold gave rise to much speculation until it was finally resolved by Muddiman.[8] He placed it, after much consideration, on the western side of the Banqueting House, which still stands in Whitehall. As it was to hold a number of guards and other people and have room for the executioners to work, it was large, probably extending along most of the western wall of the hall, its floor level with the sills of the large windows. Some prints of the event show the scaffold placed in the middle of the wall, with access to it through the central window of the seven large ones along the wall. Muddiman believed that entry to the scaffold was through the second window from the north (from the end nearest to the present

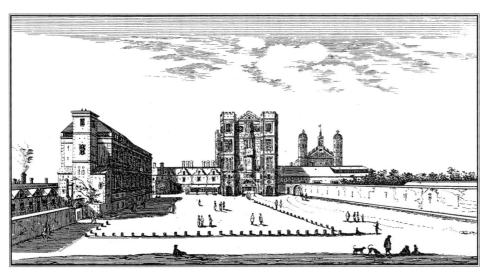

The area outside the Banqueting House, the scene of the execution.

Trafalgar Square), even if the execution block itself was nearer the central window.

The area in front of the building, normally enclosed by low posts, was railed off to keep back the expected crowds and, at 9 a.m. on the morning of the execution, the Court Commissioners meeting at the Painted Chamber ordered that the whole of the scaffold 'be covered in black'.[9] The rails around the platform were to be draped in black cloth so that the spectators on the ground would be unable to see the actual execution, although they would be able to see the headsman, from the chest up, wielding the axe as he stood over the prostrate King.

Despite the opposition expressed by the Dutch, the Scots and many of the King's English subjects at this high-handed, illegal action, the scene was set for the death of King Charles I.

CHAPTER FOURTEEN

The Execution

He nothing common did or mean
Upon that memorable scene:
Andrew Marvell, 'Horatian Ode upon Cromwell's Return from
Ireland'

Tuesday 30 January 1649

At about 5 a.m., after his discussion with Herbert about the latter's dream, the King decided to dress. It was still two hours to dawn and the weather was so bitterly cold that the River Thames was frozen. He decided that he would wear an extra shirt against the cold, also to prevent onlookers thinking that he might be shivering with fear. He told Herbert, 'I would have no imputation of fear. I do not fear death. Death is not terrible to me. I bless my God I am prepared.'[1]

Two shirts made of linen were chosen by Herbert. One, which opened down the front, was trimmed with embroidery on the collar, sleeves and its lower edges. It was also decorated with small restrained bows of red and blue ribbon. The other shirt had a very wide lace collar and embroidered ruffles. The waistcoat the King wore was made of a rich brocade, of red with silver and yellow. The skullcap he was to wear on the scaffold was of linen, with the edge turned up to form a border on which were embroidered scrolls in gilt thread enclosing summer flowers and fruits in raised silk appliqué work.

The rest of his dress, satin doublet, breeches and short cloak, was to be black, but not, as he told Herbert, 'for mourning'. The sombre appearance would be relieved by the bright blue of the ribbon of the Order of the Garter across his chest, by the 'George' he wore around his neck and by the brilliant Garter Star of over 400 diamonds that

The 'George' that the King
always wore, containing a
miniature of his wife.

emblazoned his cloak. He would also wear his usual earrings, each of
a small pearl surmounted by a tiny golden crown.

He wanted '. . . to be as trim today as may be' and so paid some
attention to his hair and beard, which had been neglected recently as
a protest against his treatment as a prisoner. His chestnut hair was
laced by white streaks, as was his beard, no longer trimmed to a
point but now bushy, with its own growth of white hair. With more
than a touch of graveyard humour he said to Herbert, 'Though it has
not long to stand on my shoulders, take all the care you can of my
head', as the latter prepared to dress the King's hair and beard.[2]

The King's toilet preparation and his dressing lasted until dawn.
When that was completed, the faithful Dr Juxon arrived with all
that was necessary for the Holy Sacrament, a chalice, a paten, the
bread and the wine. By this time Herbert was becoming more upset
by the approaching events. He fell on his knees before the King and
'. . . humbly begged his Majesty's pardon, if he had at any time been
negligent in his duty whilst he had the honour to serve him. The
King thereupon gave him his hand to kiss, having the day before
been graciously pleased, under his royal hand to give him a
certificate, expressing, that the said Mr. Herbert, was not imposed on
him, but by his Majesty made choice of to attend him in his
bedchamber.' This the King meant as a safeguard for his attendant

should Herbert ever be accused of having been one of the King's gaolers.

At 8 a.m. the House of Commons convened to be confronted by the promised return of the Dutch emissaries bearing the English translations of the appeal from the States-General of Holland. The House referred the submission to a committee of Ireton and Henry Marten, with four others, to prepare a reply with reasons why the House could not delay the course of justice. The Commons then gave the First and Second Readings to their Act prohibiting the proclamation of anyone as King of England and against any attempts to support the claims of Charles, the Prince of Wales. The Third Reading was completed in the afternoon.

The Commissioners, who were sitting in the Painted Chamber, sent Lieutenant-Colonel William Goffe to tell the King that five ministers, including Marshall and Caryl, were on their way to St James's Palace to offer him spiritual comfort. When they arrived, as in all their previous dealings from Newcastle onwards, the King declined their help, although he again asked them to pray for him. Bishop Juxon prayed with him and read to the King Chapter 27 of St Matthew's Gospel, which told the story of the trial and death of the Lord Jesus Christ. When the King asked if he had especially chosen that reading, the Bishop replied that it was the proper reading for the day according to the Calendar. The aptness of the reading affected the King, so appropriate was it to his circumstances.

During this time His Majesty also instructed Herbert about the disposal of the few legacies he was able to leave. These, apart from the jewels from the broken insignia, were mainly books. To the Prince of Wales he left his Bible, a magnificent volume, which he had copiously annotated. With it he left a last request with the Bishop that Prince Charles should read and meditate upon it frequently. James, the Duke of York, was to receive 'his large ring Sun-dial of Silver . . . invented and made by Mr. Delamain, an able mathematician .`. . . [who] . . . in a little printed book shewed its excellent use in resolving many questions in Arithmetic and other rare operations . . . in the mathematics'. To the Princess Elizabeth he left some religious books and '. . . also a paper to be printed, in which he asserted regal government to have a divine right, with proofs out of sundry authors, civil and sacred'.[3] Prince Henry was to receive the writings of his grandfather, King James I and a catechism, while the Earl of Lindsey was to have the King's copy of *Cassandre*, an imaginary account in French of the campaigns of

Alexander the Great by La Calprenede. The King bequeathed his gold watch to the Duchess of Richmond and the faithful Thomas Herbert was to receive the silver striking clock that had hung at the King's bedside in all the places he had been imprisoned.

Just before 10 a.m. Colonel Francis Hacker knocked at the door of the royal bedchamber in St James's Palace. Thomas Herbert heard the knocking and surmising the purpose, ignored it. Hacker knocked again, more loudly and the King told Herbert to go to the door. Herbert opened it, demanding, with an almost inconsequential insolence, 'Wherefore he knocked?', to which Hacker replied that he wished to speak to the King. When King Charles told Herbert to let him in, 'The Colonel in trembling manner came near, and told his Majesty, it was time to go to Whitehall, where he might have some further time to rest. The King bade him go forth, he would come presently.'[4]

For a while the King was silent with his thoughts and then took the Bishop by the hand, saying, 'with a cheerful countenance . . . "Come let us go" and bidding Mr Herbert take with him the silver clock, that hung by the bedside, said "Open the door, Hacker has given us a second warning."' They walked through the garden and into the Park, where the King stopped, asked Herbert the time and 'taking the clock in his hand, gave it him, and bade him keep it in memory of him'.[5]

There were several companies of footsoldiers lined up on either side of the pathway and as he walked, the King was preceded by a guard of halberdiers, with another following as a rearguard, both with colours flying. The noise of beating drums was so great that 'one could hardly hear what another spoke'. The Bishop walked on the King's right, with Colonel Thomlinson on his left; Herbert was just behind the

The walk from St James's Palace to Whitehall.

King, ahead of the rearguard. Herbert recounts that the walk was uneventful, except that the King had some conversation with Matthew Thomlinson, who walked bareheaded, showing his respect. Other reports mentioned an encounter with one Tench, the man who had enthusiastically built the scaffold. He walked insolently beside the King for a short way, staring hard at him, much to the King's distaste. Tench apparently had had a brother who was executed as a Parliamentary spy at Oxford during the First Civil War and as a result bore a personal grudge. The Bishop, seeing the King's aversion, intervened and dismissed the intruder brusquely.

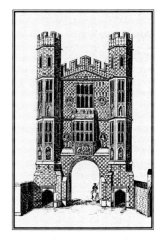

Whitehall Gate, across which the King walked into the Palace of Whitehall.

The party went up the stairs into the Whitehall Gate, through the gallery that crossed the road and into the palace. The King was taken to his usual bedchamber, where, after a short rest, the Bishop said prayers. Then the King asked Herbert to bring him some bread and wine. The King broke the small white loaf and ate a half of it, drinking a glass of claret, after which he and Juxon were together privately, awaiting the third call from Colonel Hacker.

The King had told Herbert which skullcap he would wear at the execution and had asked him to have it ready on the scaffold. Herbert, however, had confessed to the Bishop that he 'was not able to endure the sight of that violence they upon the scaffold would offer the King'. William Juxon then took charge of the cap, telling him to 'wait at the end of the Banquetting House, near the scaffold, to take care of the King's body; for (he said) that, and his interment, will be our last office'.[6]

As the King continued to compose himself, secure in his beliefs, his enemies had at least three additional reasons to be agitated. Apart from the fact that they were about to kill their King, they had not yet found anyone prepared to carry out the beheading; there was concern that there might be some attempt to free the King; and there was a suspicion that the attitudes of some of the officers they relied upon were beginning to change.

Several fanatical strangers had offered to carry out the execution, but the two officers entrusted with despatching the King, Colonels Daniel Axtel and John Hewson, preferred to make their own arrangements, using only people they knew for this important task. They had assumed that procuring a headsman and an assistant executioner would present few problems. There was, after all, an Army of regiments whose ranks contained very many officers and men whose sense of duty and detestation of the King should provide a ready pool from which to draw suitable men. Even if that should fail, there was an adequate, but not ideal, solution – the public executioner, Richard Brandon, who had succeeded his father Gregory in that role.

Hewson ordered an assembly of forty sergeants from three of the regiments on duty in London, Fairfax's, Pride's and Hacker's. When he addressed the thirty-eight men who appeared, he made them swear on the Bible that they would never talk of what they were about to hear. That done, he then offered an inducement of £100 and instant promotion to any two who would volunteer to become the King's executioner and the assistant to the headsman. No one immediately volunteered.

Colonel John Hewson, who was given the task of finding a headsman.

Axtel then sent his brother, Elisha, with an escort to bring Richard Brandon and his assistant, Ralph Jones, from their homes in Whitechapel. When Elisha Axtel explained the purpose of his visit to Brandon, the latter firmly refused to comply with his request, stating that he would rather be executed himself than do what was demanded of him. Despite this, or probably because of his attitude, he was taken to Whitehall with his equipment, which included a low headsman's block. Jones was nowhere to be found. At Whitehall, the senior officers tried to change Brandon's mind, first by offering him £200 and then, as he continued to refuse, they tried to coerce him with threats of being burnt to death if he remained unwilling. It was claimed that they did succeed in terrifying Brandon, holding him under arrest until after the execution, when he was set free.

The identities of the headsman and his assistant have, ever since the King's death, been matters of mystery and speculation. Richard Brandon, who had been the executioner of the Earl of Strafford and Archbishop William Laud, was also, in a matter of weeks, to be the executioner of Royalist leaders of the Second Civil War, the Duke of Hamilton, the Earl of Holland and Lord Capel and others. He himself was to die of natural causes in June 1649, and although he continually denied having executed the King, after his death, a 'Confession' was printed and published in which he admitted to the deed. This has been regarded as fake, intended perhaps to divert attention from the real headsman and his assistant. Conversely, if Brandon, who prided himself on his skill with the axe, was prepared to behead important Royalists after the King's death, his publicised refusals to kill the King may also have been a subterfuge to protect him from immediate Royalist revenge.

Many people were accused of having performed the execution, from Fairfax and Cromwell, who were charged by a contemporary

French writer, to Hugh Peters, George Joyce (who had kidnapped the King from Holdenby), Sergeant William Hulet, Captain Foxley, Phineas Payne, John Alured, William Walker, Colonel Foxe, Henry Porter, Lord Stair, John Bigge, Major Sydenham, Giles Dekker (an unknown trooper and an unnamed drover).[7]

This mystery is commended to the reader as a fascinating exercise. Several writers have their favourite nominations, all cogently argued, equally convincing and open to counter-argument. Few people knew the true identities of the axeman and his assistant. Among them were, presumably, Cromwell, Harrison, Ireton, Axtel and Hacker. The written order for the execution, which might have confirmed the identities of these two heavily disguised men on the scaffold, disappeared.

From the many accounts that have discussed the identities of the executioners, four people emerge as the favourites. They are Richard Brandon, the expert headsman who prided himself in the skill of despatching his victims with a single stroke; Hugh Peters, the very prominent Independent minister of religion; the former Cornet, then Captain, George Joyce; and finally, Sergeant William Hulet, who had been present at the meeting of the thirty-eight sergeants and who, shortly afterwards, received rapid, accelerated promotion to the rank of Captain, leap-frogging over two more junior commissioned ranks. Alured and Payne are said to have boasted of the act during their lives, but they were discounted as being egotistical fools during the investigations made after the Restoration of King Charles II. It is up to the reader to draw their own conclusion – they may wish to consider any two of the four men suggested, or even other individuals.

The order for the execution itself was a matter of dispute when the time came for it to be signed and delivered to the headsmen. The warrant for the King's death, signed by the Commissioners, had been addressed to Hacker, Huncks and Phayre, the senior officers delegated to carry out the execution. Soon it became time to put that warrant into practice with an order to the executioners signed by the three. In Ireton's apartment in the Palace of Whitehall, Cromwell was explaining this to the three officers as Ireton and Harrison kept warm under the bedclothes. Huncks, the rest of whose family was intensely Royalist, had qualms and refused to sign. Cromwell told him that he was 'a froward peevish fellow' (perverse and disobedient). Phayre also declined. At this Cromwell went to a little table and scribbled the authority to execute, handing the pen to Hacker, who

O horrable Murder

The King, with the execution scene shown in the background, which is how it may have appeared to the spectators.

signed and left the room with the Lieutenant-General and Axtel. The two officers who had refused to sign were then left to their own devices.

Sir Thomas, Lord Fairfax, as he had become on the death of his father some ten months previously, apparently still believed that the King's life might be saved, or at least his death postponed by reasoned argument and discussion. He was present in the Palace of Whitehall and had accepted Cromwell's suggestion of a meeting for prayer in Thomas Harrison's room. There he hoped to influence his subordinates. The course of the discussion was predictable. The disadvantages of killing the King were rehearsed and then the meeting went into prayer. Fairfax was still optimistic that the King might be saved but, apart from discarding the uncertain idea of using his regiment to effect a rescue, he relied on words, which carried little weight with the others who were determined to see the King dead.

Outside the Banqueting House the crowds had gathered. The raised scaffold, draped in black, was surrounded by ranks of soldiers lined up between it and the fencing barriers behind which the spectators waited, some distance away. The area was blanketed by soldiers, posted in case of disturbances or even a desperate last minute Royalist attempt to rescue the King.

Inside the building the executioners made their preparations, donning their disguises. They were dressed in close-fitting dark woollen frocks, similar to those worn by the sailors or, more appropriately, the butchers of the day. Their faces were covered by large false-face masks with false beards and they also wore large wigs under their headgear. The executioner had a long 'grey, grizzled periwig' that, with the large grey beard he wore, caused Hewson to call him 'Father Greybeard'. His assistant was decked out with a black beard and wig, which was topped by a broad-brimmed black hat, canted up at the front. Insolently he wore this hat throughout the proceedings, refusing to doff it in the King's presence. The executioner now had charge of the axe, endeavouring to keep its edge sharp and unbruised. A close associate of Cromwell, Captain James Berry, a former iron-worker, had inspected the blade to check the keenness of its edge.

In case it was necessary to drag the King down to the block, Hugh Peters, presumably on his own authority, had ordered Tench, the rancorous scaffold-builder, to hammer staples into the floor on either side of the block and to fix pulleys to them. These, with their threaded ropes, would enable the King to be dragged ignominiously into a prone position, if he resisted or should circumstances demand it. While this activity went on, the King and his two companions, Juxon and Herbert, were at prayer.

Eventually, at about 1.30 p.m., Colonel Francis Hacker arrived at the door of the apartment with his armed guard. There he met Colonel Matthew Thomlinson, who, on being shown the warrant for the King's death, said, 'This means that my duty is at an end.' Hacker agreed and asked Thomlinson to tell the King, to which he answered, 'No, neither I nor anyone here intends to tell him that orders for his safety are ended. You can do it yourself.' Hacker knocked at the inner door, at which Juxon and Herbert fell to their knees, in tears. King Charles gave them his hand to kiss and helped the sixty-six-year-old Bishop to his feet. Herbert then opened the door to Hacker, who began to read the warrant. His Majesty silenced him, saying that he wished Thomlinson to accompany him to the scaffold. Then he said calmly, 'Go on. I will follow.'[8] Close and prolonged contact with the King had obviously affected and softened Thomlinson's attitude towards him. Although not to be swayed from his duty and responsibility, he had developed an admiration bordering upon affection for the man he had so zealously guarded since Windsor. King Charles too had valued the Colonel's courtesy and kindness, giving him a golden toothpick as a memento of their association.

The party proceeded down the stairs into the winter air and up the outside stairs into the Banqueting House, through into that splendid room, wonderfully designed by Inigo Jones and its ceiling decorated with the brilliant paintings of Peter Paul Rubens. It was now crowded with soldiers, privileged visitors and foreign ambassadors, as Herbert noted, an '. . . abundance of men and women crowded in, though with some peril to their persons, to behold the saddest sight England ever saw . . . as his Majesty passed by, with a cheerful look, he heard them pray for him, the soldiers not rebuking any of them; by their silence and dejected faces seeming afflicted rather than insulting'.[9] When he left the Banqueting House through the window that had been removed to allow exit on to the scaffold outside, he was preceded by Hacker and the guard of soldiers, accompanied by Juxon and Thomlinson and followed by some men to take notes of what might be said and to record the event.

As he stepped on to the scaffold, the King registered concern that the block, placed in the centre, was so low. It was described as being 'about eighteen inches long and six inches in height, flat at the bottom and rounded at the top'.[10] His concern was, one presumes, that such a low block would not allow him to kneel, but would force him to adopt the far more submissive posture of lying on his stomach. He asked Hacker if there was not a higher one available, only to be told that there was not. The King also would have noted the staples, ropes and pulleys, the cheap pine coffin made of planks and covered by a black velvet cloth and, finally, the axe resting against the block. He would have glanced at the two grotesquely garbed and disguised executioners in their appropriate butcher-like dresses and trunk breeches made of Friesian wool and at the guard of soldiers deployed around the staging.

The King makes his speech
from the Scaffold.

The King looked out at the people assembled in the area, at the several ranks of footsoldiers ranged immediately around the scaffold, at the troops of horse at one side towards King Street and at the other towards Charing Cross. He saw that the citizens of London were kept beyond the barrier fences, too far away either to hear any of the words of the speech he proposed to make or to see anything that occurred below the level of the draped railings on the scaffold. The only people who might see the King die would be those who thronged the upper windows and roofs of the surrounding buildings.

King Charles took a small piece of paper from his pocket and from the notes written earlier he began his last speech to his people as the winter sun came through the clouds. He spoke, addressing his words to those on the scaffold, glancing frequently at Matthew Thomlinson.

I shall be very little heard of anybody here, I shall therefore speak a word unto you here. Indeed I could hold my peace very well, if I did not think that holding my peace would make some men think that I did submit to the guilt as well as to the punishment. But I think it is my duty to God first, and to my country, for to clear myself both as an honest man, a good king, and a good Christian.

I shall begin first with my innocency. In truth, I think it not very needful for me to insist so long upon this, for all the world knows that I never did begin a war with the two Houses of Parliament. And I call God to witness, to whom I must shortly make an account, that I never did intend for to encroach upon their privileges. They began upon me: it is the Militia they began upon. They confessed that the Militia was mine, but they thought fit for to have it from me. And to be short, if anybody will look to the dates of commissions, of their commissions and mine, and likewise to the declarations, will see clearly that they began these unhappy troubles, not I. So that as the guilt of these enormous crimes are laid against me, I hope in God that God will clear me of it. I will not; I'm in charity. God forbid that I should lay it upon the two Houses of Parliament. There is no necessity of either. I hope they are free of this guilt, for I do believe that ill instruments between them and me have been the chief cause of all this bloodshed, so that by way of speaking, as I find myself clear of this, I hope and pray God that they may too. Yet for all this, God forbid that I should be so ill a Christian as not to say that God's judgments are just upon me. Many times He does pay justice by an unjust sentence; that is ordinary. I will only say this, that an unjust sentence that I suffered for to take effect is punished now by an unjust sentence upon me. That is, so far as I have said, to show you that I am an innocent man.

After this public reference to his reluctant sanctioning of the execution of Thomas Wentworth, the Earl of Strafford, an act that he deeply regretted and which had settled heavily on his conscience, the King continued,

Now for to show you that I am a good Christian. I hope there is a good man (*pointing at Dr Juxon*) that will bear me witness that I have forgiven all the world and even those in particular that have been the chief causers of my death. Who they are, God knows; I do not desire to know. I pray God forgive them. But this is not all, my charity must go further. I wish that they may repent, for indeed they have committed a great sin in that particular. I pray God with

St. Stephen that this be not laid to their charge, nay not only so, but that they may take the right way to the peace of the kingdom, for my charity commands me not only to forgive particular men, but my charity commands me to endeavour to the last gasp the peace of the kingdom. So, sirs, I do wish with all my soul, and I do hope there is some here *(turning to some gentlemen that wrote)* will carry it further, that they may endeavour the peace of the kingdom.

Now sirs, I must show you both how you are out of the way and will put you in a way.

First you are out of the way, for certainly all the way you ever have had yet, as I could find by anything, is in the way of conquest. Certainly this is an ill way. For conquest, sirs, in my opinion is never just, except there be a good just cause, either for matter or wrong or just title. And then if you go beyond it, the first quarrel that you have to it, that makes it unjust at the end that was just at first.

But if it be only matter of conquest, then it is a great robbery; as a pirate said to Alexander the Great that he was the great robber, he [the pirate] was but a petty robber. And so, sirs, I do think the way that you are in is much out of the way.

Now, sirs, for to put you in the way.

Believe it, you will never do right, nor God will never prosper you, until you give God His due, the King his due, that is, my successors, and the people their due. I am as much for them as any of you. You must give God His due by regulating rightly His Church (according to his scripture) which is now out of order. For to set you in a way particularly, now I cannot; but only this: a national synod freely called, freely debating among themselves, must settle this, when that every opinion is freely and clearly heard. For the King, indeed I will not – *(then turning to a gentleman that touched the Axe said, 'Hurt not the Axe that may hurt me', meaning if he did blunt the edge)* – for the King, the laws of the land will clearly instruct you for that. Therefore, because it concerns my own particular, I only give you a touch of it.

For the people, and truly I desire their liberty and freedom as much as anybody whomsoever, but I must tell you that their liberty and their freedom consists in having of government those laws by which their life and their goods may be most their own. It is not for having a share in government, sirs; that is nothing pertaining to them. A subject and a sovereign are clean different things. And therefore until they do that, I mean, that you do put the people in that liberty as I say, certainly they will never enjoy themselves.

Sirs, it was for this that now I am come here. If I would have given way to an arbitrary way for to have all laws changed according to the power of the sword, I need not have come here. And therefore I tell you, and pray to God it be not laid to your charge, that I am the martyr of the people.

In truth, sirs, I shall not hold you much longer, for I will only say this to you, that in truth I could have desired some little time longer because that I would have put this that I have said in a little more order and a little better digested than I have done. And therefore I hope you will excuse me. I have delivered my conscience. I pray God that you do take those courses that are best for the good of the kingdom and your own salvations.

Dr Juxon: Will your Majesty, though it be well known Your Majesty's affections to religion, yet it may be expected that you should say something for the world's satisfaction.

King: I thank you very heartily, my Lord, for that I had almost forgotten it. In truth, sirs, my conscience in religion, I think is very known to all the world. And therefore I declare before you all that I die a Christian according to the profession of the Church of England as I found it left me by my father. And this honest man (*pointing to Dr Juxon*) I think will witness it.

Then turning to the officers, the King said: Sirs, excuse me for this same. I have good cause, and I have a gracious God. I will say no more.

Then turning to Colonel Hacker, he said: Take care they do not put me to pain. And sir, an it please you——

But then a gentleman coming near the Ax, the King said: Take heed of the Ax, pray take heed of the Ax!

Then the King speaking to the Executioner said: I shall say but very short prayers, and when I thrust out my hands . . .

Then the King called to Dr Juxon for his nightcap, and having put it on, he said to the Executioner: Does my hair trouble you? who desired him to put it all under his cap, which the King did accordingly by the help of the Executioner and the Bishop.

Then the King turning to Dr Juxon said: I have a good cause and a gracious God on my side.

Dr Juxon: There is but one stage more. This stage is turbulent and troublesome. It is but a short one. But you may consider it will soon carry you a very great way – it will carry you from Earth to Heaven, and there you shall find a great deal of cordial joy and comfort.

King: I go from a corruptible to an incorruptible crown, where no disturbance can be, no disturbance in the world.

Dr Juxon: You are exchanged from a temporal to an eternal crown – a good exchange.

The King then said to the Executioner: Is my hair well? Then the King took off his cloak and his George [his Garter insignia] giving his George to Dr Juxon, saying: Remember (*it is thought to give it to the Prince*). The King put off his doublet, and being in his waistcoat put his cloak on again, then looking upon the block said to the Executioner: You must set it fast.

Executioner: It is fast, sir.

King: It might have been a little higher.

Executioner: It can be no higher, sir.

King: When I put my hands this way (*stretching them out*) – then
. . .

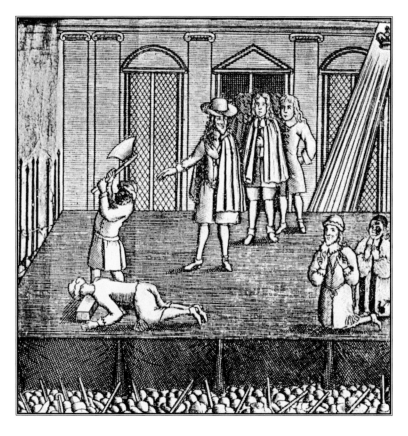

An impression of the execution, showing the King's position.

After that, having said two or three words (as he stood) to himself with hands and eyes lifted up, immediately stooping down laid his neck upon the Block, and then the Executioner again putting his hair under his cap, the King said (thinking he had been going to strike): Stay for the sign!

Executioner: Yes I will, an it please Your Majesty.

And after a very little pause, the king stretching forth his hands, the Executioner at one blow severed his head from his body . . .[11]

The time was within a minute of 2 p.m.

Then the assistant to the Executioner silently held up the King's head to the spectators, at which the crowd uttered a deep groan. Having played his part, the assistant threw the King's head down on to the planking of the scaffold, bruising the dead face.

The fact, reported by almost all the accounts, that the assistant Executioner did not utter the traditional cry of 'Behold! The Head of a Traitor!' has been interpreted in at least two ways. The first was that being inexperienced in his work, he did not know what was required of him. That is unlikely because the action and words were well-known parts of any beheading.

The second reason, which Hugh Ross Williamson accepts, was that he did not speak because his voice would have revealed his identity. Such a voice would have to be well known to be easily recognised and Williamson judged that the man concerned could have been Hugh Peters, whose voice would have been very familiar from the many and prolonged sermons he had given. A close-fitting face mask might muffle a voice enough to protect its owner from being unmasked. One wonders, however, if the swaggering, self-advertising Peters would have courted such anonymity. Reports of him indicate that he would have gloried in any part he played in the public execution of the King he hated.

CHAPTER FIFTEEN

After the Execution

Who overcomes by force, hath overcome but half his foe.

John Milton, *Paradise Lost*

Tuesday 30 January 1649

Some of the scenes which immediately followed the killing of the King were similar to the attitude and actions of the assistant to the Executioner and were appalling in their barbarity, superstition and avarice. Before the King's head and body were placed in the coffin, the soldiers on the scaffold dipped their handkerchiefs and swords in the King's blood and cut some locks from behind the severed head. So much was taken that the King's long hair at the back was left barely an inch long.

Pieces of the wooden floor of the scaffold that had soaked up some of the royal blood were prised off or split up to sell to the many who were clamouring to buy them. Even the sand spread around to absorb the blood was gathered up for profit. It is unlikely that all the purchasers wished to buy these items out of respect, although there must have been some who wanted a relic of the martyred King who had linked himself with the first Christian martyr, St Stephen, in his farewell words. In addition there was the hope that a cure for the 'King's Evil' might be even more effective if sufferers were touched by relics stained by His Majesty's blood.

Contemporary accounts convey an atmosphere of high, even hysterical, emotion. Some of this, no doubt, resulted from great sadness, some from religious fervour but much, it would seem, on the scaffold itself arose from ghoulish, vengeful delight, allied to the prospect of immediate, unearned profit. The soldiers made the most of their sales opportunities, charging whatever money they could for blood-stained bits of cloth or strands of the King's hair and even extracting money from those who wished to step on to the scaffold itself.

The prevailing general view of the King's death among the citizens of London was mentioned in a private letter written that day. It read, '. . . the King this day was beheaded before Whitehall Gate. It much discontents the citizens . . .'.[1] The spectators behind the barriers created no disturbance, and were soon dispersed by the troops of horse soldiers who flanked them. Eventually the King's body and head were put into the waiting coffin and taken from the scaffold by his grieving servants, including Herbert and the Bishop, to await the arrival of Thomas Trappam, the Army's Surgeon-General, who was charged with embalming the King for burial.

In the Long Gallery the Bishop and Herbert encountered Fairfax, who asked how the King did. Herbert, who recounted this incident after many years, seems to have misunderstood the question and assumed that the Lord General was unaware that the King was dead. Fairfax, Herbert claimed, appeared disconcerted at this news.[2] It is possible that Fairfax wished to know how the King had behaved in face of imminent death and his consternation may have arisen from his realisation that of all people, he with his reputation, might have been able to prevent or delay the King's death had he been more resolute.

There is much to commend Fairfax as a soldier and as a man, but his pusillanimous vapourings over the fate of the King, whatever the reasons he might advance for them, do him as little credit as do his actions over the execution of Sir Charles Lucas and Sir George Lisle after the siege of Colchester in 1648. Had he been as courageous in this matter as he was in battle, or even as audacious as his wife in her gallant protests at the King's trial, his efforts to obtain at least a postponement of the King's fate might have been more positive.

However, one must not give Fairfax all the discredit for failing to save the King. There were hundreds of others who also failed. There were scores of excluded Members of the Lords and Commons, who did nothing. The Militia Trained Bands of London, closely linked with the City of London and its Presbyterian leanings, did nothing. Both these interests had opposed the King but had had their influence reduced by a more powerful clique. They and the King now had a common enemy, but this situation refutes the mistaken belief that 'my enemy's enemy is, of necessity, my friend'.

Apart from the one small plot against the Commissioners of the High Court of Justice that was detected, the Royalists, many of whom were gallant, resolute and inventive, did nothing. The possible plan to rescue the King that seems to have caused most concern was the plot wrongly rumoured to have been instigated by one of the Commissioners, John Downes, who was probably thought to be active in such a plan because of his intervention at the trial.

In the Long Gallery Herbert and Juxon also met Cromwell, who told them that the orders for the King's burial would be issued very soon. This, however, was not to be the case. The embalming process needed to be undertaken soon and it was completed the following day, after which the King's body, now with the severed head re-attached by Dr Trappam, was taken from Whitehall to St James's Palace, where it was to lay while Parliament made a decision about where to bury the King.

At some time immediately after the King's death, the Council of Officers questioned the Bishop. They wanted the small piece of paper containing the notes the King had made for his speech and had handed to him. The piece of paper that Juxon ultimately pulled out of his pockets after a hurried search was challenged by the Council as being different from the one the King had handed him. Fortunately for the Bishop, a soldier who had glanced over the King's shoulder when he first consulted his notes confirmed that these were the very notes the King had used. Ireton relieved the Bishop of the 'George' the King had handed him and he also took the King's cloak, which was emblazoned with the Star insignia of the Order of the Garter. He also took two royal seals. The Bishop protested that the King had bequeathed the 'George' to his eldest son and that the seals were intended for the Princess Elizabeth. Ireton said that Parliament should decide what would happen to these items.

The Council of Officers then asked Juxon about the King's cryptic statement to him – 'Remember'. The old man explained that it was a reminder to him to ensure that the 'George' reached Prince Charles and that the King wanted his son to forgive those who had executed his father and that, finally, he should govern his subjects in a way which did not drive them to extremities.[3]

It is very likely that Juxon would also have had the text of the speech that the King was prevented from making on the day of his sentencing. The King would certainly have wanted that published, as it was his defence and the justification for his actions. Its publication was most probably the subject of the King's single word request. Hugh Ross Williamson suggested that the Bishop had the text of that speech in his pocket when questioned by Ireton and the others.[4] This is possible, but unlikely, as the King would have wanted to ensure that the text was safe and he had had several chances to pass it to Juxon between Saturday evening, when the Bishop was allowed to join him, and the Monday evening before the execution. The Bishop came to and went from the King's presence three times during that period – time enough to take the document and conceal it in his own lodgings, where it would have been safer than with the King. The King's speech was published on the Monday following his death[5] and, as with so many valuable papers of the period, was assiduously preserved by George Thomason, a bookseller, to whom all historians of the period are forever deeply in debt.

After the King's death thirteen Commissioners of the High Court of Justice met again in the Painted Chamber as a committee for 'disbursing and payment of such sums of money as they shall think fit for service of this Court, upon such bill as they shall allow'.[6] It is of interest to note that the man authorised to pay out the money was Captain John Blackwell, an officer of Cromwell's regiment who was also Deputy Treasurer for the Army. This was another example of the control the Army now exercised over the government and Parliament.

When embalmed, the King's body had been placed in a sealed lead-lined coffin, covered by a velvet pall as it waited in the

Cromwell views the King's body. A Victorian impression.

Banqueting House. Sir Roger Manley and Richard Symonds, the Royalist soldier-diarist, claimed that while the King's coffin was at Whitehall, 'Oliver Cromwell came, with one Bowtell of Suffolk, . . . and tried to open the side with his staff, but could not, then he took Bowtell's sword and with the pommel knocked up the lid and looked upon the King, showing him to Bowtell. Then at that time this Bowtell asked him what government we should have. He said "the same that is now".'[7] Symonds noted that he was told this by a 'Colonel Rolston' who had heard it from 'Bowtell'. These men would have been Major William Boteler of Cromwell's regiment and Lieutenant-Colonel William Rolleston, who was also a Suffolk man.

The King's Funeral

At St James's Palace the King's body lay in its open coffin for seven days. Many people sought permission to view their dead sovereign, but very few were allowed to do so. The King's closest noble followers kept vigil until Parliament, having rejected Westminster Abbey as a resting place, decided that Charles could be buried at Windsor. On Wednesday 7 February 'it was delivered to four of his servants Herbert, Mildmay, Preston and Joiner, who with some others in mourning equipage attended the hearse that night to Windsor, and placed it in the room which was formerly the King's bedchamber'.[8]

William Seymour, Earl of Hertford, a pall-bearer.

The King had given no instructions about his place of burial, but his four loyal followers, the Duke of Richmond, the Marquess of Hertford, the Earl of Southampton and the Earl of Lindsey, undertook the arrangements. The Duke had received permission from the Army Parliament to bury his royal kinsman at Windsor provided the cost did not exceed £500. The four Royalists wanted their sovereign to be buried in St George's Chapel according to the rites of the *Book of Common Prayer*, but the governor, Colonel Christopher Whichcote, considered that Parliament would not allow those rites to be used.

Herbert and the other royal attendants debated about where in the chapel precincts to bury the King. They considered the possibility of the Tomb House built by Wolsey, but that was not actually in the Chapel Royal and was therefore rejected. Then interment in the tomb of King Edward IV was thought of, as King Charles was descended from him and had admired the Yorkist monarch. On the arrival of the four noble Royalists and Bishop William Juxon, the

The Duke of Richmond, who arranged the King's funeral.

final decision became theirs and they searched for a suitable place to lay their King.

A gentle tapping on the flagstones in the middle of the choir produced a hollowness indicative of some sort of vault. When the stones were removed, two unmarked coffins were revealed, one large, one smaller. It was decided that they were those of King Henry VIII and his third wife, Queen Jane Seymour, the great-aunt of the Marquess of Hertford. Although Herbert was well aware that King Charles had not approved of King Henry VIII, particularly censuring that monarch's plunder of the Church's wealth, it was decided that the King should be buried there, in line with the eleventh stall of the Knights of the Garter, on the sovereign's side.

Thomas Wriothersley, Earl of Southampton, a pall-bearer.

At about 3 p.m. on the afternoon of Friday 9 February 1649 King Charles's coffin was carried solemnly and at a slow pace from the castle by soldiers of the garrison, preceded by the sombrely dressed royal servants with Herbert, Mildmay, Preston and Joiner nearest their King, ahead of the Bishop and Colonel Whichcote. The four noblemen, Richmond, Hertford, Southampton and Lindsey, dressed in mourning clothes, each held a corner of the black velvet pall above the coffin.

The Bishop, having been refused the use of the service from the *Book of Common Prayer*, but being told by the governor that he could use whatever other words he wished, remembered the King's strict adherence to the Anglican forms of service and declined the offer and said nothing. John Nalson recorded, 'And in this manner was this great King, upon Friday, the ninth of February, about three after noon, silently and without other solemnity than of sighs and tears, committed to the earth, the velvet pall being thrown into the vault over the coffin, to which was fastened an inscription in lead of these words: "King Charles, 1649".'[9]

Herbert's account of the funeral ended with, 'This is memorable, that at such a time as the King's body was brought out of St. George's Hall; the sky was serene and clear, but presently it began to snow. So went the white King to his grave in the 48th year of his age, and the 22nd and 10th month of his reign.'[10] The term 'the white King' refers to King Charles's decision to wear white to his coronation, an ominous break with tradition, which the superstitious, well after his death, confirmed as an omen of ill-fortune. Herbert's confusing calculation of the length of the King's reign was based on the Old Style calendar.

Montague Bertie, Earl of Lindsey, also a pall-bearer.

CHAPTER SIXTEEN

The Aftermath

Time, like an ever-rolling stream,
Bears all its sons away, . . .

Isaac Watts, 'O God, our help in ages past'

The general pattern of events after the death of King Charles is well known. In England the Parliament abolished the monarchy and the House of Lords on 16 March 1649 and the country became a republic as the Commonwealth. It was governed by a Council of State under the Presidency of John Bradshaw, with John Milton, the poet, as Latin (or Foreign) Secretary. This arrangement lasted until December 1653, when Oliver Cromwell set up the Protectorate, with himself as Protector.

The Scots, incensed by the death of his father, proclaimed Prince Charles as their King on 5 February 1649 and the Irish, under Ormond, rose in support of the new King, who landed in Scotland in June the following year. King Charles II, on the insistence of the Scottish Parliament, hypocritically took the Covenant, which his father had refused to do. Cromwell then invaded Scotland, defeating the Scots' Army at Dunbar on 3 September 1650. On 1 January 1651 King Charles was finally crowned King of Scotland and with a large army, swelled by English Royalists, marched into England and to defeat at Worcester, again on 3 September. After many adventures, the young King escaped to France and spent the next years in a wandering, poverty stricken exile, until he was restored to the English throne in May 1660.

Cromwell died in 1658 and was succeeded as Protector by his son Richard, 'Tumble-down Dick', who retired to exile in Europe, only to return to England in about 1680 to live quietly and unmolested as 'John Clarke' until his death in 1712.

John Milton, poet and Latin Secretary in the Commonwealth.

The Remaining Royal Family

Of King Charles I's other children, Mary, the first to hold the title Princess Royal, had married the Prince of Orange and their son eventually became the English sovereign. At first he ruled jointly with his wife, Mary, the eldest daughter of James, Duke of York, and then alone, after her death, as King William III.

In 1685 James, Duke of York succeeded his childless brother King Charles II, on the throne, as James II. His reign was fraught with religious controversy and beset by the unsuccessful Monmouth Rebellion in 1685. King James, a staunch Catholic, was faced with revolution by his Protestant subjects and fled the country in 1688. This created a unique and unprecedented situation – a living King and a vacant throne. These events became known as 'The Glorious Revolution' and James II was succeeded by William and Mary. His son, the Old Pretender, tried to regain the throne after the death of Queen Anne, the last Stuart sovereign, by fostering the failed 1715 rebellion in Scotland against the new Hanoverian King, George I. His grandson, Prince Charles Edward Stuart, 'Bonnie Prince Charlie', tried again in 1745, only to be beaten at Culloden in 1746.

The Princess Elizabeth, who with Prince Henry bade their father King Charles I such a tearful farewell the day before his execution, died on 8 September 1650 at Carisbrooke Castle, where she was held prisoner, as her father had been. It was said that she died of a broken heart. Prince Henry, who joined his mother in France and fought with distinction as a volunteer in the Spanish Army in Flanders, returned to England in 1660 at the Restoration of King Charles II, but died of smallpox that year.

King Charles I's youngest child, Princess Henrietta Anne, 'Minette', had been born in Exeter during 1644. After a perilous journey she joined her mother in Paris, where she eventually married the Duc d'Orleans, the younger brother of the French King, Louis XIV. She died in 1670. Queen Henrietta Maria had suffered much privation and poverty during her exile in France. She came to England in 1660 and stayed until 1665, when she returned to France where she died in 1669.

The Regicides

> *Revenge his foul and most unnatural murder.*
>
> Shakespeare, *Hamlet*

Most of the men who were instrumental in bringing about the King's death retained positions of authority in the newly established

King Charles II after the Battle of Worcester, 1651.

King James II, the King's second son.

Commonwealth. While somewhat apprehensive about possible vengeance from dedicated Royalist adherents, they were likely to have given little credence to even a thought that the monarchy might be restored with the dead King's son on the throne a mere eleven years later. The first man to pay the price for his involvement in the trial and execution of King Charles I was Dr Isaac Dorislaus, who had been one of the legal advisers to the High Court of Justice and had helped to draw up the charge against the King. He had been sent to Holland as an ambassador to the States-General, but barely two months after the death of the King Dorislaus was assassinated there by six men, reputedly supporters of the Marquess of Montrose.

Others who had been involved died before the Restoration and so escaped the revenge of King Charles II. Among these were Cromwell who died in 1658 and Bradshaw in 1659. Of the remainder, John Blakiston and Thomas Horton died in 1649; John Venn was said to have committed suicide in 1650, the same year that Isaac Ewer died of fever in Ireland; Henry Ireton also died of fever in Ireland in 1651; Richard Deane, as a General-at-Sea in battle in 1653; Sir John Danvers, Sir Thomas Mauleverer, Anthony Stapley and Sir William Constable in 1655; Lord Grey of Groby in 1657; Thomas Pride was purged by death in 1658, while Sir John Bouchier died in 1660 before he could be tried. In 1660, Sir Michael Livesey, denounced, was killed by some Dutchmen, in Kent.

Another who suffered death after the Restoration was Sir Henry Vane the Younger. He had disassociated himself from the King's trial

The widowed Queen Henrietta Maria.

The Restoration – King Charles II lands at Dover in May 1660. A Victorian interpretation.

and execution, concentrating on his duties as Treasurer of the Navy. His prominence in the Long Parliament cost him dearly, for although he fell out with Cromwell and some of his former colleagues, he was arrested on the orders of King Charles II and tried for High Treason on a slender charge of having conspired with the Army against the King. He was spared the dreadful hanging, drawing and quartering death of a traitor but was beheaded on 14 June 1662, the anniversary of the Battle of Naseby.

Sir Henry Vane, leading Parliamentarian and executed in 1662 for consipracy against the King.

Some escaped abroad. In 1660 Sir Michael Livesey, denounced, was set upon and killed by some Dutchmen in Holland. Others were pursued and harried by Royalist agents. These included Bradshaw's assistant William Say, John Hewson, Edmund Ludlow, John Dixwell, William Cawley, Thomas Chaloner, Thomas Wogan and, among others, William Goffe, who escaped to Connecticut in North America where, after many narrow escapes, including some from hostile native Americans, he died in about 1680. Edward Whalley also fled to the New World, as did Dixwell after a worrying time in exile across the English Channel. Even though he opposed the King's death, Algernon Sidney was not forgiven and an attempt was made on his life in Germany. John Lisle, who was also prominent as one of Bradshaw's assistants, was assassinated in Switzerland in 1664.

Although dead, Cromwell, Bradshaw, Ireton and Constable were not forgiven. They had been buried in Westminster Abbey and King Charles II ordered their bodies dug up and hanged as common criminals at Tyburn, where the Marble Arch now stands in London. Others still alive were tried, convicted and punished. Some of them, notably Thomas Harrison, John Jones, Thomas Scott, John Carew, Gregory Clement, Adrian Scroope, John Okey, John Barkestead and Miles Corbet, all of whom had signed the death warrant, were executed as traitors with all the barbarity which that entailed. Neither John Cook, the Attorney, nor Hugh Peters signed the death warrant, but their prominent roles in the affairs of the Court, and of the Army in the case of Peters, brought them to the same end. Also executed were Colonel Francis Hacker and Lieutenant-Colonel Daniel Axtel for their part in the King's death.

John Carew, a Commissioner of the High Court.

Colonel Matthew Thomlinson was impeached by Parliament before the Restoration, but he avoided punishment by either his accusers or by the restored King, who recognised his kindness to his late father. Charles II, because of this, was probably prepared to overlook Thomlinson's nomination as a member of the High Court of Justice, especially as he had not participated in the trial, despite having been recorded as present for both sessions on 27 January, the day when the King was sentenced.

Many people were imprisoned and, as few were released, most died as captives, including John Downes who had risked much supporting the King's request for a hearing before the Lords and Commons. John Hutchinson, Owen Rowe, Henry Marten, Robert Tichborne, Henry Smith, Thomas Waite, Simon Mayne, and the Temples, Peter and James, also died while still in prison. Richard Ingoldsby escaped all punishment. He had opposed Lambert's rising in 1659, capturing its leader. He supported the restoration of the King, was pardoned and, in 1661, knighted, becoming a Member of Parliament until his death in 1685. George Fleetwood was also pardoned.

Sir Thomas, 3rd Lord Fairfax, the man whose reputation might have gathered enough support to impose some sort of check on those who were determined that the King must die, did not stay long in public life after the execution. He was elected to the new forty-one-member Council of State of the Commonwealth that replaced the monarchy and was confirmed as the Commander-in-Chief of its increasingly restless soldiers. In the summer of 1649 an Army mutiny threatened and Fairfax was instrumental in quelling it, bringing the soldiers back to order. He was then concerned with administering the Army in England while Cromwell took command in Ireland.

In February 1650 Fairfax's appointment to the Council of State was renewed, as the law required annual renewals, but shortly after Cromwell's return from the pacification of Ireland, the Council considered a pre-emptive invasion of Scotland. Fairfax opposed the proposal, threatening resignation, because he believed that such an act was unjust. Despite many appeals for him to continue in command, on 25 June 1650 Fairfax resigned as Commander-in-Chief, in effect retiring from active public life. He was only involved in public affairs once more during the failing Protectorate of Richard Cromwell, when he called for a free Parliament, which was elected and then voted to restore the monarchy, inviting King Charles II to return, which he did in May 1660.

The restored King did not consider that Fairfax deserved punishment for standing aside from the trial and the execution of his father, but allowed him to live in Yorkshire in quiet retirement, beset by illness induced by arduous active service and wounds received since 1642. Lady Fairfax died in 1665 and her husband followed her to the grave on 12 November 1671, dying of a fever.

Epilogue

Clarendon, writing of King Charles I, considered that, 'There were so many miraculous circumstances contributed to his ruin, that men might think that heaven and earth conspired it, and that the stars designed it.'[1] The King's downfall stemmed not from inevitability, but from his errors of judgment. He was inflexible in his beliefs in his divine right and in religious certainty, failing to realise that among those who opposed him were men of equal determination to produce a settlement that satisfied them. He refused to recognise the intensity of the powerful urge that his principal opponents had to correct the evils which they saw in the government of their country. He failed to appreciate the need to compromise at a time when he might have retained much of his power, or at least given little away. When he did offer compromise on matters of religion, government and control of the armed forces, those with whom he made the agreement were themselves losing credibility with the people who had control of overwhelming military power.

Evidence of the divisions in Parliament were very apparent at the time of the Cromwell–Manchester quarrel in 1644–5 and the design of the Self-Denying Ordinance. The signs that moderate opinion in both Houses was losing influence were there when the Earls of Essex, Manchester and Warwick, with the others who were prepared to negotiate a peace with the King, were out-manouevred by Cromwell, Vane and those who believed that total victory was the only way to settle matters. The King recognised these divisions among his enemies, but, understandably, his exploitation of them was aimed at the total defeat of both enemy factions rather than at negotiation, a process that would have entailed concessions to the rebels, whatever views they held about the best way to end the war.

Charles's determined intransigence brought to the fore the realisation that, no matter what concessions he had made at

Newport, fundamentally he was not prepared to concede anything permanently. His views had not changed from those he had expressed in a memorandum to Sir Edward Nicholas, one of his negotiating Commissioners at the time of the Uxbridge treaty in early 1645, the tone of which was set by, '. . . I will not go one jot further than what is offered by you already'.[2]

Even though he made further concessions at Newport, these were restricted by time limits and therefore the chances of a permanent settlement were still uncertain. There were also huge differences between the interpretations placed by the King on the wording of any agreement and the meanings understood by his enemies. Added to this continual uncertainty of interpretation was the suspicion that again, as he had done all along, the King was playing for time. These factors led to the firm opinion of his more determined enemies, Ireton, Cromwell, Harrison and others, that a settlement could only be achieved without him. That decided, the prospect of an exiled King planning to recover his kingdoms was not one which appealed and, no doubt, having considered all the consequences of a choice between the King's exile or the King's death, with its attendant martyrdom, the latter appeared to offer fewer immediate problems.

One cannot but feel sympathy for the King in the last two years of his life, imprisoned by enemies, separated from his beloved family and beset by those who hectored him continually, trying to reach a settlement with him. In many ways he was an admirable man, faithful to his wife, loving to his family, deeply religious and punctilious in his devotions, as well as being a man of conscience.

The King's narrow view of situations, bolstered by his strongly held convictions, was the true 'alloy' that Clarendon observed about His Majesty's kingship, not the slowness of generosity about which he wrote. After all, he could hardly have been too highly critical of the King for whom he had sacrificed much and whose son was now on the throne as he edited his magnificent history, which was not published until 1702–4, well after the 1st Earl's death.

Much has been written, particularly by the Royalists, about the duplicity of Cromwell, whose enemies have accused him of planning the death of the King and the ultimate course of history with the determination of a far-seeing Machiavelli. Such a view assumes a long-standing omnipotence, which did not exist. Cromwell, unlike many who allied with him, was pragmatic in his approach to problems. He considered the situation as it confronted him at the time, and his experience in war would have emphasised that trait. He had no detailed blueprint for a future life of high ambition. He knew what he believed even if he was not above using his religious beliefs to justify secular actions. He was no great theorist of government, bound by rigid preconceptions.

There is an anecdote, probably spurious, that the Earl of Southampton, while keeping night vigil over the late King's body at Whitehall, observed a heavily muffled man approach the coffin and look down at the dead monarch. He was then heard to say with a sigh, 'Cruel necessity!' Although the man's features could not be seen, the Earl was reported to have said that 'by his voice and his gait, he took him to be Oliver Cromwell'. This story, first published in the eighteenth century, is likely to be fiction, as Cromwell, with Bowtell, had already inspected the King's body and was unlikely to have felt the need to view the late King yet again. There is, however, an echo of authenticity in the two uttered words – they reflected Cromwell's views.

The problems needed solving no matter how unpalatable and apparently merciless the solutions might be to any one individual, whether mutinous soldier, reluctant Earl, or inflexible King. War was, and still is, merciless to the many.

Notes

Chapter One

1. *Dictionary of National Biography.*
2. Sir R. Cary, *Memoirs* (1759). Quoted by D.R. Watson in *Charles I* (Weidenfeld & Nicholson, 1972), p. 17.
3. Watson, *Charles I*, p. 17.
4. Christopher Hibbert, *Charles I* (Readers Union and Weidenfeld & Nicholson, 1970), p. 22.
5. Edward Hyde, Earl of Clarendon, *History of the Rebellion and the Civil Wars in England*, ed. W.D. Macray (Oxford at the Clarendon Press, 1888), Book XI, 240 and 242.
6. Carola Oman, *Henrietta Maria* (Hodder & Stoughton, 1936), pp. 31–2.
7. Clarendon, *Rebellion*, Book VIII, 179.
8. *The Letters, Speeches and Proclamations of King Charles I*, ed. Sir Charles Petrie (Cassell, 1935), p. 157.
9. Ibid., p. 115.
10. Hibbert, *Charles I*, p. 156.
11. Clarendon, *Rebellion*, Book XI, 239.
12. Sir Edward Walker, *Brief Memorials of the Unfortunate Success of His Majesty's Army and Affairs . . . in 1645* (Paris, 1647), p. 134.
13. Clarendon, *Rebellion*, Book XI, 241.

Chapter Two

1. Edward Hyde, Earl of Clarendon, *History of the Rebellion and the Civil Wars in England*, ed. W.D. Macray (Oxford at the Clarendon Press, 1888), Book XI, 241.
2. Ibid., Book XI, 241.
3. *The Letters, Speeches and Proclamations of King Charles I*, ed. Sir Charles Petrie (Cassell, 1935), p. 63.
4, D.C. Coleman, *The Economic History of England 1450–1750* (Oxford, Clarendon Press, 1977), p. 64.
5. *Letters of Charles I*, p. 92.
6. Lucy Hutchinson, *Memoirs of the Life of Col. Hutchinson* (J.M. Dent, Everyman Library, n.d.).
7. *Committee of Both Kingdoms Letter Book*, 3 July 1644.

8. L. Stone, *Causes of the English Revolution 1529–1642* (Routledge & Kegan Paul, 1972), p. 143.
9. Alan G.R. Smith, *The Emergence of the Nation State* (Longman, 1984), Compendium I.
10. *Calendar of State Papers (Domestic), 1648*, vol. DXVI, p. 62.
11. *Letters of Charles I*, pp. 172–3.
12. Ibid., p. 174.
13. *The Diplomatic Correspondence of Jean de Montereul* (Scottish Historical Society), quoted in Jane Lane, *The Reign of King Covenant* (Robert Hale, 1956), p. 162.
14. Lane, *King Covenant*, p. 162.
15. Ibid., p. 166.
16. John Rushworth, *Historical Collections of Private Passages*, 7 vols (1659–1701), vol. VI, p. 272.
17. Clarendon, *Rebellion*, Book X, 33.
18. Bulstrode Whitelocke, *Memorials of the English Affairs, 1625–6* (Oxford University Press, 1853), p. 214.
19. Francis Peck, *Desiderata Curiosa* (1779), *The Examination of Dr. Michael Hudson*, XXV.
20. Clarendon, *Rebellion*, Book XI, 241.

Chapter Three

1. Thomason Tract TTE 337 (11), *'Secretary of the Scottish Army. His Relation . . . how his Majesty . . . his coming to the Scots etc'*, quoted in 'The Life and Campaigns of Alexander Leslie, First Earl of Leven' by C.S. Terry, 1899 (reprinted by Pallas Armata, Tonbridge, 1994), p. 402.
2. TTE 337 (11).
3. Sir James Turner, *Memoirs of his Own Life and Times* (reprinted by Pallas Armata, Tonbridge, Kent, 1991), p. 41.
4 *Calendar of State Papers (Domestic), 1646*, vol. DXIV, p. 433.
5. Terry, *Leven*, p. 403.
6. Ibid., p. 407.
7. Turner, *Memoirs*, pp. 41–2.
8. Quoted in 'The Quarrel between the Earl of Manchester and Oliver Cromwell', ed. David Mason, 1875, p. 72.
9. Ibid.
10. *Journal of the House of Commons* (CJ), iv 551, quoted in Terry, *Leven*, p. 412.
11. John Rushworth, *Historical Collections of Private Passages*, 7 vols (1659–1701), vol. VI, p. 274.
12. Ibid., vol. VI, pp. 303–4.
13. President of the USA, Richard Milhouse Nixon, *c.* 1970.
14. *The Letters, Speeches and Proclamations of King Charles I*, ed. Sir Charles Petrie (Cassell, 1935), pp. 179 *et seq*.
15. Ibid., p. 182.
16. Bulstrode Whitelocke, *Memorials of the English Affairs, 1625–6* (Oxford University Press, 1853), p. 234.
17. *Letters of Charles I*, p. 234 and Rushworth, *Collections*, vol. VI.
18. Rushworth, *Collections*, vol. V.
19. Ibid., vol. VI, p. 319.
20. Ibid., vol. VI, p. 328.

Chapter Four

1. *The Letters, Speeches and Proclamations of King Charles I*, ed. Sir Charles Petrie (Cassell, 1935), p. 182.
2. *Correspondence of the Fairfax Family*, ed. Robert Bell (London, 1849), pp. 235–6.
3. Alistair Cooke, *Letter from America*, Radio 4 broadcast, *c.* 1956.
4. *Calendar of State Papers (Domestic), 1644–45*, vol. DVI, p. 232.
5. D. Brunton and D.H. Pennington, *Members of the Long Parliament* (Allen & Unwin, 1954).
6. Thomason Tracts, *Perfect Occurrences* for the period.
7. P.R. Newman, *Royalist Officers in England & Wales, 1642–1660* (New York, 1981), p. 38, entry no. 161.
8. *Letters of Charles I*, pp. 214 *et seq.*
9. Ibid., p. 217.
10. Quoted in J.G. Muddiman, *The Trial of Charles I* (William Hodge and Co. Ltd, Edinburgh and London, 1928), pp. 28–9.
11. Sir Thomas Herbert, *Memoirs* (edition of 1702), *Narrative of Cromwell's Major, Huntington*.
12. Edward Hyde, Earl of Clarendon, *History of the Rebellion and the Civil Wars in England*, ed. W.D. Macray (Oxford at the Clarendon Press, 1888), Book X, 116–18.
13. Thomason Tract TTE 416 (23), *Whalley's letter to the Speaker of the Commons*.
14. Thomason Tract E. 416 (23), *Kingdom's Weekly Intelligencer*, for 9–16 November 1647.

Chapter Five

1. Edward Hyde, Earl of Clarendon, *History of the Rebellion and the Civil Wars in England*, ed. W.D. Macray (Oxford at the Clarendon Press, 1888), Book X, 22.
2. Sir Richard Bulstrode, *Memoirs & Reflections on the Reign of King Charles I & II* (1721; reprinted Pallas Armata, Tonbridge, Kent, 1997), p. 163.
3. Clarendon, *Rebellion*, Book X, 128.
4. Ibid., Book X, 129.
5. Ibid., Book X, 131.
6. Bulstrode, *Memoirs*, p. 164.
7. Sir Thomas Herbert, *Memoirs* (edition of the Folio Society, 1963 of *The Trial of Charles I*).
8. John Rushworth, *Historical Collections of Private Passages*, 7 vols (1659–1701), vol. VII, p. 1257.
9. Clarendon, *Rebellion*, Book XI, 157.
10. Old Malaysian folk tale.
11. *The Letters, Speeches and Proclamations of King Charles I*, ed. Sir Charles Petrie (Cassell, 1935), p. 239.

Chapter Six

1. Sir Thomas Herbert, *Memoirs* (edition of the Folio Society, 1963), p. 50.
2. Ibid., p. 51.
3. Ibid., p. 53.
4. Ibid., p. 55.
5. John Rushworth, *Historical Collections of Private Passages*, 7 vols (1659–1701), vol. VII, p. 1349 and also *The Moderator*, 28 November to 5 December 1648.

6. Tanner MSS, vol. LVII, p. 452, quoted in C. Markham, *Life of the Great Lord Fairfax* (Macmillan, 1870), pp. 343–4.
7. Thomas, 3rd Lord Fairfax, *Short Memorials etc* (reprinted by Pallas Armata, Tonbridge, 1990), p. 120.
8. Ibid., p. 10.
9. *Memoirs of Edmund Ludlow*, ed. C.H. Firth, 2 vols (1894), vol. 1, p. 211.
10. Herbert, *Memoirs*, p. 58.
11. Sir Richard Bulstrode, *Memoirs & Reflections on the Reign of King Charles I & II* (1721), p. 176.
12. Herbert, *Memoirs*, pp. 60–1.
13. Edward Hyde, Earl of Clarendon, *History of the Rebellion and the Civil Wars in England*, ed. W.D. Macray (Oxford at the Clarendon Press, 1888), Book XI, 222.
14. Clarendon, *Rebellion*, Book XI, 223.
15. Herbert, *Memoirs*, p. 63.
16. *The Army's Remonstrance of 12th November 1648.*
17. Herbert, *Memoirs*, pp. 65–6.
18. Ibid., p. 66.

Chapter Seven

1. Sir Philip Warwick, *Memoires of the Reign of King Charles I* (1701), p. 229.
2. Thomason Tracts, TTE 477 (18), *Several Proposals etc.*
3. Edward Hyde, Earl of Clarendon, *History of the Rebellion and the Civil Wars in England*, ed. W.D. Macray (Oxford at the Clarendon Press, 1888), Book XI, 224.
4. Clarendon MM, 2968, *Letter of John Lawrans to Sir Edward Nicholas*, 21 December, quoted in S.R. Gardiner, *History of the Great Civil War* (Longman, Green and Co., edition of 1898), p. 282.
5. *John Lawrans Letter to Sir Edward Nicholas.*
6. *Journal of the House of Lords*, X 641, quoted in Gardiner, *Great Civil War*, p. 288.
7. John Rushworth, *Historical Collections of Private Passages*, 7 vols (1659–1701), vol. VII, p. 1383.
8. Ibid., vol. VII, p. 1379.

Chapter Eight

1. Thomason Tracts, *Perfect Occurrences* of the period.
2. John Rushworth, *Historical Collections of Private Passages*, 7 vols (1659–1701), vol. VII, entry for Saturday 6 January 1648.
3. Thomas, 3rd Lord Fairfax, *Short Memorials etc*, p. 10.
4. C. Markham, *Life of the Great Lord Fairfax*, (Macmillan, 1870), p. 346.
5. *A Journal of the Proceedings of the High Court of Justice, Bradshawe's Journal*, printed in J.G. Muddiman, *Trial of King Charles I* (William Hodge & Co. Ltd, Edinburgh, 1928) dated 9 January 1648.
6. *Bradshawe's Journal*, for 12 January 1648.
7. Ibid.
8. *Mercurius Elencticus*, for 21–8 June 1646.
9. William Shakespeare, *Twelfth Night*, Act II, Scene IV.
10. *Calendar of State Papers (Domestic), 1648–1649*, vol. DXVI, pp. 345–6.
11. Ibid., vol. DXVI, p. 347.

12. *Bradshawe's Journal*, for 15 January 1649.
13. *Mercurius Pragmaticus*, 29 December 1648 – 9 January 1649.
14. *Bradshawe's Journal*, for 17 January 1649.
15. *Bradshawe's Journal*, for 18 January 1649.
16. Muddiman, *Trial*, p. 70.

Chapter Nine

1. S.R. Gardiner, *The Constitutional Documents of the Puritan Revolution* (3rd edn, Oxford, 1906), pp. 359–71.
2. *Commons Journal*, vol. 6, September 1648 to August 1651.
3. *Sidney Papers* (1825), ed. R.W. Blencowe.
4. *Bradshawe's Journal*, for 17 January 1649.
5. Edward Hyde, Earl of Clarendon, *History of the Rebellion and the Civil Wars in England*, ed. W.D. Macray (Oxford at the Clarendon Press, 1888), Book XI, 235 and John Rushworth, *Historical Collections of Private Passages*, 7 vols (1659–1701), vol. VII, p. 1395 (quoted as vol. IV in J.G. Muddiman, *Trial of King Charles I* (William Hodge & Co. Ltd, Edinburgh, 1928), p. 74).

Chapter Ten

1. *Bradshawe's Journal*, for 20 January 1649.
2. Ibid.
3. Ibid.
4. Edward Hyde, Earl of Clarendon, *History of the Rebellion and the Civil Wars in England*, ed. W.D. Macray (Oxford at the Clarendon Press, 1888), Book XI, 235.
5. *Harleian Manuscripts 3783; Nos 109, 175 and 176*, quoted in J.G. Muddiman, *Trial of King Charles I* (William Hodge & Co. Ltd, Edinburgh, 1928) p. 80.
6. John Nalson, *A True Copy of the Journal of the High Court of Justice for the Tryal of K. Charles I* (A transcript of the Journal of John Phelps, one of the two Clerks of the Court, published in 1684), entry for Saturday 20 January 1649.
7. Ibid.
8. Thomason Tract, E 1047 (3) and *The Trial of Henry Marten, 1660*; 'An Exact and Most Impartial Account of the Trials of the Regicides', p 248, quoted in J.G. Muddiman, *Trial*.
9. Nalson, *A True Copy*, 20 January 1649.
10. Ibid.
11. Ibid.
12. Ibid.
13. Johnson's letter to James Boswell, 19 September 1777.
14. Taunton, Somerset, folklore anecdote.

Chapter Eleven

Other than the Molière quotation, from *Monsieur de Pourceaugnac*, Act I sc. vii, the quotations in this chapter are taken from the contemporary accounts of Phelps and Broughton, Clerks to the Court, from *House of Commons Journal* and the account prepared after the trial by seven of the Regicides, namely Garland, Lisle, Ireton, Marten, Hardress Waller, Scott and Say. This latter text is known in Muddiman (below) as *Bradshawe's Journal*, pp. 193–230.

Extracts from John Rushworth, *Historical Collections of Private Passages*, 7 vols (1659–1701) and Sir Thomas Herbert, *Memoirs* are included in *The Trial of Charles I*, pub. by Folio Society, 1959 (below).

All these texts are included in:

J.G. Muddiman, *The Trial of King Charles I* (William Hodge and Co. Ltd, Edinburgh and London, 1928)
The Trial of Charles I, A Documentary History, ed. David Lagomarsino and Charles T. Wood (University Press of New England [Dartmouth College], 1989)
The Trial of Charles I, ed. Roger Lockyer (Folio Society, 1959)

The interpretations drawn from these texts are those of the present author.

Chapter Twelve

1. John Nalson, *A True Copy of the Journal of the High Court of Justice for the Tryal of K. Charles I* (A transcript of the Journal of John Phelps, one of the two Clerks of the Court, published in 1684), 27 January 1649.
2. Ibid.
3. Thomason Tract, E 1047 (3), *An Exact and Most Impartial Account* (Regicides Trials), pp. 189–91.
4. Sir Thomas Herbert, *Memoirs* (Folio Society, 1963), p. 119.
5. Herbert, *Memoirs*, p. 126.
6. *Bradshawe's Journal*, for 27 January, p. 226.

Chapter Thirteen

1. John Rushworth, *Historical Collections of Private Passages*, 7 vols (1659–1701), vol. VII, p. 1427.
2. *Bradshawe's Journal*, for 29 January 1649.
3. Edward Hyde, Earl of Clarendon, *History of the Rebellion and the Civil Wars in England*, ed. W.D. Macray (Oxford at the Clarendon Press, 1888), Book XVI, 225.
4. Sir Thomas Herbert, *Memoirs*, p. 124.
5. Thomason Tract, no. 669, f. 14(9), *True Relation of the King's Speech to the Lady Elizabeth and the Duke of Gloucester the day before his death*.
6. Ibid.
7. Herbert, *Memoirs* (Folio Society, 1963), p. 124.
8. J.G. Muddiman, *The Trial of King Charles I* (William Hodge and Co. Ltd, Edinburgh and London, 1928), pp. 139–43.
9. *Bradshawe's Journal*, for 30 January 1649.

Chapter Fourteen

1. Sir Thomas Herbert, *Memoirs* (Folio Society, 1963), p. 126.
2. Hugh Ross Williamson, *The Day They Killed the King* (Frederick Muller Ltd, 1957), pp. 62–4.
3. Herbert, *Memoirs*, p. 127.
4. Ibid., p. 129.
5. Ibid.

6. Ibid., p. 130.
7. Philip Sidney, *The Headsman of Whitehall* (G.A. Morton, Edinburgh, 1905).
8. Williamson, *The Day*, pp. 133–4.
9. Herbert, *Memoirs*, p. 130.
10. *The Relation of the barbarous and cruel death of the King of England* (pub. in French in Paris, 1649), quoted in J.G. Muddiman, *The Trial of King Charles I* (William Hodge and Co. Ltd, Edinburgh and London, 1928), p. 150, footnote.
11. *King Charles his Trial at the High Court of Justice* (2nd edition, London, 1650), printed in D. Lagomarsino and C.T. Wood *A Documentary History of the Trial of Charles I* (University Press of New England [Dartmouth College], 1989), pp. 138–44.

Chapter Fifteen

1. *Notes and Queries*, series vii, vol. 8, p. 326, quoted in J.G. Muddiman, *The Trial of King Charles I* (William Hodge and Co. Ltd, Edinburgh and London, 1928), p. 153.
2. Sir Thomas Herbert, *Memoirs* (Folio Society, 1963), p. 141.
3. Hugh Ross Williamson, *The Day They Killed the King* (Frederick Muller Ltd, 1957).
4. Ibid.
5. Thomason Tract, no. 669, f. 13 (81), *The King's Speech on the Scaffold*.
6. *Bradshawe's Journal*, for p.m. 30 January 1649.
7. Harleian MS 991. Quoted in Muddiman, *Trial*, p. 156.
8. Nalson, *A True Copy*, 7 January 1649, printed in D. Lagomarsino and C.T. Wood, *A Documentary History of the Trial of Charles I* (University Press of New England [Dartmouth College], 1989), pp. 147–8.
9. Ibid., p. 148.
10. Herbert, *Memoirs*, p. 146.

Epilogue

1. Edward Hyde, Earl of Clarendon, *History of the Rebellion and the Civil Wars in England*, ed. W.D. Macray (Oxford at the Clarendon Press, 1888), Book XI, 243.
2. *The Private Correspondence between King Charles I and Sir Edward Nicholas*, ed. William Bray (George Routledge & Sons Ltd), bound in with *The Diary and Correspondence of John Evelyn, FRS* [n.d.].

Bibliography

All titles were published in London unless otherwise stated.

Bell, Robert (ed.). *Correspondence of the Fairfax Family*, 2 vols, Richard Bentley, 1849

Blencowe, R.W. (ed.). *The Sidney Papers*, 1825

Brunton, D. and Pennington, D.H. *Members of the Long Parliament*, George Allen and Unwin, 1954

Bulstrode, Sir Richard. *Memoirs and Reflections of the Reign of Charles I and II*, Charles Rivington, 1721

Calendar of State Papers (Domestic), vols DXV & DXVI, 1646–1649, HMSO, 1893

Coleman, D.C. *Economic History of England*, Oxford, Clarendon Press, 1977

Dictionary of National Biography, Oxford University Press, 1993

Fairfax, Sir Thomas, 3rd Lord. *Memoirs and Other Documents including 'Short Memorials'*, reprinted by Pallas Armata, Kent, 1990

Firth, C.H. (ed.). *Memoirs of Edmund Ludlow*, 2 vols, Oxford, Clarendon Press, 1894; reprinted by Pallas Armata, Tonbridge, Kent, 1998

Gardiner, S.R. *Constitutional Documents of the Puritan Revolution*, Longman, Green & Co., 1898

Gardiner, S.R., *History of the Great Civil War, 1642–1649*, Oxford, Clarendon Press, 1928

Hibbert, Christopher. *Charles I*, Weidenfeld & Nicholson, 1968

Hutchinson, Lucy. *Memoirs of the Life of Colonel Hutchinson by his Widow*, J.M. Dent, Everyman Edition, *c.* 1900

Hyde, Sir Edward, 1st Earl of Clarendon. *History of the Rebellion and the Civil Wars in England*, 6 vols, ed. W.D. Macray, Oxford, Clarendon Press, 1888

Journal of the House of Commons

Journal of the House of Lords

Lagomarsino, D. and Wood, C.T. *A Documentary History of the Trial of Charles I*, University Press of New England (Dartmouth College), 1989, including extracts from John Nalson, *A True Copy of the Journal of the High Court of Justice for the Trial of King Charles I* (The Journal kept by John Phelps, Clerk to the Court. This is a different account from that contained in *Bradshawe's Journal*)

Lockyer, Roger (ed.). *Extracts from the Memoirs of Sir Thomas Herbert, included in The Trial of Charles I*, Folio Society, 1959

Markham, Clement R. *The Life of the Great Lord Fairfax*, Macmillan & Co., 1870

Muddiman, J.G. *Record of the Proceedings of the High Court of Justice*. The so-called *Bradshawe's Journal* – reports edited by Henry Ireton and other Commissioners of the Court, included in the appendices to *The Trial of Charles I*, William Hodge & Co. Ltd, Edinburgh and London, 1928

Newman, Peter R. *Royalist Officers in England and Wales, 1642–1660*, New York, 1981

Peck, Francis. *Desiderata Curiosa – The Examination of Dr. Michael Hudson*, 1779

Petrie, Sir Charles (ed.). *Letters, Speeches and Proclamations of Charles I*, Cassell, 1935

Rushworth, John. *Historical Collection of Private Passages of State*, 7 vols, 1659–1701

Sidney, Philip. *The Headsman of Whitehall*, G.A. Morton, Edinburgh, 1905

Thomason Tract, no. E 1047 (3), *An Exact and Most Impartial Account of the Trial of the 29 Regicides*, 1660 (other relevant Thomason Tracts listed in the references).

Turner, Sir James. *Memoirs of his own Life and Times* (1683), reprinted by Pallas Armata, Tonbridge, Kent, 1991

Walker, Sir Edward. *Brief Memorials of the Unfortunate Success of His Majesty's Army and Affairs . . . in 1645*, Paris, Walker, 1647

Warwick, Sir Philip. *Memoires of the Reign of King Charles I*, 1701

Watson, D.R. *Charles I*, Weidenfeld & Nicholson, 1972

Whitelocke, B. *Memorials of the English Affairs, 1625–1660*, Oxford University Press, 1853

Parliamentary and Royalist news-sheets of the appropriate dates as listed in the reference notes.

Further Reading

For those who wish to read about the whole period of the Civil War, the following excellent works are recommended:

Fraser, Lady Antonia. *Cromwell, Our Chief of Men*, Weidenfeld & Nicholson, 1973

Hibbert, Christopher. *Cavaliers and Roundheads*, Harper Collins, 1993

Roots, Ivan. *The Great Rebellion, 1642–1660*, 5th Edition, Sutton Publishing, 1995

Selections from Clarendon, ed. H.R. Trevor-Roper, Oxford, Clarendon Press, 1978

Underdown, David. *Pride's Purge*, George Allen and Unwin, 1985

Wedgwood, C.V. *The King's Peace*, Collins, 1955

Wedgwood, C.V. *The King's War*, Collins, 1961

Those wishing to read more about the last days of King Charles I, in addition to the works listed in the publications consulted for this book and those suggested for further reading, I would also suggest C.V. Wedgwood's *The Trial of Charles I* (Collins, 1964).

Index